# THE
# CHURCHILL
# FACTOR

# THE
# CHURCHILL
# FACTOR

## HOW ONE MAN MADE HISTORY

## Boris Johnson

RIVERHEAD BOOKS

*A member of Penguin Group (USA)*

*New York*

*2014*

**RIVERHEAD BOOKS**
Published by the Penguin Group
Penguin Group (USA) LLC
375 Hudson Street
New York, New York 10014

USA • Canada • UK • Ireland • Australia
New Zealand • India • South Africa • China

penguin.com
A Penguin Random House Company

ISBN 978-1-59463-302-7

Printed in the United States of America
1   3   5   7   9   10   8   6   4   2

BOOK DESIGN BY NICOLE LAROCHE

TO LEO F. JOHNSON

*or miscalculation*

Military, defeat can be redeemed.   The fortunes of

war are fickle and changing.   But an act of shame would

*saff*

~~rock~~ the vitals of our strength, ~~and~~ deprive us of the

respect which we now enjoy throughout the world, ~~and~~

would especially rob us of ~~the immense potent~~ hold

*During the last year*                    *a potent hold*

we have, gained by our ~~behaviour,~~ upon the sentiments

*bearing*

of the people of the United States.   In that great

*travail &*

Republic ~~across the Atlantic Ocean,~~ now in ~~great~~ stress

*such*                                    *valued*

of ~~spirit,~~ it is customary to use all the many, solid

*about of*  *the*

arguments ~~affecting~~ American interests and American

*depend upon*

safety which are ~~involved in~~ the destruction of Hitler

*even*

and ~~of Hitlerism~~ his foul gang and, fouler doctrines.

But in the long run, believe me, for I know, the action

of the United States will be dictated not by methodical

*profit*

calculations of ~~product~~ and loss but by moral sentiment

and by that gleaming flash of resolve which lifts the

hearts of men and nations and springs from the spiritual

*life itself*

foundation of human, ~~actions.   Thus it seemed to me~~

~~and to all my colleagues in our War Government, that~~

*Never
never in
our history
have we
been
~~hold~~
held
in such
admiration
& regard
by those
across
the
Atlantic
Ocean*

# CONTENTS

# A DOG CALLED CHURCHILL

When I was growing up, there was no doubt about it. Churchill was quite the greatest statesman that Britain had ever produced. From a very early age I had a pretty clear idea of what he had done: he had led my country to victory against all the odds and against one of the most disgusting tyrannies the world has seen.

I knew the essentials of his story. My brother Leo and I used to pore over Martin Gilbert's biographical *Life in Pictures*, to the point where we had memorised the captions.

I knew that he had a mastery of the art of speech-making, and my father (like many of our fathers) would recite some of his most famous lines; and I knew, even then, that this art was dying out. I knew that he was funny, and irreverent, and that even by the standards of his time he was politically incorrect.

At suppertime we were told the apocryphal stories: the one where Churchill is on the lavatory, and informed that the Lord Privy Seal wants to see him, and he says that he is sealed in the privy, etc. We knew the one where Socialist MP Bessie Braddock allegedly told him that he was drunk, and he replied, with astonishing rudeness, that she was ugly and he would be sober in the morning.

I think we also dimly knew the one about the Tory minister and the guardsman . . . You probably know it, but never mind. I had the canonical version the other day from Sir Nicholas Soames, his grandson, over lunch at the Savoy.

Even allowing for Soames's brilliance in storytelling, it has the ring of truth—and tells us something about a key theme of this book: the greatness of Churchill's heart.

'One of his Conservative ministers was a bugger, if you see what I mean . . .' (said Soames, loudly enough for most of the Grill Room to hear) '. . . though he was also a great friend of my grandfather. He was always getting caught, but of course in those days the press weren't everywhere, and nobody said anything. One day he pushed his luck because he was caught rogering a Guardsman on a bench in Hyde Park at three in the morning—and it was February, by the way.

'This was immediately reported to the Chief Whip, who rang Jock Colville, my grandfather's Private Secretary.

'"Jock," said the Chief Whip, "I am afraid I have some very bad news about so-and-so. It's the usual thing, but the press have got it and it's bound to come out."

'"Oh dear," said Colville.

'"I really think I should come down and tell the Prime Minister in person."

'"Yes, I suppose you should."

'So the Chief Whip came down to Chartwell [Churchill's home in Kent], and he walked into my grandfather's study, where he was working at his upright desk. "Yes, Chief Whip," he said, half turning round, "how can I help you?"

'The Chief Whip explained the unhappy situation. "He'll have to go," he concluded.

'There was a long pause, while Churchill puffed his cigar. Then he said: "Did I hear you correctly in saying that so-and-so has been caught with a Guardsman?"

'"Yes, Prime Minister."

'"In Hyde Park?"

'"Yes, Prime Minister."

'"On a park bench?"

'"That's right, Prime Minister."

'"At three o'clock in the morning?"

'"That's correct, Prime Minister."

'"In this weather! Good God, man, it makes you proud to be British!"'

I KNEW THAT he had been amazingly brave as a young man, and that he had killed men with his own hand, and been fired at on four continents, and that he was one of the first men to go up in an aeroplane. I knew that he had been a bit of a runt at Harrow, and that he was only about 5 feet 7 and with a 31-inch chest, and that he had overcome his stammer and his depression and his appalling father to become the greatest living Englishman.

I gathered that there was something holy and magical about him, because my grandparents kept the front page of the *Daily Express* from the day he died, at the age of ninety. I was pleased to have been born a year before: the more I read about him, the more proud I was to have been alive when he was alive. So it seems all the more sad and strange that today—nearly fifty years after he died—he is in danger of being forgotten, or at least imperfectly remembered.

The other day I was buying a cigar at an airport in a Middle Eastern country that had probably been designed by Churchill. I noticed that the cigar was called a San Antonio Churchill, and I asked the vendor at the Duty-Free whether he knew who Churchill was. He read the name carefully and I pronounced it for him.

'Shursheel?' he said, looking blank.

'In the war,' I said, 'the Second World War.'

Then he looked as though the dimmest, faintest bell was clanking at the back of his memory.

'An old leader?' he asked. 'Yes, maybe, I think. I don't know.' He shrugged.

Well, he is doing no worse than many kids today. Those who pay attention in class are under the impression that he was the guy who fought Hitler to rescue the Jews. But most young people—according to a recent survey—think that Churchill is the dog in a British insurance advertisement.

That strikes me as a shame, because he is so obviously a character that should appeal to young people today. He was eccentric, over the top, camp, with his own special trademark clothes—and a thorough-going genius.

I want to try to convey some of that genius to those who might not be fully conscious of it, or who have forgotten it—and I am of course aware that this is a bit of a cheek.

I am not a professional historian, and as a politician I am not worthy to loose the latchet of his shoes, or even the shoes of Roy Jenkins, who did a superb one-volume biography; and as a student of Churchill I sit at the feet of Martin Gilbert, Andrew Roberts, Max Hastings, Richard Toye and many others.

I am conscious that there are a hundred books a year on our hero—and yet I am sure it is time for a new assessment, because we cannot take his reputation for granted. The soldiers of the Second World War are gradually fading away. We are losing those who can remember the sound of his voice, and I worry that we are in danger—through sheer vagueness—of forgetting the scale of what he did.

These days we dimly believe that the Second World War was won with Russian blood and American money; and though that is in some ways true, it is also true that, without Churchill, Hitler would almost certainly have won.

What I mean is that Nazi gains in Europe might well have been irreversible. We rightly moan today about the deficiencies of the European Union—and yet we have forgotten about the sheer horror of that all too possible of possible worlds.

We need to remember it today, and we need to remember the ways in which this British Prime Minister helped to make the world we still live in. Across the globe—from Europe to Russia to Africa to the Middle East—we see traces of his shaping mind.

Churchill matters today because he saved our civilisation. And the important point is that only he could have done it.

He is the resounding human rebuttal to all Marxist historians who think history is the story of vast and impersonal economic forces. The point of the Churchill Factor is that one man can make all the difference.

Time and again in his seven decades in public life we can see the impact of his personality on the world, and on events—far more of them than are now widely remembered.

He was crucial to the beginning of the welfare state in the early 1900s. He helped give British workers job centres and the tea break and unemployment insurance. He invented the RAF and the tank and he was absolutely critical to the action—and Britain's eventual victory—in the First World War. He was indispensable to the foundation of Israel (and other countries), not to mention the campaign for a united Europe.

At several moments he was the beaver who dammed the flow of events; and never did he affect the course of history more profoundly than in 1940.

Character is destiny, said the Greeks, and I agree. If that is so, then the deeper and more fascinating question is what makes up the character.

What were the elements that made him capable of filling that gigantic role? In what smithies did they forge that razor mind and iron will?

What the hammer, what the chain, in what furnace was his brain? as William Blake almost puts it. That's the question.

But first let's try and agree on what he did.

# CHAPTER 1

# THE OFFER
# FROM HITLER

I f you are looking for one of the decisive moments in the last world war, and a turning-point in the history of the world, then come with me. Let us go to a dingy room in the House of Commons—up some steps, through a creaky old door, down a dimly lit corridor; and here it is.

You won't find it on the maps of the Palace of Westminster, for obvious security reasons; and you can't normally get the guides to show you. In fact the precise room I am talking about doesn't really exist any more, since it was blown up in the Blitz; but the replacement is faithful enough to the original.

It is one of the rooms used by the Prime Minister when he or she wants to meet colleagues in the Commons, and you don't need to know much about the decor, because it is predictable.

Think of loads of green leather, and brass studs, and heavy coarse-grained oak panelling and Pugin wallpaper and a few prints, slightly squiffily hung. And think smoke—because we are talking about the afternoon of 28 May 1940, and in those days many politicians—including our subject—were indefatigable consumers of tobacco.

It is safe to assume there wasn't much daylight getting through the mullioned windows, but most members of the public would easily have been able to recognise the main characters. There were seven of them in all, and they were the War Cabinet of Britain.

It is a measure of the depth of their crisis that they had been meeting almost solidly for three days. This was their ninth meeting since 26 May, and they had yet to come up with an answer to the existential question that faced them and the world.

In the chair was the Prime Minister, Winston Churchill. On one side was Neville Chamberlain, the high-collared, stiff-necked and toothbrush-moustached ex–Prime Minister, and the man Churchill had unceremoniously replaced. Rightly or wrongly, Chamberlain was blamed for fatally underestimating the Hitler menace, and for the failure of appeasement. When the Nazis had bundled Britain out of Norway earlier that month, it was Chamberlain who took the rap.

Then there was Lord Halifax, the tall, cadaverous Foreign Secretary who had been born with a withered left hand that he concealed in a black glove. There was Archibald Sinclair, the leader of the Liberal Party that Churchill had dumped. There were Clement Attlee and Arthur Greenwood—representatives of the Labour Party against which he had directed some of his most hysterical invective. There was the Cabinet Secretary, Sir Edward Bridges, taking notes.

The question before the meeting was very simple, and one they had been chewing over for the last few days, as the news got blacker and blacker. No one exactly spelled it out, but everyone could see what it was. Should Britain fight? Was it reasonable for young British troops to die in a war that showed every sign of being lost? Or should the British do some kind of deal that might well save hundreds of thousands of lives?

And if a deal had been done then, and the war had effectively ended with the British exit, might it have been a deal to save the lives of millions around the world?

I don't think many people of my generation—let alone my children's generation—are fully conscious of how close we came to it; how Britain could have discreetly, and rationally, called it quits in 1940. There were serious and influential voices who wanted to begin 'negotiations'.

It is not hard to see why they thought as they did. The news from France was not just bad: it was unbelievably bad, and there did not seem the slightest hope that it would improve. German forces were lunging towards Paris, buffeting aside the French defences with such contemptuous ease that it really looked as if they belonged to some new military master race, pumped with superior zeal and efficiency. Hitler's panzers had surged not just through the Low Countries but through the supposedly impenetrable ravines of the Ardennes; the ludicrous Maginot Line had been bypassed.

The French generals cut pathetic figures—white-haired dodderers in their Clouseau-like kepis. Every time they fell back to some new line of defence, they found that the Germans were somehow already there; and then the Stuka dive-bombers would come down like banshees and the tanks would drive on again.

The British Expeditionary Force had been cut off in a pocket around the Channel ports. They had tried briefly to counter-attack; they had been repulsed, and now they were waiting to be evacuated at Dunkirk. If Hitler had listened to his generals, he could have smashed us then: sent the ace general Guderian and his tanks into the shrinking and virtually defenceless patch of ground. He could have killed or captured the bulk of Britain's fighting forces, and deprived this country of the physical ability to resist.

As it was, his Luftwaffe was strafing the beaches; British troops were floating in the water face down; they were firing their Lee En-fields hopelessly at the sky; they were being chopped to bits by the dive-bombers. At that moment, on 28 May, it seemed very possible—to generals and politicians, if not to the wider public—that the bulk of the troops could be lost.

The War Cabinet was staring at the biggest humiliation for British armed forces since the loss of the American colonies, and there seemed no way back. It chills the marrow to look at the map of Europe as it must have appeared to that War Cabinet.

Austria had been engulfed two years earlier; Czechoslovakia was no more; Poland had been crushed; and in the last few weeks Hitler had added a shudder-making list to his portfolio of conquest. He had taken Norway—effortlessly outwitting the British, Churchill included, who had spent months elaborating a doomed plan to pre-empt him. He had captured Denmark in little more than four hours.

Holland had surrendered; the Belgian King had pusillanimously run up the white flag at midnight the previous evening; and with every hour that went by more French forces surrendered—sometimes after resistance of insane bravery; sometimes with a despairing and fatalistic ease.

The most important geostrategic consideration of May 1940 was that Britain—the British Empire—was alone. There was no realistic prospect of help, or certainly no imminent prospect. The Italians were against us. The fascist leader Mussolini had entered into a 'Pact of Steel' with Hitler, and—when it looked as though Hitler couldn't lose—would shortly join the war on his side.

The Russians had signed the nauseating Molotov–Ribbentrop pact, by which they had agreed to carve up Poland with the Nazis. The Americans were allergic to any more European wars, under-standably: they had lost more than 56,000 men in the First World War, and more than 100,000 if you include the toll from influenza.

They were offering nothing much more than murmurs of distant sympathy, and for all Churchill's wishful rhetoric there was no sign of the US cavalry coming tooting over the brow of the hill.

Everyone in that room could imagine the consequences of fighting on. They knew all about war; some of them had fought in the Great War, and the hideous memory of that slaughter was only twenty-two years old—less distant in time from them than the first Gulf War is from us today.

There was scarcely a family in Britain that had not been touched by sorrow. Was it right—was it fair—to ask the people to go through all that again? And to what end?

It seems from the cabinet minutes that the meeting more or less kicked off with Halifax. He went straight to the point: the argument he had been making for the last few days.

He was an impressive figure. He was tall, very tall; at 6 foot 5 he loomed about ten inches above Churchill—though I suppose that advantage matters less around a table. He was an Etonian and an academic star, with the domed forehead that seemed fitting in a prize fellow of All Souls. (Churchill, don't forget, had not even been to university, and got into Sandhurst only on the third attempt.) To judge by the evidence of contemporary footage, Halifax spoke in a low and melodious sort of voice, though with the clipped enunciation of his time and class. He looked through thickish round glasses, and he perhaps raised his right hand, lightly clenched, to make his case.

The Italian embassy had sent a message, he said: that this was Britain's moment to seek mediation via Italy. The information came via Sir Robert Vansittart—and that was a clever name to invoke, since Sir Robert Vansittart was a diplomat who was known to be ferociously anti-German and against the appeasement of Hitler. The message was therefore as delicately and appetisingly wrapped as possible, but the meaning was naked.

This was not just a simple overture from Mussolini: it was surely a signal from his senior partner. Coiling itself round Whitehall and penetrating the heart of the House of Commons, it was a feeler from Hitler. Churchill knew exactly what was going on. He was aware that the despairing French Prime Minister was in town—and indeed had just had lunch with Halifax.

M. Paul Reynaud knew that France was beaten; he knew in his heart what his British interlocutors could scarcely believe—that the French were possessed of an origami army: they just kept folding with almost magical speed. Reynaud knew that he was going to be remembered as one of the most abject figures in the history of France; and he believed that if he could persuade the British also to enter negotiations, that humiliation would be shared and palliated— and above all he might win better terms for France.

So that was the message: conveyed by the Italians, supported by the French, and originating from the German dictator: that Britain should see sense and come to an arrangement with reality. We don't know exactly the words with which Churchill replied; all we have is the laconic and possibly sanitised summary of Sir Edward Bridges. We don't know precisely how the Prime Minister appeared to his colleagues that afternoon, but we can have a pretty good guess.

Contemporary accounts say Churchill was by now showing signs of fatigue. He was sixty-five, and he was driving his staff and his generals to distraction by his habit of working on into the small hours— fuelled by brandy and liqueurs—ringing round Whitehall for papers and information, and actually convening meetings when most sane men were tucked up with their wives.

He was dressed in his strange Victorian/Edwardian garb, with his black waistcoat and gold watch chain and his spongebag trousers— like some burly and hungover butler from the set of *Downton Abbey*.

They say he was pale, and pasty, and that seems believable. Let us add a cigar, and some ash on his lap, and a clenched jaw with a spot of drool.

He told Halifax to forget it. As the minutes put it: 'The Prime Minister said that it was clear that the French purpose was to see Signor Mussolini acting as intermediary between ourselves and Herr Hitler. He was determined not to get into this position.'

He understood exactly what the offer implied. Britain was at war with Germany, and had been since 1 September the previous year. It was a war for freedom and for principle—to protect Britain and the empire from an odious tyranny, and if possible to repel the German armies from the subjugated states. To enter 'talks' with Hitler or his emissaries, to enter 'negotiations', to get round the table for any kind of discussion—it all meant the same.

The minute Britain accepted some Italian offer of mediation, Churchill knew that the sinews of resistance would relax. A white flag would be invisibly raised over Britain, and the will to fight on would be gone.

So he said no to Halifax, and some may feel that ought to have been enough: the Prime Minister had spoken in a matter of national life or death; in another country, the debate might therefore have been at an end. But that is not how the British constitution works: the Prime Minister is *primus inter pares*—first among equals; he must to some extent carry his colleagues with him; and to understand the dynamics of that conversation we must remember the fragility of Churchill's position.

He had been Prime Minister for less than three weeks, and it was far from clear who were his real allies round the table. Attlee and Greenwood, the Labour contingent, were broadly supportive— Greenwood perhaps more than Attlee; and the same can be said for

Sinclair the Liberal. But their voices could not be decisive. The Tories were by some way the largest party in Parliament. It was the Tories on whom he depended for his mandate—and the Tories were far from sure about Winston Churchill.

From his very emergence as a young Tory MP he had bashed and satirised his own party; he had then deserted them for the Liberals, and though he had eventually returned to the fold, there were too many Tories who thought of him as an unprincipled opportunist. Only a few days earlier the Tory benches had conspicuously cheered for Chamberlain, when he entered the Chamber, and were muted in their welcome for Churchill. Now he was sitting with two powerful Tories—Chamberlain himself, Lord President of the Council, and Edward Wood, First Earl of Halifax and Foreign Secretary.

Both men had clashed with Churchill in the past. Both had reason to regard him as not just volcanic in his energies, but (to their way of thinking) irrational and positively dangerous.

As Chancellor of the Exchequer, Churchill had deeply irritated Chamberlain with his plan to cut business rates—which Chamberlain thought would unfairly curb the revenues of Tory local government—to say nothing of the systematic monstering Churchill had given Chamberlain, for months and years, over the failure to stand up to Hitler. As for Halifax, he had been viceroy of India in the 1930s, and borne the brunt of what he saw as Churchill's bombastic and blimpish opposition to anything that smacked of Indian independence.

Then there was a further aspect to Halifax's political position that gave him—in those grim May days—an unspoken authority, even over Churchill. Chamberlain had sustained his fatal wound on 8 May, when large numbers of Tories refused to back him in the Norway debate; and in that key meeting of 9 May, it was Halifax who had been the departing Prime Minister's choice. Chamberlain had wanted Halifax. King George VI wanted Halifax. Many in the Labour Party, in the House of Lords, and above all on the Tory benches would have preferred to see Halifax as Prime Minister.

In fact the only reason Churchill had finally got the nod was because Halifax—following a ghastly two-minute silence after Chamberlain offered him the job—had ruled himself out of contention; not just because it would be hard to command the government from the unelected House of Lords, but as he explicitly said, because he didn't see how he would be able to cope with Winston Churchill rolling around untethered on the quarterdeck.

Still, it must give a man a certain confidence to think he had momentarily been the King's preferred choice as Prime Minister. In spite of Churchill's clear opposition, Halifax now returned to the fray. What he offered was, with hindsight, shameful.

The gist of it was that we should enter a negotiation with the Italians, with the blessing of Hitler, at which our opening gambit would be the surrender of various British assets—and though he did not spell these out in the meeting, they are thought to have been Malta, Gibraltar and a share of the running of the Suez Canal.

It says something for Halifax's nerve that he felt able to offer this to Churchill as a course of action. Reward aggression by entering talks? Hand over British possessions to a ludicrous jut-jawed and jackbooted tyrant like Mussolini?

Churchill repeated his objections. The French were trying to get us on a 'slippery slope' towards talks with Hitler and capitulation. We would be in a much stronger position, he argued, once the Germans had tried and failed to invade.

But Halifax came back again: we would get better terms now, before France had gone out of the war—before the Luftwaffe had come over and destroyed our aircraft factories.

It makes one cringe, now, to read poor Halifax's defeatism; and we need to understand and to forgive his wrong-headedness. He has been the object of character assassination ever since the July 1940 publication of the book *Guilty Men*, Michael Foot's philippic against appeasement.

Halifax had been over to see Hitler in 1937—and though he at one stage (rather splendidly) mistook the Führer for a footman, we must concede that he had an embarrassing familiarity with Goering. Both men loved fox-hunting, and Goering nicknamed him 'Halali-fax'—with emetic chumminess—because *halali* is a German hunting cry. But it is nonsense to think of him as some kind of apologist for Nazi Germany, or a fifth columnist within the British government. In his own way, Halifax was a patriot as much as Churchill.

He thought he could see a way to protect Britain and to safeguard the empire, and to save lives; and it is not as if he was alone. The British ruling class was riddled—or at least conspicuously weevilled—with appeasers and pro-Nazis. It wasn't just the Mitfords, or the followers of Britain's home-grown would-be *duce*, fascist leader Sir Oswald Mosley.

In 1936 Lady Nelly Cecil noted that nearly all of her relatives were 'tender to the Nazis', and the reason was simple. In the 1930s your average toff was much more fearful of Bolshevism, and communists' alarming ideology of redistribution, than they were fearful of Hitler. Indeed, they saw fascism as a bulwark against the reds, and they had high-level political backing.

David Lloyd George had been to Germany, and been so dazzled by the Führer that he compared him to George Washington. Hitler was a 'born leader', declared the befuddled former British Prime Minister. He wished that Britain had 'a man of his supreme quality at the head of affairs in our country today'. This from the hero of the First World War! The man who had led Britain to victory over the Kaiser!

Now the snowy-haired Welsh wizard had been himself bewitched, and Churchill's former mentor had become an out-and-out defeatist. It wasn't so very long ago that the media had been singing the same tune. The *Daily Mail* had long been campaigning for Hitler to be given a free hand in eastern Europe, the better to beat up the bolshies. 'If Hitler did not exist,' said the *Mail*, 'all western Europe might now be clamouring for such a champion.'

*The Times* had been so pro-appeasement that the editor, Geoffrey Dawson, described how he used to go through the proofs taking out anything that might offend the Germans. The press baron Beaverbrook himself had actually sacked Churchill from his *Evening Standard* column, on the grounds that he was too hard on the Nazis. Respectable liberal opinion—theatre types like John Gielgud, Sybil Thorndike, G. B. Shaw—were lobbying for the government to 'give consideration' to talks.

Of course, the mood had changed in the last year; feelings against Germany had unsurprisingly hardened and grown much more widespread. All we are saying—in mitigation of Halifax—is that in seeking peace, he had the support of many British people, at all levels of society. And so the argument went on, between Halifax and the Prime Minister, for that crucial hour.

Outside it was a warm and gorgeous May day; the chestnut candles were out in St James's Park. Inside it was a game of ping-pong.

Churchill told Halifax that any negotiation with Hitler was a trap that would put Britain at his mercy; Halifax said he couldn't understand what was so wrong with the French suggestion.

Chamberlain and Greenwood both chipped in with the (useless) observation that both options—fighting on and entering negotiations—were risky.

As it got to five o'clock, Halifax said that nothing in his suggestion could be remotely described as ultimate capitulation.

Churchill said that the chances of Britain being offered decent terms were a thousand to one against.

It was a stalemate; and it was now—according to most historians—that Churchill played his masterstroke. He announced that the meeting would be adjourned, and would begin again at 7 p.m. He then convened the full cabinet of twenty-five, ministers from every department—many of whom were to hear him as Prime Minister for the first time. Consider his position.

He could not persuade Halifax, and nor could he simply crush or ignore him. Only the previous day the Foreign Secretary had been so bold as to accuse him of talking 'frightful rot'. If Halifax resigned, Churchill's position would be weak: it was hardly as if his first efforts as war leader had been crowned with triumph—the Norway campaign, for which he was overwhelmingly responsible, had been a considerable fiasco.

The appeal to reason had failed. But the bigger the audience, the more fervid the atmosphere; and now he made an appeal to the emotions. Before the full cabinet he made a quite astonishing speech—without any hint of the intellectual restraint he had been obliged to display in the smaller meeting. It was time for 'frightful rot' on steroids.

The best account we have is from the diary of Hugh Dalton, the Minister of Economic Warfare, and there seems to be no reason not to trust it. Churchill began calmly enough.

I have thought carefully in these last days whether it was part of my duty to consider entering into negotiations with That Man [Hitler].

But it [is] idle to think that, if we tried to make peace now, we should get better terms than if we fought it out. The Germans would demand our fleet—that would be called disarmament—our naval bases, and much else.

We should become a slave state, though a British Government which would be Hitler's puppet would be set up—under Mosley or some such person. And where should we be at the end of all that? On the other side we have immense reserves and advantages.

He ended with this almost Shakespearean climax:

And I am convinced that every one of you would rise up and tear me down from my place if I were for one moment to contemplate parley or surrender. If this long island story of ours is to end at last, let it end only when each one of us lies choking in his own blood upon the ground.

At this the men in that room were so moved—according both to Dalton and to Leo Amery—that they cheered and shouted, and some of them ran round and clapped him on the back. Churchill had ruthlessly dramatised and personalised the debate.

It was not some diplomatic minuet. It was a choice between protecting their country or dying, choking in their own blood. It was an eve-of-battle speech, and it appealed to them in some primeval and tribal way. By the time the War Cabinet resumed at 7 p.m., the debate was over; Halifax abandoned his cause. Churchill had the clear and noisy backing of the cabinet.

Within a year of that decision—to fight and not to negotiate—30,000 British men, women and children had been killed, almost all of them at German hands. Weighing up those alternatives—a humiliating peace, or a slaughter of the innocents—it is hard to imagine any modern British politician having the guts to take Churchill's line.

Even in 1940, there was no one else who could conceivably have given that kind of leadership—not Attlee, not Chamberlain, not Lloyd George, and certainly not the most serious alternative, the 3rd Viscount Halifax.

Churchill punningly nicknamed Halifax the 'Holy Fox', partly because he was churchy, and partly because he loved riding to hounds, but mainly because he had a mind of foxy subtlety. But if the fox knew many things, Churchill knew one big thing.

He was willing to pay that butcher's bill, because he actually saw more clearly than Halifax. He had the vast and almost reckless moral courage to see that fighting on would be appalling, but that surrender would be even worse. He was right. To understand why, let us imagine May 1940 without him.

# CHAPTER 2

# THE
# NON-CHURCHILL
# UNIVERSE

L et's go back to that moment on 24 May 1940, when Heinz Guderian, one of the most audacious tank commanders in history,
is on the verge of an extraordinary triumph. After vicious fighting,
his panzers have crossed the Aa canal in northern France. They pause
in their exertions, their engines pinking gently in the sun, and Guderian prepares for a final assault on the British.

His prey is now less than twenty miles away—the 400,000 men of
the British Expeditionary Force: flinching, fearful, bracing themselves for the ignominy of surrender. All Guderian needs to do is
rev up those mighty Maybach engines, plunge onwards towards
Dunkirk, and the British army will be shattered. Back home, the islanders' ability to resist will be gone. And then he gets a message
from Berlin—a decision that he will later denounce as a disaster.

For reasons that are not entirely clear, Hitler wants him to stop; to
wait; and in an ecstasy of frustration, Guderian obeys. For the next

few days—because the evacuation is agonisingly slow—the British jugular is pitifully exposed, pulsing beneath the Nazi knife.

In this horrific context, the British War Cabinet ponders what to do: to deal, or to fight. Now let us take Churchill out of the equation.

Let's send down one of those giant Monty Python hands and pluck him from the smoke-filled room. Let us suppose that he'd copped it as a young man, on one of those many occasions when he had set out so boisterously to cheat death. Let's imagine that his preposterous luck had run out years earlier, and that he had been skewered by a Dervish spear or plugged by a ten-rupee jezail or that he had crashed one of his rope-and-canvas flying machines or died in the trenches.

We leave the fate of Britain and the world in the hands of Halifax, Chamberlain and the representatives of the Labour and Liberal parties. Would they have treated with Hitler, as the Foreign Secretary was proposing? It seems overwhelmingly likely.

Chamberlain was already physically feeble, and was to die of cancer only a few months later: and the whole purpose of his removal from the Premiership was that it was impossible to see him as a war leader. Halifax's position we know: he wanted to negotiate. The others had neither the parliamentary clout nor the bellicose flair to lead the country, in defiance of Hitler, at a moment of terrifying danger.

It was Churchill—and only Churchill—who had made resistance to the Nazis his political mission. There was a sense in which his objections to Halifax were selfish.

He was fighting for his political life and credibility, and if he gave in to Halifax he was finished. His prestige, his reputation, his prospects, his ego—all those things that matter to politicians—were engaged in the cause of fighting on; and this has led some historians to make the mistake of thinking that it was all about him, and not about the British interest.

In the last few years there has erupted an unsightly rash of revisionist accounts, suggesting that Britain should indeed have done what so many people—in all walks of society—were hoping and praying for: struck a bargain with Nazi Germany. The argument goes that the British Empire and the Nazi Reich were capable of peaceful coexistence—and there is no doubt that Hitler had said plenty of things to encourage that idea.

In the 1930s he had sent Ribbentrop over to schmooze the Establishment, and with considerable success. In 1938 Halifax was allegedly so incautious as to declare to Hitler's adjutant that he would 'like to see as the culmination of my work the Führer entering London at the side of the English king amid the acclamation of the English people'.

As we have seen, there were members of the upper and middle classes who had exhibited an unfortunate feeling for Hitlerism—including the former monarch, Edward VIII. And even now, in these evil days of 1940, Hitler would sometimes proclaim his admiration for the British Empire, and his view that it was not in Germany's interest to crush Britain—since that would only benefit rival powers, such as America, Japan and Russia.

We English were also members of the Aryan race, we gathered—though perhaps not as genetically special as the Teutonic variant. Britain and her empire could survive as a sort of junior partner—full of historical interest but fundamentally effete: the Greeks to the Nazi Rome.

Many thought that indignity a price worth paying for the preservation of the empire, and to avert slaughter. It was not just that people wanted a deal with Hitler: many thought it was inevitable.

The French did: Admiral Darlan of the French fleet was convinced that Britain would lose, and in 1940 he prepared to join forces with Germany.

So did many Americans: the ambassador of the day was the

egregious Irish-American Joe Kennedy: bootlegger, crook and father of JFK. He was endlessly requesting meetings with Hitler and sending lip-smackingly gloomy messages to Washington. 'Democracy is finished in England,' he proclaimed towards the end of 1940, shortly before he was recalled.

He was wrong, of course, just as Halifax was wrong, and the appeasers were wrong, and all the revisionists are wrong today. But to do battle with their nonsense, we have to try to understand what might have happened if their wishes had come true.

I am always nervous of 'counterfactual' history, since it strikes me that the so-called chain of causation is never really clear. Events aren't like billiard balls, with one obviously propelling the next—and even billiards can be deceptive.

Take out one spillikin from the heap of factors, and you can never tell how the rest will fall. But of all the 'what ifs' of history, this is about the most popular. Some of our best modern historians have conducted this thought experiment—and they overwhelmingly reach the same conclusion: that if you end British resistance in 1940, you create the conditions for an irredeemable disaster in Europe.

Hitler would almost certainly have won. That is, he would have been able to launch Operation Barbarossa—the attack on Russia—much earlier than June 1941. He would not have had those pesky Brits causing trouble for him in the Mediterranean and in the North African desert, and tying up men and weapons.

He would have been able to direct his full fury at Russia—as he had always intended when, fingers crossed behind his back, he agreed to the Nazi–Soviet pact—and he would almost certainly have pulled it off, before the campaign was reduced to a frozen hell. As it was, the achievements of the Wehrmacht were astonishing: they captured millions of square miles and millions of men. They captured Stalingrad and reached the outer stations of the Moscow metro.

Imagine if they had captured Moscow, decapitated the communist regime, and sent Stalin into a funk from which he did not recover (he had already had a nervous collapse when the German tanks rolled across his frontier).

Historians have envisaged the swift implosion of the communist tyranny—assisted, perhaps, by middle-class victims of collectivisation—and the installation of some pro-Nazi puppet regime. And then what?

Hitler and Himmler and the rest of the satanic crew would have been able to use this vast canvas—from the Atlantic to the Urals—to paint their hideous fantasies of government. With Britain out, there was no one to stop them, no one to interrupt them, no one with even the moral standing to denounce them.

In America, the isolationists would have won: if Britain wasn't going to risk the lives of its people, why should they? In Berlin, Albert Speer would have got on with his deranged plans for a new world capital, to be called Germania.

At its heart was to be the Hall of the People—a demented granite version of the Pantheon of Agrippa; a building so vast that you could fit the dome of London's St Paul's through the oculus—the circular hole at the top of the dome. It was intended to seat 100,000 people, and the chanting and the shouting were expected to be so prodigious that they were planning for rainfall in the building itself, as the warm exhalations rose, condensed, and precipitated on the heads of the fervent crowds of fascists.

This nightmarish structure was surmounted by a mammoth eagle, so that the whole thing looked a bit like some cosmic Prussian helmet 290 metres high—almost as tall as the Shard skyscraper in Southwark; and around it radiated other vast symbols of dominance: an arch twice the size of the Arc de Triomphe; colossal railway stations from which double-decker trains would zoom at 190 kmh, conveying

German settlers to the Caspian and the Urals and the other tracts of eastern Europe from which the Slavic *Untermenschen* had been expelled.

The whole European landmass, with the exception of Switzerland (though there was a secret plan to invade that, too), was to consist either of the Reich or of client fascist states. As many counterfactual novelists have spotted, there were all sorts of plans to convert the territory into a sinister edition of the European Union.

In 1942, the Reich economics minister and president of the Reichsbank, Dr Walter Funk, wrote a paper calling for a Europäische Wirtschaftsgesellschaft—a European Common Market. He proposed a single currency, a central bank, a common agricultural policy, and other familiar ideas. Ribbentrop proposed a similar-sounding scheme, though, to be fair, Hitler opposed this on the ground that it wasn't sufficiently beastly to the rest of the Nazi European Union.

In this Gestapo-controlled Nazi EU, the authorities would have been free to pursue their hateful racist ideology. The Nazis had begun their persecutions in the 1930s, and long before Churchill came to power—before the decision to fight on—they were moving populations of Jews and Poles.

They were creating ghettos near railway hubs as a prelude to 'deportation'—and as Eichmann later admitted at his trial, deportation meant liquidation. Unchecked and for the main part uncriticised, the Nazis would have got on with the job of massacring those of whom they disapproved—Jews, gypsies, homosexuals, the mentally unsound and the disabled.

They would have let their imaginations roam as they performed their experiments on human flesh: horrible, detached, inhuman and arrogant beyond belief. When Winston Churchill spoke later that summer of 1940 about Europe sinking into 'the abyss of a new Dark

Age, made more sinister and perhaps more protracted by the lights of perverted science', he was exactly right.

That is the most likely alternative world, then; but even if Hitler had not succeeded in Russia—even if Stalin had beaten back his assault—would life have been much better?

We would have been looking at a division of Europe between two forms of totalitarianism: on one side a world terrorised by the KGB or the Stasi; on the other side the subjects of the Gestapo—everywhere a population that lived in fear of the knock in the night, arbitrary arrest, the camps, and no way to protest.

Of the roughly two hundred countries in the world today, about 120 can claim to be democracies of some kind or other—to uphold the right of voters to determine their own fate. Most of the world pays at least lip-service to the idea that democracy is, as Churchill once put it, the worst system of government in the world, except for all the others. But if Hitler and Stalin had prevailed—or if one or the other had prevailed—does anyone seriously believe that democracy would be on her throne today?

With their superstitious habit of imputing justice and rightness to the course of history, human beings would have absorbed a dismal lesson: that the gods had smiled on the tyrannies, and that tyranny was therefore what our incompetent species required.

We in Britain would have acquiesced in this moral bankruptcy—and it is all too easy to imagine how Halifax (or Lloyd George, or whoever) could have persuaded the electorate that this was the peace they were yearning for—and yet there, surely, they would have been kidding themselves.

Do you think that by this cowardice Britain could have bought peace from the Nazis? As Churchill pointed out to the War Cabinet, any deal struck with Hitler must mean disarmament of the fleet, and a fatal weakening of Britain's long-term ability to defend herself or to fight back.

And the crucial point was surely this: that there was no deal with Hitler that could conceivably be relied upon. Churchill had been proved crushingly right in his warnings about Nazism—made since the early 1930s, when he had been out to Germany to see the parades of gleaming-eyed youths. In countless newspaper articles and speeches he had identified a spiritual evil that so many others chose not to see: the fundamental revanchism and aggression of the Nazi regime. Now he had been massively vindicated, about the Rhineland, and about Czechoslovakia, about Poland and about the desperate need for Britain to rearm.

Many counterfactual historians have pointed out that the Nazis were a long way ahead of their rivals in developing some of the most lethal weapons of the twentieth century: they had the first jet fighters; they had the first rocket-propelled missiles. Imagine if those German scientists had been so desperate to defeat the Soviets that they had been the first to produce an atomic weapon.

Think of that fate for Britain, all you who are tempted by the revisionist argument, you who secretly wonder whether the country might have done better to do a deal. Britain would have been alone, facing a hostile continent united under a bestial totalitarianism, and with nuclear-armed rockets bristling on the V2 launching pads at Peenemünde. It would have been a new slavery, or worse.

Hitler didn't tell Guderian to stop his tanks on the Aa canal because he was some closet Anglophile. He didn't stay his hand because of some fellow-feeling for those of the Aryan race. Most serious historians agree with Guderian: that the Führer simply made a mistake—that he was himself taken aback by the speed of his conquest, and feared a counter-attack.

The truth is that he saw Britain not as a potential partner, but as the enemy, and though he sometimes burbled approvingly of the British Empire, he also called for the complete annihilation of British forces. He didn't call off his extensive plans to invade Britain (Operation 'Sea Lion') because he wanted in some way to spare the British.

He did so because it had become too risky, and because one man was telling the rest of the country to fight on the beaches and the hills and the landing grounds, and was even telling his own cabinet that rather than surrender he would die choking in his own blood upon the ground.

Hitler's Operation Sea Lion was a project not just of invasion but of subjugation. He was going to carry off Nelson's column from Trafalgar Square, and install it in Berlin. Goering had plans to pillage the entire collection from the National Gallery. They were even going—infamy of infamies—to send the Elgin Marbles back to Nazi-controlled Athens. The Nazis had already drawn up a blacklist of British figures who were known to be particularly anti-Nazi, who would presumably have been either imprisoned or shot; and at one stage Himmler proposed killing or enslaving 80 per cent of the British population.

Such were the potential fruits of the deal that Halifax offered. Not only would the British have been complicit in the totalitarian tyranny that was to engulf Europe; it seems at least possible, if not likely, that they would eventually have been overrun themselves.

If Britain had done a deal in 1940—and this is the final and most important point—then there would have been no liberation of the continent. The country would not have been a haven of resistance, but a gloomy client state of an infernal Nazi EU.

There would have been no Polish soldiers training with the British army, there would have been no Czech airmen with the RAF, there would have been no Free French waiting and hoping for an end to their national shame.

Above all there would have been no Lend-Lease, no liberty ships, no Churchillian effort to woo America away from isolationism; and of course there would have been no prospect of D-Day, no heroism and sacrifice at Omaha Beach, no hope that the new world would come with all its power and might to rescue and liberate the old.

The Americans would never have entered that European conflict, if Britain had been so mad and so wrong as to do a deal in 1940. It is incredible to look back and see how close we came, and how well supported the idea was.

I don't know whether it is right to think of history as running on train tracks, but let us think of Hitler's story as one of those huge and unstoppable double-decker expresses that he had commissioned, howling through the night with its cargo of German settlers.

Think of that locomotive, whizzing towards final victory. Then think of some kid climbing the parapet of the railway bridge and dropping the crowbar that jams the points and sends the whole en-terprise for a gigantic burton—a mangled, hissing heap of metal. Winston Churchill was the crowbar of destiny. If he hadn't been where he was, and put up resistance, that Nazi train would have car-ried right on. It was something of a miracle—given his previous career—that he was there at all.

CHAPTER 3

# ROGUE ELEPHANT

These days it is probably fair to say that thrusting young Tories—and especially males—will regard Winston Churchill as a sort of divinity. These honest fellows may sport posters on their teenage bedroom walls: Churchill in a pinstripe suit and toting a tommy gun, or just giving two fingers to the Hun.

On entering university they may join Churchill Societies or Churchill Dining Clubs that meet in Churchill Rooms where his portrait grimly endures their port-fuelled yacketing. They may even wear spotty bow ties.

When they make it to Parliament they piously trail their fingers on the left toecap of the bronze effigy that stands in the Members' Lobby—hoping to receive some psychic charge before they are called on to speak. When they in due course become Tory Prime Minister, and they find themselves in a bit of a corner (as inevitably happens), they will discover that they can make a defiant speech in St Stephen's Club, where the cameras will capture them in the same frame as the image of the old war leader—pink, prognathous and pouting down at his successor with what we can only assume is pride.

The Tories are jealous of their relation with Churchill. It is a question of badging, of political ownership. They think of him as the people of Parma think of the *formaggio parmigiano*.

He is their biggest cheese, their prize possession, the World-Cup-winning hat-trick-scorer and greatest ever captain of the Tory team. So I wonder sometimes whether people are fully aware of the suspicion and doubt with which he was greeted by Tories when he became Prime Minister in 1940—or the venom with which they spat his name.

To lead his country in war, Churchill had to command not just the long-faced men of Munich—Halifax and Chamberlain—but hundreds of Tories who had been conditioned to think of him as an opportunist, a turncoat, a blowhard, an egotist, a rotter, a bounder, a cad, and on several well-attested occasions a downright drunk.

We have seen how they cheered for Chamberlain, and only murmured for Churchill, when he entered the Commons for the first time as PM on 13 May 1940 (an event that rattled Churchill: 'I shan't last long,' he said as he left the Chamber). They sustained their hostility. From his seat in the parliamentary press gallery, Paul Einzig, the correspondent of the *Financial News*, was able to study the Tories—and he could see the ill-will that formed above them like a vapour.

For at least two months after he took office Einzig recorded that Tory MPs would sit in 'sullen silence' when he rose to speak, even after he had completed one of his historic speeches. When the Labour benches cheered, the Tories were still plotting to get rid of him. On about 13 May, William Spens, the chairman of the 1922 Committee of Tory backbenchers, said that three-quarters of his members were willing to give Churchill the heave-ho and put Chamberlain back.

From about the same time we have a letter from Nancy Dugdale, the wife of a Chamberlainite MP, that sums up the mood of fastidious horror. She wrote to her husband, Tommy Dugdale, who was already serving in the armed forces:

> WC they regard with complete distrust, as you know, and they hate his boasting broadcasts. WC really is the counterpart of Goering in England, full of the desire for blood, Blitzkrieg, and bloated with ego and over-feeding, the same treachery running through his veins, punctuated by heroics and hot air. I can't tell you how depressed I feel about it.

In the view of these respectable folk the Churchillians were nothing but 'gangsters'. They were men like Bob Boothby, MP, bisexual bounder and later a friend of the Kray twins; Brendan Bracken, the carrot-topped Irish fantasist and later proprietor of the *Financial Times*; Max Beaverbrook, the deeply unreliable proprietor of the Express group: all together a rabble of disloyal and self-seeking 'glamour boys' led by a 'rogue elephant'. They tut-tutted about Churchill's drinking ('I wish he didn't give the impression of having *done himself too well*,' said Maurice Hankey, a senior civil servant, his nose almost visibly twitching) but not out of some zeal for temperance—more because they enjoyed the feeling of moral disapproval.

Some of the most virulent anti-Churchillians went on to have great careers: had he not been knifed by Harold Macmillan in the 1960s, Rab Butler might have been Prime Minister. In 1940 he was a junior minister, and a strong supporter of appeasement. Here is what he had to say about the ascent of Churchill:

'The good clean tradition of English politics has been sold to the greatest adventurer of modern political history,' he was heard to say. 'Surrendering to Winston and his rabble was a disaster and an unnecessary one', mortgaging the future of the country to a 'half-breed

American whose main support was that of inefficient but talkative people of a similar type'.

That is strong stuff. You can understand why people might have felt loyalty to Chamberlain, widely seen as an honourable man, who was actually polling ahead of Churchill among the public in early 1940; you can see that they felt disconcerted by the arrival of the Churchill gang—in what was effectively a palace coup; Churchill wasn't actually elected Prime Minister, by the public at large, until 1951. But there is a fascinating malevolence about some of the language.

Lord Halifax deplored the experience of listening to Churchill's voice, which 'oozes with port, brandy and the chewed cigar'. One observer stated that he looked like a 'fat baby' as he swung his legs on the government front bench, and tried not to laugh at Chamberlain's struggle.

So that was what the Respectable Tories thought of Winston S. Churchill: a Goering, an adventurer, a half-breed, a traitor, a fat baby and a disaster for the country. It is like the shrieking from the ballroom when a pirate comes on the tannoy from the bridge.

How to explain this hysterical rejection of our greatest twentieth-century hero?

From the strictly Tory point of view I am afraid it is all too understandable. In the course of his forty-year parliamentary career Churchill had shown a complete contempt for any notion of political fidelity, let alone loyalty to the Tory Party.

From the very moment when the bumptious and ginger-haired twenty-five-year-old entered Parliament in 1900—when Queen Victoria was still on the throne—he made disloyalty his watchword and his strategy for self-promotion. He bashed the Tory front bench for spending too much on defence ('Is there no poverty at home?' he asked). He bashed them over protection—then a left-wing cause, because it meant cheaper food for the working man. He peeved his elders so badly that at one stage the front bench all got up, as he began to speak, and stalked huffily from the Chamber.

By January 1904 he was facing the first Tory attempts to remove him as the official Conservative candidate for his Oldham constituency. By April he had already decided to switch parties—and he was pretty honest about his motives. He thought the Tories were heading for disaster. 'My prognostication', he said in October 1904, 'is that [the Tory leadership] will cut their own throats and bring their party to utter destruction . . . and that the Liberals will gain a gigantic victory at the Election.'

In other words he wasn't what people thought of as a man of principle; he was a glory-chasing goal-mouth-hanging opportunist. He crossed the floor of the House, sat down next to Lloyd George, and was deservedly called 'the Blenheim rat'.

He seemed to reciprocate the feeling. 'I am an English Liberal,' he now wrote. 'I hate the Tory party, their men and their methods.' A couple of decades later he of course switched back again—when his Liberal mount had more or less expired beneath him—in the niftiest piece of circus-style saddle-swapping ever seen in Parliament; and for much of the 1930s he lived up to his reputation by continuing to bash his own Tory Party leadership with whatever stick or knobkerry he could find, in a blatant attempt to advance his own cause.

No wonder there was scepticism on the Tory benches—and around the whole political world. If you were an anti-Churchillian in 1940, you had a long charge-sheet before you.

EVEN WHEN he was at Sandhurst, he was accused of nefarious deeds. First he and his fellow subalterns were charged with fixing their pony races. Then there was the rum business of poor Allan Bruce, a subaltern whom Churchill and his colleagues allegedly tried to freeze out of the regiment. There was even some suggestion (from Bruce) that Churchill had been engaged in practices of the Oscar Wilde variety—baseless allegations that were dismissed in an expensive libel suit brought by his mother; but mud has a way of sticking.

Then there was that dodgy affair in Pretoria, when he had escaped the Boers by breaking his parole and leaving his chums behind. As for his political career—my word, what a feast of bungling! If you were an anti-Churchillian you might start your prosecution by citing his handling, as Home Secretary, of the violent strikes of 1910–12. Actually, you could attack him from almost any perspective, since the Tories thought on the whole that he had been too wishy-washy with the strikers, while he entered Labour's demonology as the man who had 'fired on' unarmed miners in the Welsh town of Tonypandy—when in fact the police had used nothing more lethal than rolled-up mackintoshes.

Then in 1911 there was the farce of the Sidney Street siege, when he had gone down to take personal charge of an East End gun battle between the police and a mysterious gangster called 'Peter the Painter', who was never found and in fact may never have existed.

Churchill can be seen in the photographs of the event, peering round a corner in the direction of the supposed anarchist terrorists, and looking thoroughly conspicuous in a top hat.

'I understand what the photographer was doing,' a languid Balfour told the House of Commons, 'but what was the honourable gentleman doing?' Cue roars of laughter. The answer, as everyone knew, was that he was trying to get himself into the photograph.

This was nothing, though, to what an anti-Churchillian would see as his epic misjudgements during the First World War. First there was the Antwerp 'blunder' or 'fiasco' of October 1914, when Churchill had taken it into his head that Antwerp must be saved from the Germans and that he alone could save it.

For four or five days he masterminded the defences of the port, and even had nominal control of the whole of Belgium. One journalist captured the Napoleonic demeanour of this 'man enveloped in a cloak and wearing a yachting cap. He was tranquilly smoking a large cigar and looked at the progress of the battle under a rain of shrapnel . . . He smiled and looked satisfied.'

Antwerp surrendered shortly thereafter, and it became an accepted view that Churchill's intervention was a pointless ego-trip that rendered him—in the words of the *Morning Post*—'unfit for the office he now holds'. Unfit or not, he persisted in that office, First Lord of the Admiralty, long enough to engineer what an anti-Churchillian would say was an epic and unparalleled military disaster—a feat of incompetent generalship that made the Charge of the Light Brigade look positively slick. It was an attempt to outflank the stalemate on the Western Front that not only ended in humiliation for the British armed forces; it cost the lives of so many Australians and New Zealanders that to this day their 1915 expedition to Turkey is the number-one source of pom-bashing and general anti-British feeling among Antipodeans.

Gallipoli, or the Dardanelles, was perhaps the most pungent of all the charges against Churchill; and the memory would certainly have been strong enough in 1940 to infect people's feelings about him and whether or not he was the right man to lead the country in war. Even those who thought he was brilliant—and most people could see that—were often dismayed by his seeming lack of judgement, his tendency to hyperbole, to overexcitement, even to hysteria. In 1931 he became so worked up about the prospect of Indian independence that he called Mahatma Gandhi a 'half-naked fakir'—in words that have certainly not been forgotten in India.

He had misread public feeling in his attitudes towards the Abdication in 1936, seemingly taking the view that the King of England could marry whatever filly he damn well pleased, American divorcee or not, or else what was the point of being King? At one stage he was making a speech in defence of Edward VIII—who was, paradoxically, a pro-Nazi, and who would have presented all kinds of problems to Churchill had he remained on the throne—when he was howled down by his audience and lost control of the House.

His enemies detected in him a titanic egotism, a desire to find whatever wave or wavelet he could, and surf it long after it had dissolved into spume on the beach. When the anti-Churchillians heard him rail portentously about Hitler, and the dangers of German rearmament, they heard a man who had railed before and would rail again, and whose railings had just become part of the landscape— like the railings of Hyde Park.

We have to acknowledge that this reputation didn't just come from nowhere. There was a reason he was thought to be arrogant and 'unsound', and that was because to a certain extent it was true: he did behave with a death-defying self-belief, and go farther out on a limb than anyone else might have thought wise. And why did he behave in this way?

Throughout his early career he was not just held to be untrustworthy—he was thought to be congenitally untrustworthy. He had been born under a wonky star.

The other day I found myself in the very room, and looking at the very bed, where this momentous event had taken place. Down the corridor—several corridors, in fact—a huge party was getting under way to honour the sixtieth birthday of a twenty-first-century hedge fund king.

'Wait,' I said, as we were ushered towards the first phalanx of waitresses bearing champagne. 'Can you show us the room where Churchill was born?' A nice housekeeper led us down a side corridor, into a little square ground-floor room.

As the door closed, the noise faded—and it was possible to imagine that we had gone back 140 years, to the climax of another great party. You could screw up your eyes and see gaslights instead of electricity, but the same chintzy wallpaper, the same cheery little fire, the same bowls and ewers with the Marlborough crest.

I could see it perfectly in my mind's eye: the coats of the revellers hastily pushed off the bed, the ewers filled with hot water—and on the bed the sinuous shape of Jennie Churchill, too far gone in labour to try to make it upstairs. She was only twenty years old, but already famous as one of the most beautiful young women on the London scene.

Everyone had been out shooting all day, and by some accounts she had slipped and fallen earlier; others say that she had whirled too enthusiastically at the dancing. At 1.30 a.m. on 30 November 1874 she was delivered of a baby her husband described as 'wonderfully pretty and very healthy'.

To understand the psychological make-up of Winston Leonard Spencer-Churchill, we should be attentive to both the place and the time. The room was in the heart of Blenheim Palace—the superfluously colossal home of the Duke of Marlborough. This house has 186 rooms and the structure alone spreads over 7 acres (to say nothing of the lakes, mazes, columns, parkland, triumphal arches, etc.). It is the only non-royal or non-episcopal building in Britain that is called a palace.

Though it has its detractors it is for my money by far the greatest masterpiece of English baroque architecture—with its vast wings rising and falling in minutely symmetrical and wonderfully pointless parapets and finials of honey-coloured stone. Blenheim is an architectural statement, and that statement is: I am big; bigger and grander than anything you have ever seen.

It was given to one of Churchill's dynastic forebears, John Churchill, Duke of Marlborough, for what was seen as his excellent work in thrashing the French and helping to make eighteenth-century England top nation in Europe. Churchill was born there for the very good reason that it was his home: he was the grandson of the seventh Duke, nephew of the eighth Duke and the first cousin of the ninth Duke—and if that beloved cousin had not himself produced an heir, as seemed likely for quite some time, then Churchill would himself have been the Duke of Marlborough.

That is important: he was not just posh; he was ducal—and always at the forefront of his sense of self was the knowledge that he stood in dynastic succession to one of this country's greatest military heroes.

As for the time of his birth—well, that is also revealing; because it looks as though he appeared two months ahead of schedule, only seven months after the wedding. This has always raised eyebrows. Although it is possible that he was born prematurely, the simplest explanation is that he was in fact born at full term, but was conceived out of wedlock.

If that is so, it would not be surprising—because his parents, in their own way, were about as self-willed and unconventional as their son. Their most important contribution to civilisation is that they were both neglectful of the child.

His mother was the daughter of a successful American businessman called Leonard Jerome, a man who at one stage had a majority share in the *New York Times*, owned racehorses and an opera house and made love to female opera stars. Jennie had (allegedly) a small dragon tattooed on her wrist and (indubitably) a voluptuous hour-glass figure. She is credited with the invention of the Manhattan cocktail, and was so admired for her wit and her dark and 'panther-ine' good looks that she attracted scores of lovers, including the Prince of Wales. She eventually had three husbands, some of whom were younger than her son.

'She shone for me like the Evening star,' Churchill later wrote. 'I loved her dearly—but at a distance.' His letters from his schools are full of plaintive entreaties for love, money and visits. But it was his father who really moulded him—first by treating him abominably and then by dying prematurely.

When you read Randolph's letters to his son, you wonder what the poor kid had done to deserve it. He is told to drop the affectionate 'Papa'. 'Father' is better, says Randolph. He can't seem to remember whether his son is at Eton or Harrow, and prophesies that he will 'become a mere social wastrel, one of the hundreds of public school failures, and you will degenerate into a shabby unhappy and futile existence'.

Perhaps the most tragic example of Winston trying to please his father is the story of the watch. Randolph had given his son a new watch when he was a cadet at Sandhurst, and one day he lost it in a deep river pool. Churchill dived in repeatedly to get it, but was frustrated by the icy water. He then tried to dredge the river, and when that failed he hired twenty-three fellow cadets—at a cost of £3—to dam the stream, divert it into a new path, and actually drain the river bed. The watch was found.

None of this Herculean exertion impressed the crazed Randolph, who said that his son was a 'young stupid' and 'definitely not to be trusted'. There was perhaps a medical reason for this extreme be-haviour: Lord Randolph Churchill was dying of syphilis.

Recent scholarship has attempted to remove the venereal stigma and to suggest that it was actually a brain tumour—but even so, he believed it to be syphilis, his wife thought it was syphilis, and so did his doctor. So did Churchill, who spent his adolescence watching the awful political implosion of his father—from supernova to black hole—and then his death, by inches, in public, from a shameful disease.

So he grew up with two powerful and simultaneous feelings about his father: that he was a disappointment to Randolph, and that Randolph himself had been cheated of the greatness that should have been his. He wanted therefore to do two things: to prove himself to his father, and to vindicate him.

It is only when you dig into the relation with Randolph—and Randolph's mesmerising example—that you start to see how Churchill could have behaved as he did. He had to emulate him—how else could he properly prove himself to Randolph? And he had to imitate his life and even his pattern of behaviour, because that was the only way to vindicate him in the eyes of everyone else.

'He is completely untrustworthy, as was his father before him,' said Lord Derby in 1916. Theodore Roosevelt said they were both 'cheap fellows'.

There was a reason he had that reputation—and that is that to a large extent Churchill set out deliberately to make his father's life the programme and template for his own.

# CHAPTER 4

# THE RANDOLPH FACTOR

A t the age of seventy-three Winston Churchill wrote a curious little essay that he did not intend for publication—at least not until after his death. It is all about a spooky experience that he had in the winter of 1947. The glory days of the war and the premiership are over, and he finds himself in his studio in the cottage at Chartwell.

He is getting ready to paint, when he feels an odd sensation—and turns round to see his father sitting in an armchair. Randolph's eyes are twinkling and he is fiddling with his amber cigarette holder, just as Churchill remembers him from those rare moments when he was both charming and loving to his son.

There then takes place a poignant conversation. The conceit is that in the fifty-two years since he died—in political isolation and syphilitic despair—Randolph does not know what has happened in the world. So Churchill fills him in.

He tells him that King George VI is on the throne, and that they still race the Derby, and that the Turf Club is 'OK' and that 'OK' is a new American expression. He tells Randolph how the former Tory leader Arthur Balfour eventually came a cropper—a pleasing reflection, since neither of them really got on with snooty old Balfour. He relates the rise of socialism. He explains that there have been two world wars in each of which about thirty million people have died, and how the Russians have a new type of tsar, more fell and murderous than any that has gone before.

The trick of the piece is that Randolph never quite understands what his son has accomplished. The father gathers that the son is now a part-time painter, of indifferent ability, that he appears to live in a small cottage, and that he never rose above the rank of major in the yeomanry.

At the end of Churchill's grim exposition of the modern world, Randolph seems vaguely impressed with how much his son seems to know about current affairs. He says, with deafening irony, 'Of course you are too old now to think about such things, but when I hear you talk I really wonder that you didn't go into politics. You might have done a lot to help. You might even have made a name for yourself.'

At this he smiles and strikes a match, and in the flash the apparition vanishes. Many historians have taken this sketch—which Churchill's family called 'The Dream'—to be immensely and deliberately revealing about the psychological make-up of Winston Churchill. So it surely is.

It is elegiac; it is wistful; it is in one sense a great sorrowful sigh of yearning from a man who always wanted to impress his father and never succeeded. As Winston Churchill used to tell his own children, he never had more than five conversations with his father—or not conversations of any length; and he always had the feeling that he didn't quite measure up to expectations.

He spent his youth in the certainty, relentlessly rubbed in by Randolph, that he must be less clever than his father. Randolph had been to Eton, whereas it was thought safer to send young Winston to

Harrow—partly because of his health (the air of the hill being deemed better for his fragile lungs than the dank air by the Thames) but really because Harrow, in those days, was supposed to be less intellectually demanding.

Randolph had been to Merton College, Oxford, and had almost got a first in law. He could quote Horace with fluency. Churchill, on the other hand, had flunked his exams and only scraped into Sandhurst.

As Winston had struggled on his duffer's career path, he had watched his father's meteoric ascent, his rise to the Chancellorship, how he dominated the Tory Party; and then it was the cruel fate of young Winston also to watch his father's decline. He scoured newspapers for accounts of his speeches. He was furiously loyal. He refused to accept that his faculties were dimming, that his diction was slurred and that he lacked his former oratorical fire; and when once he was in the audience and someone let out a catcall, the teenage Churchill whirled round and hissed, 'Stop that now, you snub-nosed radical!'

When Churchill was twenty his relations with his father had a last golden moment. He found himself invited to lunches with great and famous men such as Joe Chamberlain, Herbert Henry Asquith and Lord Rosebery, and performed creditably. 'He has much smartened up,' noted his father, 'and he has got steadier . . . Sandhurst has done wonders for him.' By his own account, Churchill dreamed of being politically useful to his old man, of joining him in Parliament, of rallying to his cause—and then he was gone, dead at forty-five, before his son had the chance.

So here he is now in 'The Dream', with his father before him, and the moment has finally come to explain to his wrathful parent that the cosmic Head Master has a new end-of-term report for Winston; that he is no longer a wastrel and an idler but the Greatest Living

Englishman and the Saviour of his Country—and, puff, Randolph has gone again before he can hear the good news.

We end the piece in a state of melancholy. Churchill feels too tired to go on painting. His cigar has gone out and the ash has fallen among the paints. On the face of it we are meant to feel sorry for him and the hyper-Victorian distance of his relationship with Randolph. But I can't help thinking that there is also a bit of smugness in this essay.

He is not only seeking his father's posthumous approval. He is surreptitiously boasting—to Randolph and to the reader—of how he defied those miserable expectations, and actually exceeded his father in virtually every respect.

So there! says Winston Churchill to the vanished shade of Randolph. Put that in your cigarette holder and smoke it, you gooseberry-eyed and walrus-moustached demagogue. You had no right to be so critical—that is the message to Randolph and the subtext of the essay.

What was Churchill trying to do in that studio at Chartwell, when the ghost of his father appeared? He was actually repairing an old oil painting of Randolph, one that had been damaged in some Ulster club. He was taking that image, and he was using his own paints and his own skill to tart it up.

There, surely, is the metaphor that sums up the whole exercise. Churchill said that he set out to 'vindicate' his father, and that is true. But he also means to go one better. He takes that battered and nicotine-stained canvas and he embellishes it.

It was Randolph who began the family tradition of making money from journalism. As Churchill notes in 'The Dream', Randolph went off to South Africa for the *Daily Graphic*, and earned the colossal sum of £100 an article. So how does Churchill launch himself upon the world?

He goes off to South Africa, among other places, and becomes the most highly paid journalist of his age; and like Randolph, he makes a bit of a habit of cheesing off the people who help him in his ambitions.

And what kind of lesson did Randolph offer his son, about how to get on in Parliament? He displayed a shocking disloyalty to the Tories, and set up a group called the 'Fourth Party', whose mission was to bash Gladstone but also to wind up the Tory Party leadership, in the form of Sir Stafford Northcote.

Randolph and chums called him 'the goat', and after a while the goat could take it no more, and wrote to Randolph, begging him not to be such a tosser. Randolph wrote back, with blissful condescension, saying: 'Since I have been in parliament I have always acted on my own account, and I shall continue to do so.'

There, too, is young Churchill's cue: and when he gets to Parliament in 1900 he begins by setting up his own group of rebellious young Tories—called the Hughligans, in honour of Hugh Cecil, one of their number—and razzes the Tory high command, with Randolphian brio and insolence.

It was Randolph who showed the first and programmatic disdain for the very idea of party loyalty. As his son later described it, his father's preferred strategic position was 'looking down on the Front Benches on both sides and regarding all parties in the House of Commons with an impartiality which is quite sublime'.

So how does Churchill treat his political parties? As he once said—with the kind of candour that would be simply intolerable in today's desiccated politics—choosing a political party is like choosing a horse: you just go for the nag that will take you farthest and fastest. As we have seen, he chooses one, and leaps off just before it is about to die; leaps on a Liberal horse; and when that, too, is obviously about to cark it (or possibly dead on its feet), he leaps back on a new Tory steed. No one, before or since, has been so magnificently and unrepentantly disloyal.

Churchill decides from very early on that he will create a political position that is somehow above left and right, embodying the best points of both sides and thereby incarnating the will of the nation. He thinks of himself as a gigantic keystone in the arch, with all the lesser stones logically induced to support his position. He has a kind of semi-ideology to go with it—a leftish Toryism: imperialist, romantic, but on the side of the working man.

And he gets it from Randolph. Randolph's formula was called 'Tory Democracy'. The idea was a bit vague (asked to define it, Randolph said it was 'opportunism, mostly'). But Tory Democracy galvanised and invigorated the Tory Party in the 1880s, and the idea certainly invigorated the career of Randolph Churchill.

His son takes up the theme. Randolph campaigned for servants to be entitled to compensation for industrial accidents, and in the same spirit Winston is the author of important social reforms: bringing the pension age down to sixty-five, setting up Labour Exchanges, giving workers the tea break, and so on—while always remaining, on the whole, a steady defender of free markets.

Churchill inherits his political positioning from Randolph; and above all he inherits his style, his self-projection. Randolph became the most famous orator of his day, the man who could clear the tea rooms when he stood up to speak, and whose working-class fans called him 'Little Randy' and 'Cheeky Randy'. 'Give it to 'em hot, Randy!' they cried, when the shrimp-like fellow worked himself up into a frenzy of pop-eyed invective—a snarling version of the P. G. Wodehouse character Gussie Fink-Nottle in the great prize-giving speech at Market Snodsbury Grammar School.

He was a phrase-maker of note, who said that Gladstone was 'an old man in a hurry'. Speaking of Gladstone's habit of relaxing by chopping wood at Hawarden Castle, he said, 'the forest laments in order that Mr Gladstone may perspire'. Churchill adopts the same speaking techniques—mostly writing out the whole text in full, before trying to declaim as much as possible from memory—and becomes the most glorious political speaker not just of his age but perhaps of any age.

But where, you may ask, did Randolph get it all from? Who was his inspiration?

Both Churchills, father and son, are avowedly working in the tradition of that greatest of all Tory magicians and opportunists, Benjamin Disraeli. Randolph was Disraeli's disciple and his vicar on earth. When Disraeli died, Randolph helped to establish the 'Primrose League' in his memory, because the primrose was the favourite flower of the great Victorian leader and dandy.

As Randolph tells his son in 'The Dream', 'I always believed in Dizzy, that old Jew. He saw the future. He had to bring the British working man into the centre of the picture.' The two Churchills— father and son—were, as Winston put it, the 'bearers of the mantle of Elijah', the heirs of Disraeli.

The continuities are indeed very striking, and go way beyond an interest in social reform. Disraeli and the Churchills also have in common the journalism (and in Winston's case, the novel), the love of show, the rhetorical flourishes, the sense of history, the imperialism, the monarchism, the slight air of camp and the inveterate opportunism.

These days it seems that Disraeli is in danger of some sort of eclipse. Douglas Hurd has produced a fine but slightly finger-wagging biography, demanding to know what Disraeli actually achieved by comparison with 'effective' plodders like Peel.

This is unfair on Disraeli, of course, but also on a crucial tradition in modern British politics. If it hadn't been for Disraeli, we would not have had Randolph Churchill, and if it hadn't been for the example and model provided by Randolph, we would never have had Winston Churchill. What was Churchill's delighted reaction, when Prime Minister Stanley Baldwin made him Chancellor of the Exchequer? 'I still have my father's robes!'

I do not mean to suggest that Churchill was identical to his father, or some kind of mini-me. In all sorts of important ways, he was very different, and a very much better man.

Randolph was a serious cad, in a way that Churchill never quite managed. It is hard to imagine Winston contracting syphilis. Both his parents were 'famous for sex', in the phrase of Muriel Spark, in a way that Churchill wasn't.

You can't see Churchill getting so deranged with anger as to assault his valet, as Randolph did, and you can't imagine him writing such dreadful letters to his children. And Winston would never have behaved in the demented way that Randolph did in 1873, when he tried to blackmail the Prince of Wales, and then challenged him to a duel.

This bizarre and revolting story has now faded into a dusty crevice of the library; but when Winston Churchill was beginning his career, there were people who remembered it—and they must have wondered how far the apple had fallen from the tree.

It all began because Randolph's older brother, the Earl of Blandford, was having a major extramarital affair with a woman called Lady Edith Aylesford. This Edith seems from her photo to have had a longish nose, but she must have been a sex bomb. She was simultaneously involved with Blandford, with her husband, and with 'Bertie'—the portly and underemployed heir to the throne. That was how they carried on in those days, you see.

Edith decided that she wanted to divorce her husband, Lord

Aylesford, and shack up with Blandford. For reasons that are not quite clear, Randolph decided that his older brother should be party to no such thing. It would bring disgrace on the family even to be cited in a divorce case, he said.

So he came up with a wheeze to get the Prince of Wales—who set the moral tone for society—to forbid the divorce. He found some letters from Prince Bertie to Edith. They were hot stuff, said Randolph. They implied intimacy between the Prince and Lady Edith, and if they were exposed—why, then Bertie would never sit upon the throne!

He threatened to publish. An epic scandal impended. The Queen was informed. Disraeli, then Prime Minister, had to step in. An incandescent Bertie challenged Randolph to a duel, to which Randolph wrote back by figuratively sticking up two fingers to the heir to the throne, by pointing out that no subject could be asked to risk the life of a future monarch.

In the end the whole Churchill family had to be banished to Ireland, with the Duke of Marlborough going as Viceroy and Randolph serving as his Private Secretary; which is why Winston spent his early years in Dublin. As for the various marriages and love affairs, they all came to grief in one way or another.

I dig up this unhappy tale as evidence of that quality of Randolph's that Winston certainly did inherit—and that is not the caddishness, but the recklessness, or rather, the willingness to take risks. It was loopy of Randolph to think he could stop the divorce of his brother by blackmailing the Prince of Wales.

It was loopy of him, at the end of his career, to think that there was no one who could replace him as Chancellor of the Exchequer, and that he was safe to threaten to resign. 'I had forgotten Goschen,' he said, once they put Goschen in instead. (Indeed, George Goschen, the first Viscount Goschen, is only remembered for being forgotten by Randolph.) But that gambler's temperament he passed on to his son—and it is vital that he did.

By the time Winston Churchill came to power in May 1940, there were many people who were amazed, and many who were appalled—but also many who thought it was inevitable. In 1936—even as he was denying him a place in the cabinet—Stanley Baldwin remarked that they would need to keep Churchill in reserve to serve as a war prime minister.

By 1939 there were poster campaigns in London, with the slogan 'What Price Churchill?' Candidates began to stand in by-elections on a 'Bring Back Churchill' ticket. In May 1940, shortly before the Norway debate, his acolyte Harold Macmillan approached Churchill in the lobby and said, 'We must have a new Prime Minister and it must be you.'

As Churchill said about the moment when he finally took over, 'I felt as though I was walking with destiny. All my life was a preparation for this hour and this trial.' He did indeed seem somehow predestined for the job, and not just in his own eyes.

No one else had such long experience of fighting—both as a politician and a soldier. No one else seemed built on the same scale as Churchill, or equal to the level of events—and there was a further reason why so many people looked at him in this way, as the natural man for the moment.

They knew that throughout the amazing snakes-and-ladders of his life he had followed the pattern of Randolph not just in his ducal disdain for party or his Homeric desire for glory but in his willingness to back himself and his ideas—to take risks that no one else would take.

In peacetime, such behaviour can be disastrous. But you can't win a war without taking risks, and you won't take risks unless you are brave. That, finally, was the quality that people sensed in Churchill; that was why some people yearned for him in 1940, in spite of all the sneering of the Tory establishment and the appeasers.

His whole career so far had been a testament to that primordial virtue—the virtue, as he pointed out himself, that makes possible all the others. Of the immense physical and moral courage of Churchill there can be no doubt.

# CHAPTER 5

# NO ACT TOO DARING
# OR TOO NOBLE

It was a glorious evening in Croydon, on 18 July 1919. The war was over, and Churchill was back in government—long since restored after the disgrace of Gallipoli. He had put in a hard day as Secretary of State for War and Air, and now he hankered for excitement. It was time for one of his flying lessons.

With several hours of daylight left, he had driven down to the aerodrome south of London. Together with his instructor, Captain Jack Scott, he clambered into the biplane—a De Havilland Airco DH4, with its brass fittings and fine wooden propeller. Scott sat in the front seat of the dual-control machine, Churchill behind him. Though he had no formal pilot's licence, Churchill was experienced enough to perform the take-off himself.

For a while, things seemed to go according to the book. They chuntered down the field; the engine pulled well; they ascended to 70 or 80 feet above the upturned faces of the ground crew. They must have made a fine sight—one of Britain's most famous statesmen, his big head sheathed in leather flying cap and goggles, soaring heavenward in what was then a cutting-edge piece of British

technology—one of the very first people since Icarus to master the skies, to defy gravity in a machine that was heavier than air.

Just as they reached a fatal distance from the ground, things started to go wrong.

In those days Croydon Aerodrome was bordered by clumps of tall elm trees. In order to avoid these trees the ascending pilot was obliged to make two banked turns, first to the right and then to the left. Churchill made his first turn—no problems. The wind sang through the struts. The speedometer registered 60 knots, healthy enough to avoid a stall.

He turned left, and the delicate fins and ailerons obeyed his touch. Slowly and gently he now centred the joystick—as he had been taught—to bring the machine back on an even keel. He brought it all the way back; he moved the head of the joystick about a foot. He noticed something funny.

The plane remained banked, at 45 degrees. The machine showed no sign of responding to his commands. In fact, it started to list even more to the left. The speedo was falling fast. It was instantly obvious to Winston Churchill that he and Captain Scott were in trouble.

'She is out of control,' said Churchill to Scott—a highly experienced and capable man, who had already endured one bad crash, and had the injuries to show for it. In that moment Churchill felt Scott overriding him, taking control of the joystick and pedals—yanking and pushing to perform the only manoeuvre that you can, in such situations: pointing the nose downwards so as to pick up enough speed to get out of the side-slip. Any higher, and it might have worked. They were only 90 feet off the ground. Disaster was at hand.

As they descended, out of control, Churchill saw the sunlit aerodrome beneath him, and had the impression that it was bathed in a baleful yellowish glare. In a flash—and he didn't have much longer than a flash—the thought formed in his head: 'This is very likely death.' And so, very likely, it was.

Let us leave our hero there for a second or two, hurtling headlong towards the packed earth of Croydon. Let us look back at the risks he had already run. Consider the way he had loaded the statistical dice against himself—not just in his career as an aviator, but in his exhibitionist lust for glory of all kinds.

Churchill had begun his obsession with flying before the First War, when he was still First Lord of the Admiralty. At the beginning of 1913 he went to visit the naval air station at Eastchurch on the Isle of Sheppey. He was captivated by the atmosphere: young Biggles-like characters nervelessly hurling themselves about the ether as they tested the world's first seaplane (a word that Churchill was credited with coining). Apart from the moustaches, it must have been like the early days of the US space programme: the Right Stuff exuding from every pore.

Churchill immediately saw the potential of what they were doing. He wanted a proper division, with its own identity and *esprit de corps*: and so began what was to become the Royal Air Force. 'We are in the Stephenson age of flying,' he proclaimed, referring to the inventor of the steam locomotive. 'Now our machines are frail. One day they will be robust, and of value to our country.' He was so excited, in fact, that he wanted to take off himself—and to learn how to fly.

To see how bonkers this was, remember that it was then just ten years since the very dawn of flight. It was only in 1903 that Orville and Wilbur Wright had finally taken off at Kitty Hawk, in their bizarre contraption. Here was Churchill, a not-especially-fit thirty-nine-year-old, asking for tuition in flying these objects that—to modern eyes—are barely recognisable as planes. They look like weird giant canvas box kites mounted on pram wheels with a lawn-mower engine shoved on one end, and the whole thing lashed together with ropes or leather straps.

They look lethal. They were. It has been calculated that in 1912 one flight in five thousand ended in death. By modern standards, that is insanely dangerous. Compare another mode of transport that is sometimes—irrationally—held to be dangerous, such as cycling in London, where one journey in about 14 million ends in a fatality; and you see the risk that Churchill was running.

These days no one would be allowed aloft in one of those planes, let alone a senior government minister. One of Churchill's first instructors was a twenty-three-year-old sprig of the aristocracy called Spenser Grey—until Spenser had to bow out, after having a serious prang and suffering life-changing injuries.

Churchill's friends begged him to stop. His cousin Sunny, the Duke of Marlborough, said: 'I do not suppose I shall get the chance of writing you many more letters if you continue your journeys in the Air. Really, I consider you owe it to your wife, family and friends to desist from a practice or pastime—whichever you call it—which is fraught with so much danger to life. It really is wrong of you.' F. E. Smith told him he was being 'foolish' and 'unfair to his family'.

His cousin Lady Londonderry said he was 'evil'. His wife, Clementine, was distraught—and sometimes Churchill would steal away without even telling her. 'I have been very naughty today about flying,' he confessed on 29 November 1913, as though he had been to the larder and eaten the children's pudding.

His next instructor was another dashing young captain, Gilbert Wildman-Lushington. On 30 November—his birthday—Churchill spent the whole day with Lushington, much of it in the air. The captain wrote to his fiancée, Miss Airlie Hynes, about his exuberant pupil. 'I started Winston off on his instruction about 12.15, and he got so bitten with it I could hardly get him out of the machine, in fact except for about ¾ of an hour for lunch we were in the machine till 3.30. He showed great promise, and is coming down again for further instruction and practice.'

The brief lunch had taken place in Lushington's cabin, where Churchill spotted a photo of the young woman. When was the wedding? he asked. Captain Lushington replied that he was saving up for it—and you can imagine that teaching Churchill was a useful freelance income. Alas, the wedding never took place. Three days later Lushington himself was killed, side-slipping in the very plane he had used for the lesson.

There is an eerie letter from Churchill to Lushington, presumably written on the evening of the day they had spent together. He asks why he couldn't seem to make the rudder work, and why it seemed so stiff. 'Probably the explanation is that I was pushing against myself,' he says, cryptically. Lushington writes back, confirming that this is indeed probably the case. He has tried the rudder and it seems fine: 'You were pushing against yourself,' says Lushington, before taking off again for his last doomed flight.

We might ask: how can you push against yourself? What does that mean? Did Churchill really understand what was happening with these primitive flaps and levers? Did anyone?

He swore to Clementine that he would give up, after the death of Lushington. Then in 1914 he swore again that he would do so, after he invited French air ace Gustav Hamel to come over the Channel from Paris, and give a display to the Royal Flying Corps.

Hamel took off from Paris and was never seen again. And yet on Churchill went with his flying. He was constantly nipping over to France, glorying lark-like in the high places, boasting about the speed and the convenience of the air. By 1919 he was back at the controls, and in the immediate run-up to this fateful episode at Croydon he had been given all sorts of presentiments of doom.

On one occasion he had got completely lost in a storm over northern France, and had to descend until he could see a railway line by which to steer his course. Only the previous month he had sustained a serious smash at the Buc aerodrome near Paris. The long grass had slowed his take-off, so that the plane's skis hit the edge of a concealed road at the end of the runway.

The plane did a somersault—like a shot rabbit, he said—and he ended up hanging upside down by his harness. Now he was about to be violently and involuntarily reunited with the soil of Croydon, and if his life had flashed before him he might have reflected that he had behaved recklessly for years.

When we look at the prodigious bravery of his early military career, we are driven to the conclusion that he actively courted danger. It is as though he hungered—like Achilles or some Arthurian knight—for the prestige that goes not just with being in the thick of battle, but above all for being seen in the thick of battle.

His exploits began in Cuba at the age of twenty, when he first found himself in that ambiguous role that was to serve him so well: at once an officer of the British army, and yet also a front-line reporter. Sandhurst had ended satisfactorily, in the sense that he became a bold and skilful horseman and graduated twentieth out of a class of 130, before enlisting as a cornet in the 4th Queen's Own Hussars. The army was expensive, however, and he saw journalism as an ingenious way of supplementing his income and personally burnishing his own reputation.

When the Cubans rebelled against their Spanish colonial masters, Churchill wangled himself into the Spanish forces. Ostensibly he was there to report for the *Daily Graphic*; in reality he hoped to get as close as possible to a live bullet without actually being hit.

He got lucky quickly. On his twenty-first birthday he was in the jungle, when shots rang out. The horse behind him copped it; a red stain spread over his chestnut coat, and he died. Churchill's account quivered with excitement, as he described how the bullet had come 'within a foot of my head'. The next day he was bathing in a river and more shots were heard. 'The bullets whizzed over our heads,' he said with pride.

All this was glorious in its way, but it could hardly be described as a full-scale battle. He wanted active service in the British army. He wanted to do some shooting himself—and preferably against Her Majesty's enemies. Thanks to some nifty lobbying by his mother (who is said to have used all her resources of feminine charm to bend the generals to her will) he got himself a billet, two years later, with the Malakand Field Force, commanded by Sir Bindon Blood.

The mission of this well-moustachioed imperialist was to make life tough for some Afridi rebels—Muslim tribesmen on India's North-West Frontier, the borderland between what is now Afghanistan and Pakistan. They had risen against the British Empire, in a region that still shelters some of the world's most hardened fanatics and terrorists. Then as now, the operation was no picnic.

The Afridis fought back ferociously. Churchill's hankering for action was answered—and how. It is pretty hair-raising to read his accounts of the engagements: men cut to pieces next to him; tribesmen charging towards him until he shoots them; British infantry scattering in panic, leaving a wounded officer to be carved up on his stretcher by the fanatical Afridis. He was under fire for hour after hour.

On one occasion he blazed away with his pistol, then dropped it and picked up a rifle. He later reported, 'I fired 40 rounds with some effect at close quarters. I cannot be certain, but I think I hit four men. At any rate, they fell.' Sometimes he seemed to be positively swanking about the way he exposed himself to fire. 'I rode my grey pony all along the skirmish line when everyone else was lying down in cover. Foolish perhaps, but I play for high stakes and given an audience there is no act too daring or too noble.'

He behaved, all in, with the kind of suicidal daring displayed by those 1980s millennialist tribesmen of northern Kenya, who believed that they could ward off bullets by smearing themselves with nut oil. His exploits in Malakand would earn a modern soldier the Victoria Cross, or at least some pretty serious gong. And then he repeated and excelled them.

In 1898, at Omdurman in the Sudan, he took part in the last full cavalry charge by the British army. Once again, Churchill was in the role of colonial suppressor, helping to put down a revolt by Sudanese Muslims who resented British rule and, among other grievances, the attempt by London to abolish the slavery of black Africans. Once again, Jennie had been instrumental in getting him the position as a hybrid soldier-cum-reporter—much to the disgust of the army top brass. This time he was a more important player—a scout who at one point actually told the even more lushly moustachioed General Kitchener the whereabouts of the Sudanese Islamic army.

The objective of the mission was to defeat the Muslim leader, and to avenge the killing of General Charles Gordon—whose frenzied skewering at Khartoum, thirteen years earlier, had shocked the Victorian world. At 8.40 a.m. on 2 September 1898 Churchill found himself riding towards the 60,000-strong Dervish army, admittedly after they had been pounded for an hour or more by British guns. Churchill and his men thought they were taking on a bunch of 150 native spearmen—only to find they were riflemen.

The Dervishes suddenly knelt and started shooting at the detachment of lancers. What could they do? Beat it, or charge? They charged. Churchill had covered about a hundred yards in the direction of the

Dervishes when he realised that he was about to rush into a ravine full of 'closely packed spearmen', twelve deep.

What did he do? He kept charging. There was a terrific melee; many of the Dervishes were knocked over like skittles. Churchill fired the ten shots of his Mauser pistol's magazine and came through without a scratch, either to himself or his horse. Having broken through the ravine, he then trotted around the scene, where Dervishes and British were hacking away at each other.

He 'rode up to individuals, firing my pistol in their faces and killing several—three for certain—two doubtful—one very doubtful'. When it is put like this, you might get the impression that these battles were a bit one-sided. After all, we had got the Maxim gun, and they had not.

That is totally to underestimate the risk. Of the 310 men in the charge, 21 had been killed and 49 wounded. As Churchill put it later, it was 'the most dangerous two minutes I shall live to see'.

Or was it? He then fought in the Boer War, and came under fire on many occasions from these tough Dutch farmers—who were better shots, and had better weapons, than either the Afridis or the Dervishes. We have no space here to repeat the whole drama of Churchill and the Boers; there have been books on it, not least two of them by Churchill himself.

In summary, he went out as a twenty-four-year-old reporter to this unfortunate war, in which the might of the British Empire was all but humiliated by bearded and glottally challenged characters from the pages of a veld novel by Wilbur Smith. In 1900 he managed to get himself into a colossal scrape that launched him finally on to the front page.

He was taking a train to a place called Colenso, in Natal, when it was ambushed by the enemy and derailed. He then showed great coolness under fire, and disregard for his own safety, in organising resistance. As usual, he was shot at, and as usual he survived as if by a miracle. He was captured and escaped from prison; he jumped on a goods train; he hid in a wood; he was spooked by a vulture; he hid in a coal mine; he emerged to a hero's welcome at Lourenço Marques in what is now Mozambique.

He later cycled through Pretoria with a price on his head; he was shot at again and very nearly killed at a place called Dewetsdorp; he showed 'conspicuous gallantry' at a battle called Diamond Hill . . . I hope I am beginning to make my point.

I could go on: I could add that when he joined the army in 1915, after Gallipoli, he went and served with the troops on the Western Front, and went out into no man's land thirty-six times, sometimes going so close to the German lines that he could hear them talking. I could tell you about his disregard for the shells and the bullets— but I believe that the reader may be getting the message.

As a young man, and indeed throughout his life, Churchill showed the courage of a lion. How many bullets and other missiles were fired in his general direction? A thousand? How many men did he kill, with his own hand? A dozen? Maybe more. No prime minister since Wellington had seen so much active service, or been so personally homicidal to any inhabitants of the developing world who offered him violence, and to some, no doubt, who did not.

He has the unique distinction, as a prime minister, of having been shot at on four continents. By this stage the sensitive reader may be willing to accept this overwhelming evidence of Churchill's bravery—but want to know more about the psychology behind it. Why was he like this?

What wound his spring so tight? One of the great joys of Churchill's character—and one of the reasons for his mental robustness—

is that he is capable of great honesty about his motives. He knows that he is playing to the gallery, he tells his mother, as he explains his conduct in Malakand. He needs the audience for the daring and the noble acts—because he has something to prove.

As he admits. 'Being in many ways a coward—particularly at school—there is no ambition I cherish so keenly as to gain a reputation for personal courage.' The child is father to the man, and gingery young Churchill was a pretty runty sort of kid.

He was not in the team for Harrow football, the violent and hearty game that is a peculiarity of the school. He didn't even play much cricket, and on one occasion the other boys threw cricket balls at him—and he scarpered and hid in the woods. The memory stuck with him; he felt judged and found wanting by his peers, just as he felt judged and found wanting by Randolph.

As it happens, I think he erred in this self-criticism. He wasn't a coward as a young schoolboy. He was hellish brave. He was first sent away to school at the age of seven, to the care of a sadistic whacker called Herbert Sneyd-Kynnersley. This man was a High Anglican old perv who used to give the boys twenty strokes of the cane—drawing blood after the third—for the slightest infraction.

Though he was miserably unhappy at the school, Churchill never complained about this barbarism, and indeed it wouldn't have been exposed had not the family doctor noticed the weals. But you know what young Churchill did?

One day Sneyd-Kynnersley had given him a thrashing for taking some sugar, and Churchill went and got the old boy's straw hat—and kicked it to pieces. I love him for that. He wasn't really anything like a coward at school: he may not have been much good at muddy team games, but he was the inter-schools fencing champion. He famously pushed older boys into the swimming pool, and if you want a final proof of his sheer raw courage, as a teenager, I give you the famous occasion when he was playing hare and hounds with his brother and cousin in Dorset.

They trapped him on a bridge, one at either end, and beneath the bridge was a chasm. Then Churchill noticed a fir tree whose top came up to the level of the bridge, and in a second his ingenious mind had conceived a project.

He would leap on to the tree, and slide down, using the branches to slow his descent. Nice idea in theory, disastrous in execution. It was three days before he regained consciousness and three months before he was out of bed.

In that episode we see so many elements of his character—the imagination, the bravado, and the ability to take a decision in a flash. Churchill's bravery wasn't something he just put on. It wasn't a mask he struggled with. He was made like that. The spirit of derring-do just pumped through his veins, like some higher-octane fuel than the one the rest of us run on.

Nothing could stop him, not even that accident in Croydon, where we have rejoined the plane as it fell fast towards the ground. Now it went smack into the runway at 50 mph. The left wing went in first, smashed to pieces, while the propeller was buried in the earth.

Churchill was whacked forward. He was crushed. The pressure seemed unendurable. Streams of petrol shot past him and he thought—again—that he was going to die. But it turned out that the good Captain Scott had turned off the electric current, shortly before he was knocked out.

Churchill got out and vowed that he would never pilot himself in the air again—a vow he kept, more or less, until the middle of the Second World War, when he needed, again, to show what he was made of; and when his general willingness to take the risk of getting in a plane became vital to British resistance.

---

OF COURSE he enjoyed showing off—not just to his mother, or to the press, or to the public, but above all to the person who chronicled his deeds most lovingly and faithfully: himself. Whatever Churchill said or did, he had an eye, like Julius Caesar, to the way he would report it.

But that didn't make him any less lion hearted. And it was precisely because he was so unambiguously and irrefutably brave that he was able, from 1940, to demand so much bravery from others. Others—Attlee, Eden—had certainly fought in the war; but their reputations were not quite the same.

There was one thing the public could say for certain about Churchill: that there was nothing that he was going to ask the British armed forces to do that he would not have done himself.

And then Churchill had one further advantage over the others. He not only inspired by his personal example and career. He had the gift of language to put heart into people, and to breathe some of his own courage into others.

# CHAPTER 6

# THE GREAT
# DICTATOR

A ha, I am thinking, as I stand at last in Winston Churchill's study. So this is how he did it. By special leave of the staff at Chartwell I have come right up to the desk—beyond the rope barrier. I am looking at the very same pair of round black John Lennon-ish Bond Street spectacles that he used; and there are his hole-punches. There is the bust of Napoleon, rather bigger than the bust of Nelson, and there are the paperweights that you see in some of the photographs.

As I stoop to examine the deep scuffing in the right arm of his desk chair—a reminder of the odd way Churchill used to clutch it, perhaps because of his dislocated shoulder—I am politely asked to step back. I think they are worried I am going to test the chair with my weight.

I comply unhesitatingly. I have seen enough.

This is not just an English country house, with a stunning view of the weald of Kent, with fish ponds and croquet lawn and a cinema and painting studio and every civilised amenity that could be devised by a gentleman of leisure. No, no: this much-amended Elizabethan manor is no scene of repose. This is a machine.

It is no wonder that the design of this house proceeded from the same teeming brain that helped invent the tank and the seaplane and which foresaw the atom bomb. Chartwell Manor, Westerham, Kent, was one of the world's first word processors. The whole house is a gigantic engine for the generation of text.

Downstairs there is a room with green lamps hanging from the ceiling, and maps on the wall, and a telephone exchange: and here he kept his researchers—about six of them at once, junior Oxford dons, research fellows, some of them destined for high academic honours. There they were, filleting, devilling, rootling around in books and documents in search of stuff that might be of use.

They were his Nibelung, his elves, the tinkling dwarves in the smithy of Hephaestus. Or, to compare them with their modern equivalent, they were Winston Churchill's personal search engine—his Google. When they needed more books, they would pad down the corridor to the library—with its 60,000 mainly leather-bound volumes. This was his data bank. When he needed some fact or text, he would figuratively hit the 'execute' key, and summon them; and up they would go—only one at any time. They would go into the study, and there they would find him in the act of composition.

One of the many reasons for feeling overawed by Churchill is that he could not only discharge his duties as a minister of the Crown by day. He would then have a slap-up dinner, with champagne, wine and brandy. Only then, at 10 p.m., refreshed and very jovial, would he begin to write.

I KNOW THAT I speak for many journalists—and many others— when I say that it is perfectly possible to write after lunch, even if, or particularly if, you have had a bottle of wine. It is simply not possible to do this after dinner; not after booze. I don't know anybody else who is capable of knocking out first-class copy after a long day and a drunken dinner.

There must have been something unique in his metabolic pathways; and what makes it even more astonishing is that most of the time he didn't even write. He dictated. He would gather his thoughts and then, wreathed in tobacco and alcohol—and perhaps wearing his monogrammed slippers and the peculiar mauve velvet siren suit made for him by Turnbull and Asser—he would walk the wooden floorboards and growl out his massively excogitated sentences. And that was barely the beginning of the word-processing system.

Typists would struggle to keep up, but on he jawed, even into the small hours of the night, licking and champing his unlit cigar. Sometimes he would take them with him into his tiny and austere bedroom, and then while they blushed and squeaked he would disrobe and submerge himself in his sunken Shanks bath and continue to prose on, while they sat on the floor and pitter-pattered away on the specially muffled keyboards that he preferred.

The sheaves of typewritten paper he would then correct and amend by hand—and we have innumerable examples of his cursive blue-inked marginalia—and then the results would be typeset as they would appear on the page; and even that was not the end.

Now I pace across the room to an upright sloping bureau that is set against the wall, like a newspaper-reading slab in a club. It was here that he engaged in the final exercise of word-processing, a ritual that we would now perform effortlessly with our Microsoft programmes. He would fiddle with the text. He would switch clauses around for emphasis, he would swap one epithet for another and in general he would take the utmost delight in the process of polishing his efforts; and then he would send the whole lot off to be typeset again.

It was a fantastically expensive method of working, and yet it enabled Churchill to produce not just more words than Dickens, or more words than Shakespeare—but more words than Dickens and Shakespeare combined. Go into so many respectable middle-class English homes, especially of the older generation, and you will see them there, bulking out the bookshelves next to the *Encyclopaedia Britannica*: *The World Crisis*; *A History of the English-Speaking Peoples*; *The Second World War*; *Marlborough—His Life and Times*, and many others— and then ask yourself which ones have actually been read.

There are some people—faced with this vast quantity of text— who may be tempted to dismiss or downplay the virtuosity of Churchill as a writer. Indeed, he has always had his detractors. Evelyn Waugh, that inveterate Churchill-basher, said he was a 'master of sham-Augustan prose', with 'no specific literary talent but a gift of lucid self-expression'. After reading Churchill's life of his father Randolph, Waugh dismissed it as a 'shifty barrister's case, not a work of literature'.

By the late 1960s his historical gifts were being pummelled by the likes of J. H. Plumb, the Cambridge University pioneer of 'social history'. 'There is no discussion of the labouring classes and industrial technology,' complained Plumb of *A History of the English-Speaking Peoples*. 'He had an ignorance of economic, social and intellectual history of staggering proportions.' His prose style was 'curiously old-fashioned and somewhat out of place, like St Patrick's cathedral on 5th avenue'.

As for his amazing achievement in winning the Nobel prize for literature, it is conventional to treat this as a joke—an embarrassing attempt by the Swedes to make up for their neutrality in the war. Even relatively sympathetic historians, such as Peter Clarke, have dismissed the possibility that there was any merit involved. 'Rarely can an author's writings have received less attention than those of the winner of the Nobel prize for literature in 1953,' he says. This is not just a little bit snooty, but surely untrue.

Look at the list of Nobel winners in the last century. Avant-garde Japanese playwrights. Marxist-feminist Latin Americans. Polish exponents of the concrete poem. All of them are no doubt meritorious in their way, but many of them are much less read than Churchill.

Why did Evelyn Waugh sneer at Churchill's writings? Notice that he—Waugh—had actually tried to emulate Churchill in the 1930s, and got himself sent out to cover a war in Abyssinia. He produced *Scoop*, of course, one of the great stylistic landmarks of the twentieth century. But his reporting had nothing like the same journalistic impact as Churchill's.

Is it that Waugh was a teensy bit jealous? I think so; and the reason was not just that Churchill had become so much more famous than Waugh had been, by the time he was twenty-five, but that he had made such stupendous sums from writing. And that, for most journalists, alas, is the truly sensitive point of comparison.

By 1900 he had not only written five books—some of which had been best-sellers—but he had become just about the highest-paid journalist in Britain. For his Boer War coverage he was paid £250 per month—the equivalent of £10,000 a month today. He was commissioned to write the life of his father in 1903, and given a staggering payment of £8,000. To give you the scale of those riches, consider that there were then only a million people in the country who had the privilege of paying income tax, and that was because they earned £160 per year.

These publishers didn't pay him this kind of money because they liked his blue eyes. They paid him handsomely because he was popular with the public, and helped boost circulation, and the reason he was popular was that he wrote so well, with a rich and rollicking readability. He was a superb reporter. Try this account from the *Morning Post* of April 1900.

We take up the story as Churchill and his fellow mounted scouts are trying to beat the Boers to secure a kopje, a rocky outcrop in the South African plain.

It was from the very beginning a race, and recognised as such by both sides. As we converged I saw the five leading Boers, better mounted than their comrades, outpacing the others in a desperate resolve to secure the coign of vantage. I said, 'We cannot do it'; but no one would admit defeat or leave the matter undecided. The rest is exceedingly simple.

We arrived at a wire fence 100 yards—to be accurate 120 yards—from the crest of the kopje, dismounted, and, cutting the wire, were about to seize the precious rocks when—as I had seen them in the railway cutting at Frere, grim, hairy and terrible—the heads and shoulders of a dozen Boers appeared; and how many more must be close behind them?

There was a queer, almost inexplicable, pause, or perhaps there was no pause at all; but I seem to remember much happening. First the Boers—one fellow with a long, drooping, black beard, and a chocolate-coloured coat, another with a red scarf round his neck. Two scouts cutting the wire fence stupidly. One man taking aim across his horse, and McNeill's voice, quite steady: 'Too late; back to the other kopje. Gallop!'

Then the musketry crashed out, and the 'swish' and 'whirr' of the bullets filled the air. I put my foot in the stirrup. The horse, terrified at the firing, plunged wildly. I tried to spring into the saddle; it turned under the animal's belly. He broke away, and galloped madly off. Most of the scouts were already 200 yards off. I was alone, dismounted, within the closest range, and a mile at least from cover of any kind.

One consolation I had—my pistol. I could not be hunted down unarmed in the open as I had been before. But a disabling wound was the brightest prospect. I turned, and, for the second time in this war, ran for my life on foot from the Boer marksmen, and I thought to myself, 'Here at last I take it.' Suddenly, as I ran, I saw a scout. He came from the left, across my front; a tall man, with skull and crossbones badge, and on a pale horse. Death in Revelation, but life to me.

I shouted to him as he passed: 'Give me a stirrup.' To my surprise he stopped at once. 'Yes,' he said, shortly. I ran up to him, did not bungle in the business of mounting, and in a moment found myself behind him on the saddle.

Then we rode. I put my arms around him to catch a grip of the mane. My hand became soaked with blood. The horse was hard hit; but, gallant beast, he extended himself nobly. The pursuing bullets piped and whistled—for the range was growing longer—overhead.

'Don't be frightened,' said my rescuer; 'they won't hit you.' Then, as I did not reply, 'My poor horse, oh, my poor horse; shot with an explosive bullet. The devils! But their hour will come. Oh, my poor horse!'

I said, 'Never mind, you've saved my life.' 'Ah,' he rejoined, 'but it's the horse I'm thinking about.' That was the whole of our conversation.

Judging from the number of bullets I heard I did not expect to be hit after the first 500 yards were covered, for a galloping horse is a difficult target, and the Boers were breathless and excited. But it was with a feeling of relief that I turned the corner of the further kopje and found I had thrown double sixes again.

This isn't Gibbon. This isn't sham-Augustanism. It is more like something from the pages of Victorian adventure novelist H. Rider Haggard: crisp, punchy, full of the kind of wham-bam short sentences that keep the reader moving down the page. Churchill could do action reporting better than many of the greatest modern exponents—and he had the inestimable advantage of being able to use the first person.

He could do the *Boy's Own* stuff. He could sound, when he chose, like an extract from *The Wonder Book of Daring Deeds*. But Churchill had so many more shots in his journalistic locker. He could do the meditative passages as well: the evils of Islamic fundamentalism; the horrors of war. Sometimes he was angry—and angry at his own side.

His description of the aftermath of Omdurman, where he made that famous charge, is one that lives in the eye and in the nostrils: the machine-gunned corpses lying three deep, men still living but already putrefying; men dying of thirst but crawling pathetically towards the Nile; here a man with one foot who has covered a mile in three days; here a man with no legs who is making 400 yards a day.

It has long been a theme of imperial writing—since the ancient Romans—to dwell tearfully on the sufferings of the subject peoples, and thereby to intensify the triumph of the conquering race. But Churchill takes it a stage farther, actively bashing the British authorities and their bland assurances. 'The statement that "the wounded dervishes received every delicacy and attention" is so utterly devoid of truth that it passes into the realms of the ridiculous,' he wrote.

He publicly abuses Kitchener for his conduct of the war. He slates him for desecrating the tomb of the Mahdi, and for keeping his head as a trophy—allegedly in a tin of kerosene. Churchill's criticism was justified, but it was outrageous and hubristic.

Kitchener was his Commander-in-Chief, the man he had personally assisted, on the morning of the battle (though there is some doubt as to whether Kitchener knew that the officer he was talking to was the notorious Churchill). Kitchener was not some has-been; he was to go on and command British forces in the First World War.

Here he was—being rubbished by some jumped-up young officer in his own army. Churchill infuriated the generals because he seemed to be riding at once with the hare and the hounds. He was using his military status to get into the action—and then slagging them off. Mind you, Kitchener should have known better. Churchill had done it before—and everyone knew it.

This is how he repaid Sir Bindon Blood for his kindness in taking him on with the Malakand Field Force. He blasted the expedition in a letter to his mother, saying 'financially it is ruinous, morally it is wicked, militarily it is an open question and politically it is a blunder', and the important thing is that he said more or less the same in public. He ended his final *Daily Telegraph* article, a dispatch from Nowshera on 16 October 1897, with this gloomy analysis: 'It is with regret that I do not see any sign of permanency in the settlements that have been made with the tribesmen . . . They have been punished, not subdued; rendered hostile, but not harmless. Their fanaticism remains unshaken, their barbarism unrelieved.'

How was that supposed to cheer up the *Telegraph* reader? At other points he is more gung-ho about the whole business; but no wonder his superior officers never recommended him for a Victoria Cross— in spite of all his ostentatious and sometimes lunatic bravery. No wonder Kitchener was so leery of having him along to the Sudan—only giving way, it seems, in 1898, when a friend of Jennie's wrote to him, saying: 'Hope you will take Churchill: guarantee he won't write.' Ha! That was a good one, eh?

Who knows what shameless undertakings Jennie gave to this woman, or to her friends in the British military—but her son passed the first and most important test of a journalist. He put the reader first.

He told the story as he saw it. He opened his heart. Of course, he wasn't some anti-imperialist and anti-Western campaigner—some precursor of the famously anguished reporters of the Vietnam War. He was a passionate believer in empire. But that did not mean he could ignore what he saw: the superior fighting spirit and marksmanship of the Boers; the evil of the Maxim gun.

No one has ever unpicked the essential honesty of his accounts. Harold Nicolson was later to say of him, in another context, that it was among his many virtues that he 'cannot really tell lies'. That verdict needs some qualification: he certainly sometimes stretched things in wartime. But in his journalism there was a genuine determination to get to the heart of things.

I say: stuff his snobbish detractors. When did Evelyn Waugh write a dispatch that was half as good as Churchill's reports from Malakand or the Sudan? The reason Churchill has lasted, and the reason his phrases are still on people's lips, is that he could deploy so many styles: not just the pseudo-Gibbonian periods, but Anglo-Saxon pith.

Some chicken, some neck. Fight them on the beaches. Blood, toil, tears and sweat. Never in the field of human conflict has so much been owed by so many to so few.

Often he is orotund and Augustan, but the phrases for which he is remembered are masterpieces of compression. He loved new words as much as he loved new machines. He was entranced, for instance, on first hearing the word 'stunt', imported from America. 'Stunt. Stunt,' he kept saying, rolling it around his mouth and announcing that he would use it at the earliest opportunity.

He was one of the great linguistic innovators of recent times. When world leaders meet to discuss a crisis they might have a SUMMIT at which they discuss the MIDDLE EAST or possibly the risk that Russia will create a new IRON CURTAIN. All three are neologisms either invented or championed by Churchill. Sometimes he could be Gibbonian; sometimes he was more of a funky Gibbon; but he was always fertile, and he was fast.

It began very early. Indeed, it is one of the myths about Churchill that he was always backward at school. Even at his prep school in Brighton, in 1884, he came top in classics. Take his first ever essay at Harrow, on the subject of Palestine in the time of John the Baptist. Here he is on the Pharisees. 'Their faults were many. Whose faults are few? For let him with all the advantages of Christianity avouch that they are more wicked than himself, he commits the same crime of which he is just denouncing them.'

That is pure Churchill. The Pharisees were famously savage in their judgements of others; but if we judge them harshly we are ourselves pharisaical! Paradox! Even at the age of twelve or thirteen he is groping for epigrams. Long before he went to India and spent his long afternoons reading Gibbon and Macaulay, he had memorised 1,200 lines of the *Lays of Ancient Rome*.

He had all the rhythms of English imprinted on his silicon chip, and together with a vocabulary that has been estimated at 65,000 words—most people have a half or a third of that number—he had an unbeatable tool to serve all his interconnected purposes and ambitions.

It was a way of dramatising and publicising himself; he could operate his own spotlight. Unlike any other young hussar, he could ensure that there was a long and gripping account of his bravery, because he would supply it. And like his father, he could use his facility with words to deal with a financial position that was almost always precarious.

THE CHURCHILLS WERE not poor. That description would be absurd. But as ducal families go, they hadn't much ready income—the fortune being more or less tied up in Blenheim. In spite of her long list of male admirers (her conquests have been reckoned to number 200, though Roy Jenkins thinks this number 'suspiciously round'), Jennie was not especially good at converting their attentions into cash; and at one stage Churchill was forced to take legal action against his mother to stop her squandering his—and his brother Jack's—inheritance.

Sure, his income from writing was vast by the standards of the day. His early success was continued, with average earnings of £12,883 between the years 1929 and 1937—about ten or twelve times what a prosperous professional could hope to make. But his outgoings were epic.

The bill from his wine merchant alone was three times the earnings of a male manual worker of the time. He had to pay for the upkeep of Chartwell, whose comforts included a Neronian circular outdoor pool that he kept heated, all year round, to a temperature of 75 degrees—a feat that necessitated a coke-fuelled boiler on the same scale as that of the House of Commons.

There is something gloriously unstingey about his approach to life: he once boasted that there had never been a time when he had not been able to order a bottle of champagne for himself and one for a friend. Sometimes, though, he was driven to all kinds of hack work, just to pay the bills. At one stage the *News of the World* commissioned him to condense and rehash a series of classic novels, under the title *Great Stories of the World Retold*.

It was not, as he himself confessed, an 'artistic' success. But what the hell: he was paid £333 per piece; or rather, he was paid £333, while his long-suffering secretary Eddie Marsh, who really did them, was paid £25. And then there were the awful depredations of the taxman—and here the scholarship of Peter Clarke has unearthed some spectacular manoeuvres.

As he was perfectly entitled to do, Churchill believed in keeping up the writing even when he was a minister of the Crown. He kept working on *A History of the English-Speaking Peoples*, for instance, even when he had become Chancellor of the Exchequer in 1924. But he nonetheless decided (or some brilliant accountant decided) that for tax purposes he had ceased, at the moment of putting on his father's Chancellor's robes, to be an 'author', and that the huge payments he was receiving—totalling £20,000—should be classified not as income but as 'capital gains'.

Which had the preposterous result that he didn't pay a penny of tax! Pol Roger all round.

No man but a blockhead ever wrote except for money, he would often say, quoting Dr Johnson; but of course in his case that was far from true. He also wrote because his temperament demanded it.

His creative-depressive personality meant that writing (or painting, or bricklaying) was a way of keeping the 'black dog' of depression at bay. He wrote for that sensation of release that comes with laying 200 bricks and writing 2,000 words a day.

Above all, he wrote his journalism and history and biography because for Winston Churchill writing was—to adapt Clausewitz on war—the continuation of politics by other means. These torrential literary efforts were his most potent weapons in his various campaigns, whether against Indian independence or against complacency about Hitler.

He could dramatise events and personalities in a way that was given to few other politicians, adding the emotion and colour that suited his cause. Neville Chamberlain fatefully said that Czechoslovakia was a faraway country of which we know little. Churchill had the literary and imaginative skill to bring the tragedy home—even to people who had never thought much about Czechoslovakia at all.

By the time he came into Downing Street in May 1940 he had written and read so much history as to have a unique understanding of events, to see them in context, and to see what England must do. J. H. Plumb mocked what he saw as Churchill's simplistic understanding and complacent belief in British greatness.

'The old Whig claptrap echoes in chapter after chapter,' he said— and by that he means to attack the central idea that guided Churchill all his life: that there was something special about the rise of England, and of liberty in England: the process by which freedoms were won from the Crown, the growth of a sovereign and democratic Parliament.

Huh, said J. H. Plumb: 'The past is a pasteboard pageant that indicates nothing and does not signpost the future.' Well, I look at the world today, and I think Plumb is wrong about that. Look at the fringes of the former Soviet Union, look at what is happening in the countries of the Arab Spring—I think most people would say that those ideals are still being fought for and are still worth fighting for.

It was greatly to the advantage of this country and the world that Churchill was able to articulate that vision with such confidence. He knew what England, for all her faults, had given the world—and that gave him his certainty of eventual victory.

There are two final ways in which his literary exertions made Churchill the only man for 1940. As even Plumb admits, in his study of Marlborough, there is something orchestral about Churchill's ability to deploy and coordinate his material: switching from Holland to Paris to London and to the Seven Seas. He knew instinctively which subject needed attention and when, while driving the central narrative along. Which was more or less how he ran the war.

Finally, let us go back to that figure in the study in Chartwell, pacing up and down and dictating to Mrs Pearman or Eddie Marsh. It takes prodigious mental effort to assemble the right words in your head, and then ensure that they are loaded on to the conveyor belt of the tongue so as to emerge in an order fit for printing.

Surely it was that endlessly repeated oral discipline which improved him not just as a writer but as a speaker. We may not read enough of his books today, but it was his speeches which galvanised the nation.

As we shall now see, the greatest orator of the modern era did not always speak fluently or well.

# CHAPTER 7

# HE MOBILISED
# THE ENGLISH
# LANGUAGE

Wjoin our hero on his feet in the House of Commons. He's
rhythmically thumping out a speech he will never forget. It's
an occasion that will be imprinted in his memory—the time he
found a new way to leave his listeners breathless and stunned.

It is 22 April 1904, and the young thruster is at the top of his
game. He is twenty-nine, pink in the cheek, with a downy corona of
gingery-brown hair still adhering to his head. He almost bursts with
brio. This year alone he has spoken dozens of times, yo-yoing up and
down to catch the eye of the Speaker on debates ranging from the
Army Estimates to the Brussels Sugar Convention to Chinese Inden-
tured Labour; and he is starting to get a bit of a name.

His portrait has been regularly published in the papers, complete
with admiring captions. He is seen pounding his fist into his palm, or
with hands on hips, or making his famous double-handed chopping
motion—and with his impudent attacks on his own party, and with
the Tories seemingly swirling towards the electoral oubliette, he is a

man on the up. The Liberals are about to find him a seat; he scents the prospect of office . . .

So he slashes away at the Tories on the benches in front of him—as an energetic rambler might thwack a row of thistles gone to seed. The Tories are a 'sham', he says. They have forgotten the precepts of Tory Democracy, he tells Balfour, who has already spoken in the debate—and one can imagine Balfour listening and looking inscrutable from beneath his vulturine eyelids.

Around him the Tories are hissing and scratching and fitfully trying to put him off his stroke. It is the Labour benches which are cheering him—and not surprisingly, in view of the kind of thing he is saying.

This isn't anything a Tory would today recognise as Conservatism. It would send Margaret Thatcher wild. In fact there isn't even a modern Labour government that would agree to the kind of thing that Churchill seems to be advocating. He is making a case to allow big groups of striking workers to go to the homes of those who are not on strike—and effectively to bully them into joining in. He wants unions to be protected from legal action, so that they can't be fined even if their members break the law in the course of their agitations.

It's not so much socialism as neo-anarcho-syndicalism—though before any of today's Tories get too upset, they should remember the context: Churchill was speaking when poverty was far deeper, and when the working man could still suffer oppression at the hands of the bosses, of a kind that is unknown today. Churchill has been going for forty-five minutes, and going well.

He comes to the climax of his remarks, and lambasts the entire House of Commons for its flagrant lack of proper class representation. Where are the working men? demands this scion of Blenheim. Look at the influence of the company directors, the learned professions, the service members, the railway, landed and liquor interests, he says—and we can imagine his ducal arm sweeping round to take in the balefully staring Tories.

It must be admitted, he says, that the influence of the labouring classes is ludicrously small. 'And it rests with those who . . .' he says; and then he stops.

A few eyes turn enquiringly his way. With whom does it rest? What is it that rests? What rests on whom? The House waits.

A whole second elapses. Churchill tries again. 'It rests with those who . . .' But by now it is clear that something is up.

It seems he is the victim, ironically, of some kind of mental sabotage—a sudden wildcat industrial action in his memory.

In the vast cargo hold of his brain the baggage handlers have gone on strike. The conveyor belt of his tongue flaps vacantly. No words come out. He tries again, but it is no use. He can't for the life of him remember what he was going to say next.

For three whole minutes he stands there, while the Tories cachinnate, and the opposition benches try to make noises of sympathy. Three minutes! The House of Commons at the best of times is an unforgiving ecosystem: lose your way for just a few seconds, and you will feel the scorn of the Chamber. By now Churchill has been unable to pronounce a word for longer than you have been reading this chapter.

This is disaster, a living death. People are starting to whisper and look at the floor. This is what happened to Randolph, they say; poor young chap, going the way of his father—overwhelmed by a horrible premature senility. At last he sits down. 'I thank the House for having listened to me,' he says in despair, and covers his head with his hands.

The following day the papers are full of Mr Churchill's shipwreck, and a famous nerve specialist is called upon to diagnose the cause. It is a case, says the doctor, of 'defective cerebration'. Well, there can't be a person in the world who hasn't at some time suffered from defective cerebration—a useful-sounding disorder—but that wasn't really the problem with Winston Churchill that day.

If we have one unshakeable and instinctive conviction about him, it is that he was the greatest public speaker of the last hundred years; definitely the greatest orator Britain has produced, and perhaps even knocking Martin Luther King off the global number-one spot. He is the only politician whose speeches and speaking style can still be parodied by people of all ages.

Ah, Churchill! we say, and we jut our chins and recite something, in that familiar sing-song growl, about fighting them on the beaches. He stands in relation to oratory as Shakespeare stands to the writing of plays: the top performer, a mixture of Pericles and Abraham Lincoln with a small but irrefutable dash of Les Dawson.

We think of him as somehow supernaturally gifted, as if he had sprung from a union of Zeus and Polyhymnia the very Muse of Rhetoric. I am afraid we are only partly right.

The truth is that he was a genius in his own way, but he wasn't really a natural. He was no Lloyd George; he was no Luther King, at least in the sense that he could not improvise as some born speakers can; and when he spoke it certainly did not pour from his full heart in profuse strains of unpremeditated art.

Churchill's speeches were a triumph of effort, and preparation, in which phrases were revised and licked into shape as a she-bear licks her cubs. Dancing before him like a will-o'-the-wisp was always the ghostly luminescence of his father's reputation, and as he grows up we can feel him straining and yearning in emulation.

We catch him at Harrow, speaking up noisily in a debate with senior boys. As a Sandhurst subaltern, he makes a passionate defence of the right of some prostitutes to frequent the bar of the Empire in

Leicester Square. 'Ladies of the Empire,' says the nineteen-year-old virgin, rising on a stool amid his guffawing comrades, 'I stand for liberty!'

It is not immediately obvious why this subject—the freedom of prostitutes to ply their trade—should have prompted the first public speech by Britain's greatest statesman.

There is no evidence of any reward for his intervention, carnal or otherwise. The answer is surely that it was a jape. He wanted to draw attention to himself—and he succeeded. The speech was reported in the papers.

By the age of twenty-three he thought himself a sufficiently experienced orator to write an essay on the subject called 'The Scaffolding of Rhetoric'. This is a splendidly portentous and self-confident document—never published in his lifetime—in which he seems to be analysing what he obviously considers to be his own success. 'Sometimes a slight and not unpleasing stammer or impediment has been of some assistance in securing the attention of the audience,' he says—a point that may not be unconnected with his lisp, and what he claimed was an obstructive ligament in his tongue, unknown to the anatomy of any other human being.

He goes on to describe the effects of his prescribed methods on the human herd: 'The cheers become louder and more frequent; the enthusiasm momentarily increases; until they are convulsed by emotions they are unable to control and shaken by passions of which they have resigned all direction.' That is certainly a trick that some orators have been able to perform. That was the skill that fate had given his greatest adversary—the German dictator against whom he would have to wage rhetorical war in 1940 and beyond.

But was it really Churchill's skill? Did his audience quiver like aspens? Were they convulsed by emotions they were unable to control? His maiden speech in the Commons is generally held to have been a success; and yet at least one observer thought he looked a bit weedy—'scholarly and limp'. People inevitably drew comparisons with Randolph, and they were not always kind.

'Mr Churchill does not inherit his father's voice—save for the slight lisp—or his father's manner. Accent, address, appearance do not help him,' said one review. Another journalist noted, in an essentially friendly piece, that 'Mr Churchill and oratory are not neighbours yet. Nor do I think it likely they ever will be.'

This kind of criticism was perhaps frustrating for Churchill. He took enormous pride in his speeches, and in his novel *Savrola*— written when he was in India—he paints a gloriously self-aggrandising picture of his (aka Savrola's) methods of composition.

What was there to say? Successive cigarettes had been mechanically consumed. Amid the smoke he saw a peroration, which would cut deep into the hearts of a crowd; a high thought, a fine simile, expressed in that correct diction which is comprehensible even to the most illiterate, and appeals to the most simple; something to lift their minds from the material cares of life and to awake sentiment. His ideas began to take the form of words, to group themselves into sentences; he murmured to himself; the rhythm of his own language swayed him; instinctively he alliterated. Ideas succeeded one another, as a stream flows swiftly by and the light changes on its waters. He seized a piece of paper and began hurriedly to pencil notes. That was a point; could not tautology accentuate it? He scribbled down a rough sentence, scratched it out, polished it, and wrote it again. The sound would please their ears, the sense improve and stimulate their minds. What a game it was! His brain contained the cards he had to play, the world the stakes he played for.

As he worked, the hours passed away. The housekeeper entering with his luncheon found him silent and busy; she had seen him thus before and did not venture to interrupt him. The untasted food grew cold upon the table, as the hands of the clock moved slowly round marking the measured tread of time. Presently he rose, and, completely under the influence of his own thoughts and language, began to pace the room with short rapid strides, speaking to himself in a low voice and with great emphasis. Suddenly he stopped, and with a strange violence his hand descended on the table. It was the end of the speech. . . .

A dozen sheets of note paper, covered with phrases, facts, and figures, were the result of the morning's work. They lay pinned together on the table, harmless insignificant pieces of paper; and yet Antonio Molara, President of the Republic of Laurania, would have feared a bombshell less. Nor would he have been either a fool or a coward.

I like this sketch, because I am sure it shows his early speech-making methods; and it shows the absolute primacy of his interest in language. It is the words which count, and the pleasure of assembling them to get the rhythm he wants, and the effect that he wants.

It's all about the music of the speech, more than the logic or the substance. It's the sizzle not the sausage.

And that was the charge against him—the fatal suggestion that he did not quite believe what he was saying. There is a very simple reason why he crashed and burned that day in April 1904. He was not speaking from the heart; he was not speaking from profound and intimate knowledge of the matter acquired over years of dealing with trade unions.

He was speaking from memory. He had written the speech in the *Savrola* manner, and then he had learned it parrot fashion, word for word. And after forty-five minutes of sledging from the Tories he just forgot what came next—or possibly succumbed to some subconscious repulsion at the socialist sentiments he was expressing.

He never made that mistake again. He kept his sheaf of typewritten notes, pinned together, and had no shame whatever in peering down at them through his black horn-rims. Churchill's speeches were Ciceronian in their essentially literary nature: they were declamations of text.

He had great triumphs in the Commons—see his speeches as Chancellor, compendious and lucid expositions of economics as he understood it—and yet for most of his career his listeners would report that there was something missing. Yes, he was good at the verbal pyrotechnics: but where was the feeling, where was the truth, where was the authenticity? Lloyd George said in 1936 that Churchill was 'a rhetorician and not an orator. He thought only of how a phrase sounded and not how it might influence crowds'. In 1909 the Liberal MP Edwin Montagu wrote to Asquith: 'Winston is not yet Prime Minister, and even if he were he carries no guns. He delights and tickles, he even enthuses the audience he addresses—but when he has gone, so also has the memory of what he has said.'

Even his keenest supporters saw this flaw in his make-up. Lord Beaverbrook was one of those who helped propel him to power in 1940; but in 1936 he observed that 'he lacks the proper note of sincerity for which the country listens'.

As so often, Churchill was more than willing to acknowledge his own defects. He knew that he got carried away with words, and he admitted it. 'I do not care so much for the principles I advocate as for the impression which my words produce,' he once said.

That is perhaps how he might now be remembered—as an old-fashioned and hyperbolical merchant of bombast; the kind of speaker who thinks it droll to refer to an untruth as a 'terminological inexactitude'; or to remark, with unthinking and jaw-dropping prejudice, that the Hindus were a 'foul race protected by their pullulation from the doom that is their due'.

He might be thought of as a man whose love of lush language exceeded his good sense, who lacked that vital note of sincerity—and therefore who lacked the final power to persuade.

All that changed in 1940, because by then events themselves had reached their own pitch of hyperbole. The crisis facing Britain attained the exalted level of Churchill's speeches. At once he seemed neither over the top nor archaic in his manner, because he was required to evoke ancient instincts—the deep desire of the islanders to beat off an invader; and the danger was so intense and so obvious that there could be no question about his sincerity.

Churchill responded to history with some of the most sublime speeches ever made. It is not that they were necessarily masterpieces of oratorical theatre. Set Hitler and Churchill side by side; look at the recordings of their speeches on YouTube—and it is obvious that for sheer demagogic power the Nazi leader is way out in front.

It is true that he used Goebbels as his warm-up act, whipping the audience to an anti-Semitic frenzy; and he used tricks of staging: searchlights, music, torches, all designed to accentuate the mood. But that wasn't the secret. Look at Hitler, if you can bear it, and see his hypnotic quality. First the long, excruciating pause before he speaks; and then see how he begins so softly—with his arms folded— and how he uncoils them as his voice starts to rise, and then the awful jabbing fluidity of his gestures, perfectly timed to intensify the crescendos of his speech.

He has some paper on the table in front: but he hardly refers to it. He seems to be speaking entirely without notes. See the effect on his audience: the happy beams on the faces of the young women, the shouts from the men, and the way their arms rise as one to salute him like the fronds of some huge undersea creature.

Listen to the way he brings them all to their collective climax: with short verbless phrases—grammatically meaningless, but full of suggestive power. It was to become a highly influential technique, copied, among others, by Tony Blair.

Look at good old Churchill, on the other hand. There he is—notes in hand, organised like a series of haikus on the page, though every one is a full and grammatical sentence, complete with main verb. His gestures seem wooden by comparison, and slightly mistimed: now and then an arm thrown out in a disjointed way.

As for the delivery: well, the sad thing is that we don't have his Commons performances, and must make do with recordings he made for broadcast. There is plenty of growl—but he certainly neither rants nor raves, and if anything some of his phrases have a downward slide, a dying fall. Perhaps he gave things a bit more oomph in the Commons, but you can see why he didn't always get good reviews.

In fact, as Richard Toye has recently shown in his excellent survey *The Roar of the Lion*, it is a bit of a myth to think that the country 'rallied behind Churchill'. Here is our old friend Evelyn Waugh, taking the opportunity of his death in 1965 to put the boot in again. 'Rallied the nation indeed! I was a serving soldier in 1940. How we despised his orations.'

Churchill was a 'radio personality' who had outlived his prime, said Waugh. Some people complained that he was drunk, or tired, or too old, or that he was trying too hard for effect. Toye has unearthed the verdict of A. N. Gerrard, a clerk from Manchester, who said of Churchill that 'he gives the impression, when he speaks, of knowing he is expected to "deliver the goods" and of endeavouring to make his speeches of such quality that they will be handed down to posterity, as in Lincoln's Gettysburg Address, for instance. I think he fails miserably.'

Toye finds soldiers listening to him in hospital wards, and shouting 'fucking liar' or 'fucking bullshit'. At the end of one of his radio addresses, the aunt of a diarist by the name of M. A. Pratt said, 'He's no speaker, is he?'

There were people who disliked him for being too Tory, or too anti-communist, or too bellicose. They gave their opinions freely to a government-financed social research exercise called Mass Observation—and it is when one thinks of all these dissenters, innocently knocking the great war leader in the country's hour of maximum peril, that one is tempted to turn Toye's argument on its head.

Surely it doesn't really detract from Churchill's reputation that he had robust criticism from a sizeable slice of the British public. What was the war all about—at least, according to him? What were we fighting for?

Churchill's whole pitch to the nation was that we were fighting for a series of old English freedoms—and high up among those freedoms was the right to say what you think of the government, without the fear of arbitrary and extrajudicial arrest. Of course some people found some of his speeches irritating. But that is true of virtually every great speech ever made.

Someone might have reminded the waspish A. N. Gerrard, who compared Churchill unfavourably to Lincoln, of what *The Times* had said in 1863. 'The ceremony at Gettysburg was rendered ludicrous by some of the luckless sallies of that poor president Lincoln.'

The reality is surely that the bashers and the knockers were there in numbers, and quite rightly, in a way that the Nazis would never have allowed. But look at the statistics at the end of Toye's book: the massive audiences for his broadcasts, the stratospheric approval ratings. People were buoyed, bucked, energised by what he said.

They felt the nape of their necks prickle and tears in their eyes, and when Vita Sackville-West heard him one night on the radio she felt a shiver down her spine—not of disgust or embarrassment, but of excitement and the knowledge that he was right.

He found in the war the words to speak directly to people's hearts—in a way that had perhaps eluded him in his previous career. He didn't always tell the exact truth. At one stage, said Harold Nicolson, his estimates for the size of the British navy included some steamers on the Canadian lakes.

Group Captain A. G. Talbot was responsible for the anti-U-boat campaign at sea. He got the following response, when he had the effrontery to question Churchill's statistics for the sinking of the German submarines: 'There are two people who sink U-boats in this war, Talbot. You sink them in the Atlantic and I sink them in the House of Commons. The trouble is that you are sinking them at exactly half the rate I am.' But in the main people felt he was straight with them, and certainly frank about the challenge facing the country.

They liked his jokes, because laughter gave them release from the anxieties of their lives. His fellow MP Chips Channon was among those who thought his 'levity' was out of place—but the public generally enjoyed the way he called the Nazis 'Narzis' and Hitler 'Herr Schickelgruber' and Pétain 'Peetayne'. Above all he spoke to people in language that was instantly understandable. Harold Nicolson summed it up in 1943. 'The winning formula was the combination of great flights of oratory with sudden swoops into the intimate and conversational. Of all his devices it is the one that never fails.'

He was going back to one of the key precepts of his essay of 1897, on the Scaffolding of Rhetoric—the use of short words. We hear the youthful Churchill speaking down the decades to the old war leader, whispering in the wrinkly ear of his sixty-five-year-old avatar.

'Audiences prefer short homely words of common usage,' he says. 'The shorter words of a language are usually the more ancient. Their meaning is more ingrained in the national character and they appeal with greater force to simple understanding than words recently introduced from the Latin and the Greek.'

It is a lesson that infuses the great speeches of the war. If you look at the manuscript of the 'finest hour' speech, you can see that he has actually crossed out 'liberated' and put 'freed' in its place.

For a perfect example of that combination mentioned by Nicolson, the swoop from the lofty to the plain, look at that immortal line about the Battle of Britain. It is 20 August 1940, and the war for the skies is at its height. In fact, the point has come where Britain has no reserves left; virtually every single aircraft is up there trying to fight the Germans off.

General Hastings 'Pug' Ismay, his military secretary, described being with Churchill. 'I felt sick with fear. As the evening closed in the fighting died down, and we left by car for Chequers. Churchill's first words were, "Don't speak to me. I have never been so moved." After about five minutes he leaned forward and said, "Never in the field of human conflict has so much been owed by so many to so few."'

Now Churchill was not just asking for silence so that the emotion could wash over him, but so that he could do what all good journalists do in such circumstances: he wanted to verbalise and articulate his feeling.

We begin with the elevated diction—'the field of human conflict' is a pompous and typically Churchillian circumlocution for war. Then we go to those short Anglo-Saxon zingers. Look how much work those six words are made to do.

'So much'. What is this thing that is owed in such quantity? He means gratitude: for protecting England, for warm beer, suburbia, village cricket, democracy, public libraries, everything that makes the country special and that had been placed in mortal peril by the Luftwaffe.

'So many'. Who are the many? He means the whole country, and those beyond England who depend on her to survive; the subjugated French; the Americans; everyone who hopes that Hitler will not win.

'So few'. It is a very ancient idea that there is a particular heroism in the struggle of few against many. We few, we happy few, says Shakespeare's Henry V, and in Churchill's mental hard drive there are the 1,200 lines of Macaulay's *Lays of Ancient Rome*, including the speech of Horatius Cocles, who held off the Etruscan hordes. 'In yon straight path a thousand may well be stopped by three,' he cried.

In this case every listener understood him to be referring to the tiny number of the RAF pilots—relative to the millions of people then under arms—who went up into the skies, and so often failed to come back, but who determined the course of the war.

It is a perfect epigram, in that you can remember it as soon as you hear it, tightly compressed; and it is rhythmically perfect. To use technical rhetorical terms, it is a classic descending tricolon with anaphora, or repetition of key words. Each leg, or colon, is shorter than the last.

(Never in the field of human conflict has)
    So much been owed by
    So many to
    So few.

If you want a classic ascending tricolon, then try his peerless line from 1942, after the victory at El Alamein.

Now this is not the end.

It is not even the beginning of the end.

But it is, perhaps, the end of the beginning.

When he uncorks this one at the Lord Mayor's Banquet, you hear his audience laugh with pleasure and surprise. That is because in this case the last colon is varied by chiasmus, in that he swaps 'beginning' and 'end' so as to make the mind race and, again, to create an instant quotation that is entirely etymologically Anglo-Saxon.

I dwell on these rhetorical tricks, because it is important to recognise that all great speeches to some extent depend on them. Since the days of Gorgias the sophist there have been those who have argued that all rhetoric is suspect, that it makes the weaker argument the stronger, that it bamboozles the audience.

If you listen to Hitler on YouTube, you will find him making a speech that is distressingly similar—in theme and structure—to Churchill's 'fight them on the beaches' speech. 'We shall never slacken, never tire, never lose faith', etc., etc. And yet you have only to make the comparison to watch it disintegrate.

What does Hitler want? Conquest and revenge. What emotions do his speeches provoke? Paranoia and hate. What does Churchill want? Well, that is a good question—because, apart from survival, there is a wonderful vagueness about his teleology, uplifting though it is.

He wants 'broader lands and better days', he says, or 'broad sunlit uplands'. He likes the idea of a 'definitely larger period'. A larger period? What's that? Sounds like something to do with obesity. And what does he mean by 'broader lands'? Norfolk?

I think he doesn't really know what he wants (a problem that was to become politically acute once the war was over), except a general sense of benignity and happiness and peace and the preservation of the world he grew up in. As for the emotions that his speeches provoked—they were entirely healthy.

Yes, there were plenty of sceptics. But for millions of people—sophisticated and unsophisticated—he deployed his rhetorical skills to put courage in their hearts and to make them believe they could fight off a threat more deadly than any they had ever known.

Hitler showed the evil that could be done by the art of rhetoric. Churchill showed how it could help to save humanity. It has been said that the difference between Hitler's speeches and Churchill's speeches was that Hitler made you think he could do anything; Churchill made you think you could do anything.

The world was lucky he was there to give the roar. His speeches were to earn him an undying reputation, and undying popularity. He loved that applause, of course; and to some extent making a speech was like his constant search for physical excitement.

He wanted the risk, the exposure, the adrenalin—and the acclaim. Many people are made like that, and many are performers who exist only for their public. They are loved by the multitude; and often they turn out to be monsters in private.

That was emphatically not the case with Churchill. He not only took the wider public with him, he earned the devotion of those who were closest.

# CHAPTER 8

# A PROPER
# HUMAN HEART

It is not raining in London 94 per cent of the time. This, alas, is not one of those times. I am soaked. My blue suit is black and shiny with water and there is a sucking noise in my shoes as I get off my bike and enter the impressive Portland stone gateway.

All the way up the Romford Road I have cycled, through neighbourhoods whose languages and culture have changed a bit since Churchill came this way—past mosques and shops selling saris and kebabs and all the paraphernalia that goes with mobile phones. I am here at the burial-grounds of the City of London, at Wanstead.

'I have come to find a grave,' I tell them at the gate. They assure me I have plenty of choice. 'Dame Anna Neagle's buried here,' says the chap in the peaked cap, helpfully. 'And Sir Bobby Moore, and a couple of Jack the Ripper's victims.' And so are thousands of others.

As far as the eye can see there are the tombs and monuments of the Victorians in marble and porphyry and granite. The names have been in some cases eroded by time and sulphurous rain, and for a few minutes I worry that this is going to be one of those airport car park nightmares, and that I will spend hours pacing the well-kept paths, and getting wetter and wetter.

And then I see it—or a grave exactly matching the description. I squelch towards it over the grass, and yes, surely this is it: a simple cross on a square plinth, and before it a rectangle of freshly tilled earth and a couple of alliums. It occurs to me that someone has been looking after it, a bit. I lean down to read the name at the foot of the plinth.

Winston Spencer Churchill, it says.

Except, of course, that it isn't Churchill's body mouldering underneath. He's somewhere else—at Bladon in Oxfordshire. This is the resting-place of someone he is said to have loved very dearly indeed.

I stand for a moment. It has stopped raining, and drops are falling slowly from the chestnut trees above. I brood on the person below, and her passionate relationship with Churchill; and Churchill's feelings for her.

I am here on a mission, to try to answer the important question about any famous person; the key question, in fact, about any human being. In Churchill's case the question is critical, because there are so many people (and by no means just politicians or journalists) who have secretly or openly regarded his life as the pattern, example, inspiration and role model for their own. That is why we need to dig into his essential nature.

One night I was explaining Churchill to some friends: his bravery, his genius for language, his indomitable energy. 'Yes,' said one friend, leaning back in a languid way, 'but what do you think he was like to meet? I mean: was he a nice guy?'

Well, I can tell you about what he was like to meet—because a few months previously I had virtually met him.

As soon as I walked into the Churchill archive in Cambridge I bit back a yelp of alarm. Allen Packwood, the director, was there to greet me, and he seemed to be holding out an artificial hand. Manners, of course, got the better of me, and I shook his prosthesis; and then I realised that it was made of bronze.

'You have just shaken the hand of Winston Churchill,' he said. I examined the cast, and was struck by how dainty it seemed. The fingers were shapely, but not long or large. This was the hand that so fiercely swung polo mallets until the age of fifty-two, that fired Mausers, that steered seaplanes, that pulled apart the barbed wire of no man's land.

This was the hand that signed the paper that felled the city, five sovereign fingers that put a regime to death. 'He had small hands,' confirmed Allen. I would say that Churchill's hands were about the same size as his mother's—and if you doubt me, have a look at the cast of Jennie's hand in a glass case at Chartwell. Churchill's hands look rather finer.

'And they were very pink,' said Allen, 'because he liked baths so much.' It wasn't just that his hands were small. We all know that statue in Parliament Square, of Churchill hunched forward with his stick. You have the impression of a physical colossus with raking arms and bison-like shoulders. In fact Martin Gilbert says he was 5 foot 8, while other authorities—William Manchester, Norman Rose—say he was at best 5 foot 6½.

There are some photos of him walking across Horse Guards—leg swinging in his butler's trousers—and I swear there is a touch of the Tom Cruise about the heel. When I told Andrew Roberts, that most eminent Churchillian, of Churchill's vertical sub-eminence, he was not entirely surprised. 'I knew we would have seen eye to eye!' he exclaimed.

Who else was 5 foot 6 or under? Some of the biggest tyrants and creeps in world history: Augustus (5 foot 6), Napoleon (ditto), Mussolini (ditto), Stalin (teensy at 5 foot 4). Hitler was only 5 foot 8. All these characters have been associated with the over-compensatory aggression that is sometimes referred to as 'short man' syndrome; and there is some evidence, at least on the face of it, that Churchill suffered from this, too.

He could certainly be—how shall we say—short with people. Roberts has daringly observed that, of the two men, Hitler was probably kinder and more solicitous to his staff. Churchill would not only keep them up all night while he dictated; he could get quite testy if they got things wrong. 'Where were you educated?' he would shout. 'Why don't you read a book?'

Mind you, he didn't only shout at underlings. We have a description of him from the 1920s, marching about Baldwin's room during a dispute with Neville Chamberlain, ranting and shaking his fist. Let us therefore now assemble the whole case against his character. Let us follow the example of the modern showboating district attorney, and create a kind of insinuating hodge-podge or collage of all the evidence—trivial or otherwise.

The case against him is that he was not only the greatest man of modern British history but also, in his own sweet way, something of a tosser in his treatment of others.

Here are the things that his enemies (and sometimes his friends) would say, and the reasons they gave for saying them. They said that he behaved like a spoilt child; and we must accept that he was used to getting his way—and from a very early age. Read the emetic and manipulative letters he writes to his mother at the age of twelve, begging her to let him go to see Buffalo Bill.

. . . I want to see Buffalo Bill and the Play as you promised me. I shall be very disappointed, disappointed is not the word I shall be miserable, after you have promised me, and all, I shall never trust your promises again. But I know Mummy loves her Winny too much for that . . .

And so on in a similar vein. This was the first of three such letters about Buffalo Bill, and they show not just his iron determination but his sense of entitlement. By the age of fourteen he had already persuaded one of his schoolchums—one Milbanke—to take down his dictation while he reclined in the bath. Poor Milbanke was later to die at Gallipoli, but he was the first of many bathside amanuenses.

As Churchill's sister-in-law Lady Gwendoline 'Goonie' Bertie put it, he had a tendency to 'orientalism', and was never so happy as when a servant was pulling on his socks. He may have shown outstanding bravery when he went to the trenches, but his luxuries were astonishing.

To the front with Churchill went a private bathtub, large towels, a hot-water bottle, food boxes from Fortnum and Mason, large slabs of corned beef, Stilton cheeses, cream, ham, sardines, dried fruit, and a big steak pie, not to mention peach brandy and other liqueurs. 'You must remember,' his wife once told his doctor, 'he knows nothing of the lives of ordinary people.'

He never took a bus in his life, she said, and had only once been on the London Underground; one of the few modern technical marvels that defeated him. He got lost, and had to be helped to find his way out.

Ladies and gentlemen of the jury, there are those who will tell you that he was not only irascible, and spoilt, but that he was a bully. Remember the murky affair at Sandhurst, and the way the young officers all ganged up on the subaltern called Bruce—so that he was effectively forced to leave.

There is no sign that Churchill did the Christian thing, and tried to reassure the anxious soldier. On the contrary, there were those who said Churchill was the positive ringleader of the bullying.

What is worse than being a spoilt and irascible bully? How about the general charge that he didn't really have real friends—only people he 'used' for his own advancement. In the recent docudrama *The Gathering Storm* we see the way a young Foreign Office man called Ralph Wigram was persuaded to go down to Chartwell and brief Churchill about the reality of German rearmament—information that Churchill was to use ruthlessly and effectively in his attacks on Stanley Baldwin's government.

In taking these documents from Whitehall, Wigram put his career on the line. He was eventually suspected of leaking to Churchill, and sidelined within the Foreign Office. In the telly drama we see the toll this takes on his family, the threats from his superiors; and then he appears to commit suicide. Poor fellow—the drama seems to say—sacrificed for the sake of Churchill's ambition.

Or what about the charge of ratting on his friends—in many people's eyes the ultimate crime? When he made his famous escape from the Boer jail in Pretoria, there were two men who were meant to go with him, called Haldane and Brockie. The suggestion was that Churchill had welched on the agreement, and scooted off by himself.

An aggressive, spoilt, bullying double-crosser: what else can we add? The final charge is just that he was too self-interested, too wrapped up in himself to be properly human.

Suppose you were a young woman ushered into a dinner party, and found yourself sitting next to the great man. The allegation against Churchill was that he was really fascinated by only one subject, and that was Winston Churchill. As Margot Asquith put it: 'Winston, like all really self-centred people, ends up by boring people.' So that is the case for the prosecution, Your Honour.

Winston Leonard Spencer-Churchill is accused of being a spoilt, bullying, double-crossing, self-centred bore, and a bit of an all-round brute. Let's now call the counsel for the defence—a role I am also happy, for the sake of argument, to play myself.

Take first the assertion that he was a tyrant to his staff. Yes, of course he pushed people hard, and it is certainly true that poor Alan Brooke, his military adviser, was driven more or less round the bend in the war—silently snapping pencils in an effort to control his feelings. But think of the stress that Churchill was under, coordinating a war that we showed no sign of winning.

It was not as if Churchill was always unaware of his behaviour. 'I wonder that a great many of my colleagues are on speaking terms with me,' he said. He would sometimes break out of his marathon dictation sessions, realise that his assistants were getting cold, and make the fire himself.

On the death of Violet Pearman, one of his most faithful and put-upon secretaries, he made sure that her daughter got money from his own pocket. He sent money to the wife of his doctor, when she got into difficulties. When a friend of his was injured in the Boer War, Churchill rolled up his sleeve and provided a skin graft himself—without anaesthetic.

Was this the action of a selfish tosser? 'When you first meet Winston you see all his faults,' said Churchill's early love interest Pamela Plowden. 'You spend the rest of your life discovering his virtues.'

Let us turn now to the allegations of his luxury amid the squalor of the trenches—the suggestion that he somehow lorded it over the rest of the battalion. What nonsense.

It is true that there was a certain amount of dudgeon when he arrived at his command in January 1916. Who was this politician? grumbled the Scots Fusiliers. Why couldn't he find another battalion? Churchill began by launching a savage rhetorical attack on the louse, *Pulex europaeus*. The men listened, amazed, to his disquisition on the origins of the insect, its nature, its habitat, its importance in wars ancient and modern.

He then organised for unused brewery vats to be brought to Mool-enacker for a collective delousing—and it worked. Respect for Churchill climbed. He reduced punishments. He dished out his luxuries to all who visited the mess. Read *With Winston Churchill at the Front*, published by 'Captain X' (in reality Andrew Dewar-Gibb), who saw what happened with his own eyes.

If a man left that mess 'without a large cigar lighting up his molli-fied countenance, that was because he was a non-smoker and through no fault of Col Churchill'. He did the same with the peach and apri-cot brandy. Yes, there was a bath—described by Dewar-Gibb as a kind of long soap dish; but plenty of other people used it. Churchill's trenches reign was somehow both democratic and domestic, says Dewar-Gibb, and he paints a picture of the battalion at rest: Chur-chill sitting tilted in a rickety chair, reading a pocket Shakespeare and beating time to the gramophone, with other officers lounging about or reading in the sun.

Remember that these men are taking awful casualties, with shells (German and sometimes British) exploding around them virtually every day. It was Churchill who got them singing music-hall songs—some of them a bit 'robust' for Captain Dewar-Gibb's taste. It was Churchill who urged them to laugh when they could. One young of-ficer, Jock MacDavid, later recalled that 'After a very brief period he had accelerated the morale of officers and men to an almost unbe-lievable degree. It was sheer personality.'

I put it to you that this is the conduct of a leader, a man with a proper care for the welfare of his charges. This is not the behaviour of a bully; and we can likewise dismiss the old canard about the treat-ment of poor Bruce the subaltern at Sandhurst.

Almost all the allegations were peddled by a radical journalist and MP (and ocean-going creep) called Henry Labouchere, who was not only vehemently anti-Semitic but moved a horrible motion in Parliament that criminalised all homosexual activity. The allegations do not appear to have any foundation. Churchill's lawyers easily dismissed the baseless suggestion that he had indulged in 'practices of the Oscar Wilde variety' and he won very substantial damages.

Did he really 'use' young Ralph Wigram, and recklessly blight his career? It is not quite clear that Wigram did commit suicide, and in any event the Foreign Office man leaked information to Churchill because he wanted to expose the horror of what was happening in Germany, and government complacency.

He did it out of a sense of duty—not because he was cozened by Churchill. After the funeral, Churchill threw a lunch party at Chartwell for the mourners; and showed great solicitude to his wife, Ava, with whom he remained in touch for many years afterwards.

Nor does Churchill need to reproach himself for any detail of his conduct towards Haldane and Brockie, his two would-be fellow-escapees from the Pretorian jail. It is absolutely clear from all the diaries and letters that when it came down to it, on the night, they just wimped out.

Churchill went into the latrine and jumped over the wall, and then waited for them for an hour and a half in the garden, risking detection. But they never came: he can't be blamed for that! He later sent gold watches to all those who helped him escape, a present he could ill afford. Did he do it out of some sense of guilt? On the contrary; he did it out of characteristic impulsiveness and generosity.

Let us deal lastly with the general charge of selfishness: that he wasn't much interested in other people, that he wasn't much fun at parties—except when bragging about himself. Of course he was self-centred, and narcissistic—a fact that he readily acknowledged. But that does not mean he had no interest in or care for other people.

Read his letters to Clementine, worrying about such things as whether the baby is going to lick the paint off the Noah's ark animals. Think of his kindness to his mother—who had actually cheated him of his £200,000 inheritance; how he puts his arms round her on the day of her wedding to George Cornwallis-West, and tells her that her own happiness is all that matters.

Note his endless generosity towards his younger brother Jack, who lives with Churchill in Downing Street in the war. All the evidence suggests that Churchill was warm hearted to the point of downright sentimentality. He showers kindness on his menagerie at Chartwell (not conclusive, of course: Hitler liked Blondi, his Alsatian; but Churchill's love extended much farther over the animal kingdom).

He blubs at the drop of a hat. He weeps at the news that Londoners are queuing to buy birdseed to feed their canaries during the Blitz; he weeps when he tells an ecstatic House of Commons that he has been forced by fate to blow up the French navy; he weeps when he watches Alexander Korda's *Lady Hamilton*, a film he sees seventeen times. He loved cheap music, and we have plenty of vignettes of Churchill bawling out his favourites; he was no party-pooper.

He was openly emotional in a class and society that was supposed to be all about the stiff upper lip. And—most unusually for a British politician—he never bore grudges. People responded to this warmth; and if he was exhausting to work for, his colleagues nonetheless gave him loyalty and unstinting devotion.

When he came back from New York in 1932, after nearly dying under the wheels of an oncoming car, he was presented with a Daimler. The Daimler had been organised by Brendan Bracken, and financed by a whip-round of 140 friends and admirers.

Can you think of any modern British politician with enough friends and admirers to get them a new Nissan Micra, let alone a Daimler? It would be fair to say that his wife did not always approve of his friends: F. E. Smith was a boozer; Beaverbrook was said to have been dodgy in his business dealings; and Brendan Bracken—who rather played up the (absurd) suggestion that he was Churchill's illegitimate son—was positively bizarre.

Bracken lied about his age, even going back to school in order to fake it. He lied about his Irish origins, and claimed to be Australian. A fine man, you might think, to end up being Minister for Information. But Churchill stuck with them, and they with him.

Reading that account by Dewar-Gibb of Churchill in the trenches, I am struck by the favourable mention of Lord Fisher—the great naval chief who went so spectacularly wobbly over the Dardanelles in 1915, and whose inconstancy contributed significantly to the delay, and therefore to the disaster.

'Colonel Churchill amused us much by his frequent stories of Lord Fisher,' says Captain Dewar-Gibb, 'for whom he seemed to have the greatest admiration.' That shows superb generosity of soul, when you consider that Fisher's wacko behaviour had helped all but destroy Churchill's political career.

On leave from the trenches for a couple of days, he then made a speech in the Commons urging the recall of Fisher to the Admiralty—a suggestion that most people thought was final proof that Churchill had lost the plot altogether. He didn't have to defend Fisher—in fact Fisher had been spectacularly disloyal to him, telling Clementine (falsely, it seems) that the reason Churchill was always hopping over to Paris was to see a girlfriend.

There was every reason, rationally, for him to chuck the old man overboard. But Churchill didn't think like that: he liked Fisher, he admired him, and he wanted to express it.

He had what the Greeks called *megalopsychia*—greatness of soul. Churchill was not a practising Christian. He never believed in the more challenging metaphysics of the New Testament; and when some prelate benignly hailed him as a 'pillar of the church' he had the honesty instantly to demur. He was more of a 'flying buttress', he said.

His ethic was really pre-Christian, even Homeric. His abiding interest was in glory and prestige—both for himself and for the 'British Empire'. But he had a deep sense of what it was right and fitting for him to do—and remember that his self-narrator's eye was beadily following and judging him all the time.

THAT IS WHY I am here at this sodden graveyard in East London. The lady before and beneath me is—of course—Churchill's nanny. 'Erected to the memory of Elizabeth Ann Everest,' says the inscription, 'who died on 3rd July 1895 aged 62 years, by Winston Spencer Churchill and John Spencer Churchill'.

Compared to the other memorials, it is not a particularly gushing tribute. There is no mention of love, or angels singing her to rest; and indeed the two-foot cross is just about the smallest and plainest that I can see. The story of how it came to be here is in some ways an awful one, but also a physical testimonial to the fundamental goodness of Churchill's nature.

As we have seen, Churchill's mother Jennie was a remote and glamorous figure, swishing in panther-like in her skin-tight riding gear to kiss him goodnight; otherwise not much involved. It was Mrs Everest, a largish and middle-aged woman from the Medway towns, who gave Churchill the unstinting love he craved. Most Churchill biographies rightly contain a splendid picture of her looking a bit like a pudgy Queen Victoria: white lace cap and black dress, with so much bustle and petticoat that she appears as pyramidical in structure as Everest itself.

'My nurse was my confidante,' said Churchill. 'Mrs Everest it was who looked after me and tended all my wants. It was to her I poured out my many troubles.' He called her 'Woom' or 'Woomany', and we have many lovely letters from her to him: urging him to take heroin for his toothache, to watch out for the east wind, not to try to get on moving trains, to avoid the hot weather, and debt, and bad company.

On one famous occasion neither of his parents could be bothered to come to his Speech Day at Harrow; so Mrs Everest came, and Churchill walked around town with her, arm proudly in arm, while the other boys snickered. That showed moral courage; and more was to come.

When Churchill was seventeen and Jack was eleven it was decided that the nanny was no longer needed; and though there were plenty of posh English families that retained their superannuated nannies, Churchill's mother made no provision for Mrs Everest. She was to be out on her ear.

Churchill was incensed. He protested, supposedly on behalf of his brother; and as a compromise work was found for her at the London home of his grandmother, the Duchess. But two years later that job, too, came to an end. Again Churchill was angry that she was being treated in this way—dismissed by a letter! He accused his mother of being 'cruel and mean'.

It was no good. Mrs Everest went to live in Crouch End, and Churchill helped to support her from his own relatively meagre income. She continued to write to him, and while he was at Sandhurst she sent him some encouragement. 'Take plenty of open air exercise and you will not require medicine . . . Be a good Gentleman, upright, honest, just, kind and altogether lovely. My sweet old darling, how I do love you, be good for my sake.'

By 1895 Mrs Everest's health was failing, and on 2 July he received a telegram at Sandhurst, saying that her condition was 'critical'. He arrived at Crouch End, to find her only concern was for him: he had got wet on the way there. 'The jacket had to be taken off and thoroughly dried before she was calm again.'

He found a doctor and a nurse, and then had to rush back to Aldershot for the morning parade—returning to North London as soon as the parade was over. She sank into a stupor and died at 2.15 a.m., with Churchill by her side.

It was Churchill who organised the funeral and the wreaths and the tombstone, and indeed it was Churchill who paid for them all, out of his own exiguous resources. He was only twenty.

It is hard to know exactly how much the world owes Winston Churchill's nanny. But if anyone taught him to be good and kind and by and large truthful, it was surely her. She it was, I reckon, who helped him to that vast and generous moral sense.

Once, at the age of seven, he was walking with his nanny in the grounds of Blenheim. 'We saw a snake crawling about in the grass,' he wrote to his father. 'I wanted to kill it but Everest would not let me.' Chapeau, Mrs Everest.

It may be that Churchill despaired when Everest died, and thought he would never again find a woman so rock-like and dependable. If so, he was wrong there. It is time to consider his brilliant decision to marry Clementine; and, indeed, the eternal puzzle of Winston Churchill's relations with women in general.

# CHAPTER 9

# MY DARLING CLEMENTINE

So let us pause now outside the Temple of Artemis, and adopt the sibilant whisper of a TV naturalist. We have come at the height of August to the vast and rolling park of Blenheim Palace, a noted breeding-ground for the English aristocracy. A light summer shower is falling. It is mid-morning. Inside that graceful little Ionic-porticoed temple the time-honoured mating ritual is coming, in theory, to its climax.

Sitting on the bench at the back are Winston Churchill, thirty-three, President of the Board of Trade, and a lovely female with large dark eyes, called Clementine Hozier. Notice how carefully the male has chosen the location: the palace, to display the wealth and power of his family, and the genes he has to offer; the view of the lake, to inspire feelings of romance; a scrunchy gravel path on either side, to alert him to anyone who might be coming.

Any minute now he is going to pop the question. Clementine is surely aware of the significance of the temple: Artemis is the virgin goddess of hunting, and here the virgin has been brought to bay.

Let us tiptoe over the moss behind the building, and see whether we can hear what they are saying. Shhh.

Churchill appears to be talking . . . and talking. The female is still sitting with her eyes downcast. In fact, she is looking not at the animated face of the male, but at a beetle on the floor. She is watching the beetle as it moves slowly from one crack in the flagstone to the next—and she is wondering, frankly, whether Churchill is ever going to get to the point. Churchill has had her on his own, in the temple, for half an hour—and still he hasn't summoned up the courage to blurt it out.

Any biologist studying the romantic life of Winston Churchill might conclude that he makes the courtship of the giant panda look positively rash and impetuous. He first met Clementine four years ago, and made a not wholly favourable impression. He met her more recently, and things went swimmingly—and now he has sent her letters that make it pretty clear what he has in mind for her. He has plotted it all out, as he plots out so much in his life.

Five days ago, on 7 August 1908, he wrote to invite her to Blenheim, and he dropped a hint that no one could miss. 'I want so much to show you that beautiful place and in its gardens we shall find lots of places to talk in, and lots of things to talk about.' The next day he writes another letter, explaining which train she should catch, and refers to 'those strange mysterious eyes of yours whose secret I have been trying so hard to learn'.

He goes on to warn her, with tactical self-deprecation, that he has difficulties with girls, being 'stupid and clumsy in that relation and naturally quite self-reliant and self-contained'. By that path, he admits, he has managed to 'arrive at loneliness' . . . HINT! HINT! Clementine is being clearly given to understand—by all the forms and conventions of Edwardian England, where premarital sex was a no-no for respectable girls—that she is going to be made an offer.

Well, she has been here in Blenheim for three days, and nothing has happened. Churchill has not lunged; he has not pounced; he has not even coughed as they sat on the sofa, and suddenly draped an arm round her lovely shoulders. Poor thing, we feel: she must be starting to wonder whether she has failed some unspoken exam. Now is the morning when she has to leave, and Churchill has not even got out of bed. In fact (though she doesn't know this) his cousin the Duke of Marlborough himself has had to go into Churchill's room in order to rouse him, and tell him firmly that if he wants to propose to this girl, he had better get up and get a move on.

So at 11 a.m. Churchill has finally found her, and they have walked through the formal gardens, with their neatly shaven bushes and nude Greek statuary; they have turned left and wandered past the boathouse, where the water laps musically under the jetty. They have passed all sorts of bowery corners and bosky nooks of a kind that might have been specifically designed to prompt a marriage proposal.

Now they have been secluded in this temple for what must seem to the young woman to be an agonisingly long time—and still no action. She later describes watching that beetle, moving as slowly as Churchill himself. 'I thought to myself, "If that beetle reaches that crack, and Winston hasn't proposed, he's not going to."' There were plenty of people who would have put money on the beetle.

If you go behind the Temple of Diana (or Artemis) today, you will find graffiti from those who have more recently enjoyed its tranquillity. Someone has charmingly inscribed a swastika, but there are a few love hearts. I bet 'Dave' didn't sit for half an hour before announcing his feelings for 'Sarah'. Knowing us British, I expect this has been the scene of quite a lot of alfresco lovemaking—and those happy fornicators would perhaps be mildly puzzled to hear of Churchill's technique.

Some people have gone so far as to claim that there is no evidence that by the age of thirty-four Churchill had even lost his virginity; and they suggest that this may perhaps help to explain his bashfulness in the temple. There has long been a widely held view that women, or at least sexual relations with women, were less important to Churchill than they are to some other world leaders, or that he had fewer notches on his bedpost than you might expect for a man whose appetites—for praise, food, drink, cigars, excitement, etc.— were generally so titanic. By the time of his engagement one newspaper had already described him as a 'confirmed bachelor'; which didn't carry quite the implication it has these days, but reflected the way he was seen.

'I always hear that no one can nail Winston down to any particular lady,' one woman wrote to Lloyd George, 'and the opinion is that "he is not a lady's man" . . . and that he had a rather curious way of looking at a woman. Winston would become a million times more popular if it could be thought that he cared enough for some woman to risk even a little discomfort for her sake. Perhaps it will come but I doubt it.'

Was he sexist? One group of women who certainly felt that he looked at them in a curious way were the suffragettes. 'You brute!' cried prominent suffragette Theresa Garnett as she attacked him with a dog whip. 'Why don't you treat women properly?' The suffragettes could not forgive his early opposition to their cause. They punched him, knocked him to the ground, and mercilessly heckled and interrupted his speeches, sometimes by ringing bells as he reached his perorations.

Churchill responded with unvarying politeness; and most people now accept that he was a bit hard done by. His initial reservations about female suffrage appear to have been motivated not so much by male chauvinism as by a straight calculation: that polling evidence suggested women would tend to vote Tory. In any case, he eventually changed his tune, and in 1917 he supported the extension of the franchise to all women over thirty.

Nor do most historians now accept the picture of Churchill as some sort of asexual Edward Heath-like character; in fact, the notion is utter nonsense. All his life he loved the company of women, appreciated their beauty, sought them out and tried to show off to them. Even in his mid-seventies we find him doing somersaults in the sea in the south of France, and hoping to impress some Hollywood starlet—slightly to the irritation of Clementine.

For a man who is supposed not to have been much interested, he has a long list of youthful dalliances and entanglements of one kind or other. There is 'the beautiful Polly Hacket', who appears when he is eighteen. They go for walks in the park and he gives her a packet of sugar plums—who are you calling unromantic, eh?

Then he pursues a showgirl of some description called Mabel Love—though history is blushingly silent on what happened between them. He falls head over heels in love with Pamela Plowden, the daughter of the Resident at Hyderabad, and declares she is 'the most beautiful girl I have ever seen'. He takes her on an elephant; does all the right things—it is hardly his fault if she turns him down.

He has a bit of a thing with a married woman called Ettie Grenfell. He makes advances towards Ethel Barrymore, of the showbiz dynasty. He pursues one Muriel Wilson, and spends a week driving around France with her; and then there is the romance with Violet Asquith, who seems to have fallen more or less in love with him, and whose feelings were so strong that he needed to go up to see her, at

Slains castle in Scotland, and propitiate her only two weeks before his marriage to Clementine (perhaps because he feared that there would be political consequences from treating her badly: he depended on her father for promotion, after all).

There are some who now think his relationship with Violet was much more significant, and physical, than has been previously allowed. Who knows what really happened between them? Or between Churchill and the others, and women whose names we don't even know? And frankly who cares?

There are all sorts of reasons why Churchill was not held by his contemporaries to be a modern Casanova, but the most obvious is surely that he was too darned busy. In habits he superficially resembled a Bertie Wooster figure—rising late, living on his own in a flat, smoking cigars with cronies in clubs, surrounded by lissom and intelligent girls who never quite count as girlfriends, and with his devoted secretary Eddie Marsh hovering around like Jeeves. But in industry and output he is the polar opposite. (You will recall Bertie Wooster's credentials as a journalist rested entirely on a single article on 'What the Well-Dressed Man is Wearing' that once appeared in the periodical edited by his Aunt Dahlia called *Milady's Boudoir*.)

Churchill had written five books, and become a Member of Parliament, and reported from multiple war zones, and written innumerable articles, and given many well-paid lectures, by the time he was twenty-five. He was one of the half-dozen youngest people ever to hold cabinet rank. When he sat down on that bench with Clementine, he was already the author of millions of published words, many of them popularly and critically acclaimed. The miracle is that he found any time to see girls at all.

Read his correspondence, and you will find all sorts of tantalising clues about his early romantic career—what does Pamela Plowden

mean when she writes in 1940 to congratulate him on the premiership, by referring back fondly to 'our days of hansom cabs'? Was he
Not Safe In Taxis? But in the end such speculations are not only
impertinent; they are irrelevant. All that matters is that Churchill
beat the beetle; he proposed to Clementine, and, as he put it, they
'lived happily ever after'.

Clementine was twenty-two; her background was relatively impoverished and a little bit rackety—in the sense that her mother, Lady
Blanche Hozier, had enjoyed so many extramarital amours that
Clementine was not entirely sure as to the identity of her father.
Clementine had been engaged three times before, and though many
newspapers commented on her beauty, her rival Violet Asquith was
prepared to be splendidly bitchy about her other qualities.

Here is the seething Violet, writing about the impending marriage to a friend:

> His wife could never be more to him than an ornamental side-
> board as I have often said & she is unexacting enough not to
> mind being more. Whether he will ultimately mind her being
> as stupid as an *owl* I don't know—it is a danger no doubt—but
> for the moment at least she will have a rest from making her
> own clothes & I think he must be a *little* in love. Father [the
> Prime Minister] thinks that it spells disaster for them both.

There speaks a bruised young woman. Clementine was not a side-
board, but wise as a tree full of owls, and the marriage was not a disaster but a triumph. She gave Churchill nothing but the most flabber-
gasting loyalty and support; and made his achievements possible.

These days we have more or less dispensed, thank goodness, with
the concept of the political wife—the woman who serves as a kind of
proxy for her husband, a utensil for the projection of his ambitions.

But Clementine not only believed in her husband—and endlessly discussed politics with him. She believed in him so fiercely that she would go into battle for him, sometimes physically.

When a suffragette tried to push him under a train, Clementine was there to whack the woman with her umbrella. When he was laid up with appendicitis during the election campaign of November 1922, she went up to Dundee to campaign on his behalf. She bravely informed a sceptical public that her husband was not a warmonger; and though that campaign failed (as Churchill put it, he found himself 'without an office, without a seat, without a party and without an appendix'), she was at it again soon after in West Leicester. Again, she contended: 'A lot of people think he is essentially military, but I know him very well, and I know he is not that at all. In fact one of his greatest talents is the talent of peace-making.'

That was surely a well-judged appeal to every man and woman in the audience who knew the importance of the skill of peace-making, not just abroad but in the kitchen and the bedroom. If Churchill had begun his career as a Tory, and ended a Tory (and indeed was, fundamentally, a Tory), Clementine was by background and temperament a confirmed Liberal. She had nothing to do with his move to the Liberal Party—that happened long before they were married; but she has been rightly credited with softening and tempering her husband's natural aggression.

In 1921 she wrote to him warning that 'It always makes me unhappy and disappointed when I see you inclined to take for granted that the rough iron-fisted hunnish way will prevail.' She cared for him and watched him—and was sufficiently respected by him—to be able to write the following superb letter. It is 1940, the Battle of Britain is under way, and the anxiety must be terrible; and it has started to show in Churchill's behaviour.

*10 Downing Street,*
*Whitehall*

*June 27, 1940*

*My Darling,*

*I hope you will forgive me if I tell you something that I feel you ought to know.*

*One of the men in your entourage (a devoted friend) has been to me & told me that there is a danger of your being generally disliked by your colleagues and subordinates because of your rough sarcastic & overbearing manner—It seems your Private Secretaries have agreed to behave like school boys & 'take what's coming to them' & then escape out of your presence shrugging their shoulders—Higher up, if an idea is suggested (say at a conference) you are supposed to be so contemptuous that presently no ideas, good or bad, will be forthcoming. I was astonished & upset because in all these years I have been accustomed to all those who have worked with & under you, loving you—I said this & I was told 'No doubt it's the strain'—*

*My Darling Winston—I must confess that I have noticed a deterioration in your manner; & you are not so kind as you used to be.*

*It is for you to give the Orders & if they are bungled— except for the King, the Archbishop of Canterbury & the Speaker, you can sack anyone & everyone—Therefore with this terrific power you must combine urbanity, kindness and if possible Olympic calm. You used to quote:– 'On ne règne sur les âmes que par le calme'—I cannot bear that those who serve the*

*Country and yourself should not love as well as admire and respect you—*

*Besides you won't get the best results by irascibility &*
*rudeness. They <u>will</u> breed either dislike or a slave mentality—*
*(Rebellion in War time being out of the question!)*

> *Please forgive your loving*
> *devoted & watchful*
>
> *Clemmie*

*I wrote this at Chequers last Sunday, tore it up, but here it*
*is now.*

She signed off with a little drawing of a cat—an allusion to the pet names they had for each other. She was 'pussie' and he was 'pug' or 'pig', and would accordingly finish his letters with a drawing of a pig. Indeed, when Churchill opened the door at Chartwell they used to greet each other with pleasurable animal noises—he 'wow-wow' and she 'miaow'.

We have the impression of a woman totally bound up in her husband's life and career—not just loving towards him, but a positive battleaxe towards his detractors. She was travelling in a railway carriage with a group of friends in the 1930s, when someone on the radio made a derogatory remark about Churchill. One of the party was an upper-class woman who shared the widespread pro-appeasement views, and who murmured 'hear, hear'. Clementine instantly marched out of the carriage and refused to return until she had received an apology. She was at a lunch party in 1953 with Lord Halifax, who said something mildly deprecatory about the state of the Tory Party. 'If the country had depended on you,' she said, applying the sledgehammer to the old appeaser, 'we might have lost the war.'

Clementine Churchill paid a price for her commitment to Churchill's life, and she knew it. She once said that her epitaph would be 'Here lies a woman who was always tired, Because she lived in a world where too much was required'. She confided in her daughter Mary that she felt she had missed out on the joys of bringing up her own four children (a fifth, Marigold, had died in infancy).

She gave up almost all her time for Winston, who came—as Mary Churchill put it—'first, second and third'. This was a sacrifice, and it can be argued that both Clementine and her children suffered from feeling themselves to be minor celestial bodies, condemned to perpetual orbit around the *roi soleil* of Chartwell. He was so busy that sometimes she felt neglected.

He could write to her with unmistakable ardour (there is a letter about wanting to grab her naked out of the bath, for instance); but there is also a plangent letter she writes to him in March 1916, when he has gone away to the trenches. 'We are still young, but time flies, stealing love away and leaving only friendship which is very peaceful but not very stimulating or warming.' Uh-oh.

On at least one occasion she threw a plate of spinach at his head. Given his immense capacity for self-obsession, I expect there will be many people who will cheer the gesture—and be thankful that she missed. Both of them had parents who were serially unfaithful; both had grown up in households that were unhappy in one way or another. Did Churchill or Clementine ever feel the temptation to stray, in fifty-six years of marriage?

I would be surprised—whatever the occasional rumours—if we found that Churchill had done any such thing himself. He was not only devoted to Clementine, it just wasn't the way he was made. There is the story of Daisy Fellowes, described as 'a figure of panache, chic and somewhat heartless beauty', who bumped into Churchill when he was at the Versailles peace conference in 1919. She invited him round to tea 'to see my little child'. When Churchill rolled up for tea, he found no little child, but a chaise longue on which had been stretched a tiger skin, and on the tiger skin stretched his hostess. She had no clothes on. He fled.

As for Clementine, well, much has been made of the tale of the Bali dove. Such was the general stress of living with Churchill that she used to go on quite long holidays—to the south of France, or the Alps, or the West Indies. In 1934 she went on an absolute odyssey—30,000 miles across the South Seas aboard a luxurious steam yacht belonging to the Guinness heir, Lord Moyne. She went to Borneo, Celebes, the Moluccas, New Caledonia, New Hebrides and the island of Bali, from where she wrote to her husband: 'It's an enchanted island. Lovely temples embedded in green vegetation in every village. Lovely dancers. The inhabitants lead an Elysian life. They work for about two hours a day—the rest of the time they play with musical instruments, dance, make offerings in the Temples of the Gods and make love! Perfect, isn't it?'

At this time Churchill was waging hand-to-hand warfare with the government over the India Bill—struggling home exhausted after late divisions—and one can see that the life he offered Clementine back home was not always paradise; nor, perhaps, was daily lovemaking as high on the Chartwell agenda as it was among the happy tribes of Bali. Clementine had all sorts of mementoes in her luggage on her return in April 1935, having lost weight and looking well.

She had pretty seashells that they put into the ornamental ponds, and which turned a bit yellowy-green. Her prize trophy was a Bali dove. Her daughter Mary described it as an enchanting pinky-beige little bird, with coral beak and feet. 'He lived in a beautiful wicker cage rather like a glorified lobster pot. He would crou crou and bow with exquisite oriental politeness to people he liked.' The dove was a present from a chap who was with Clementine on the boat. He was an art dealer named Terence Philip.

We have a hint of the feelings this fellow aroused in Clementine, because when the dove eventually wheezed its final crou-crou, she personally designed an inscription to go on the sundial, in the rose garden at Chartwell, which serves as the grave stele.

HERE LIES THE BALI DOVE

*It does not do to wander*
*Too far from sober men.*
*But there's an island yonder.*
*I think of it again.*

The lines were not by herself, but taken—at the suggestion of the travel writer Freya Stark—from the works of the nineteenth-century literary critic W. P. Ker. Some people say it is pretty blindingly obvious what this is supposed to be driving at.

Churchill is the sober man from whom she wandered, and she admits that she was wrong. But the dove—the bird of Venus, the symbol of love—is the reminder of the other life she almost had on a tropical island half a world away. The dove has been so ceremoniously interred not just because it was a jolly little bird, but because it reminds her of the time when she was billing and cooing herself. It is a symbol of her fling—her first, her last, her only fling.

Is that right? Did she have a thing with the art dealer? Well, it is possible, I suppose—though others have pointed out that Terence Philip was in fact supposed to have homosexual leanings. We know that he came several times to Chartwell in the next two years; but whatever it was that existed between them died as dead as the dove—

and Philip himself died during the war, working for the art dealer Wildenstein in New York.

Perhaps there was something a little bit more than a flirtation between Clemmie and this suave fellow; perhaps not. But there are two points about the Bali dove business. The first is that whatever the bird signified, Churchill knew about it and understood it and forgave it: how else could he allow a shrine to this holiday romance to be erected in his own garden?

The second is that whatever Terence Philip did for Clemmie— whatever he made her feel—did absolutely nothing to affect the love affair between herself and her husband. Here she is, writing to him from the yacht, as she heads back home. 'Oh my darling Winston, the Air Mail is just flitting and I send you this like John the Baptist to prepare the way for me, to tell you I love you and I long to be folded in your arms.' Does that sound like a woman in the grip of a red-hot affair with another man? Possibly, of course—but unlikely, I think, in her case.

Here is what Churchill wrote to her:

> *I think a lot about you, my darling Pussie . . . and rejoice that*
> *we have lived our lives together and still have some years of*
> *expectation in this pleasant vale. I have been sometimes a little*
> *depressed about politics and would like to have been comforted*
> *by you. But I feel that this has been a great experience and*
> *adventure to you and that it has introduced a new background*
> *to your life and a larger proportion; and so I have not grudged*
> *you your long excursion; but now I do want you back.*

You sense from this letter that Churchill knows the awful demands he has made on his wife. We also understand that he has had more than enough of her absence, and badly needed her with him. Why did Churchill forgive her flirtation with Terence Philip, assuming there was anything to forgive? Because he loved her, that's why. The world owes her a huge debt—a point the British government recognised after Churchill's death, when they made her a peeress in her own right.

He could not have done it without her. She gave his life a pile-driven domestic foundation, and not just in supplying the management of Chartwell and its nine servants and two gardeners; and in meeting all the vast emotional and logistical demands of four children. Here, too, her efforts must be counted a success.

It cannot have been easy to bring up the four of them—Diana, Randolph, Sarah and Mary—and though they were not all of them always happy in their lives they were all to become remarkable and courageous individuals: a credit to Winston (he was a loving father, when time allowed) and above all to Clemmie.

She curbed his excesses, she made him think more of other people, and to be less self-centred, and she helped to bring out what was lovable and admirable in his character. That was important, in 1940. The country needed a leader the public could understand, and who was likeable, and who seemed wholly 'grounded' and authentic.

If Churchill was to lead his country in war, he needed to be able to relate to people, and they needed to be able to relate to him; and in Churchill's case it helped that they could go farther, and actually identify themselves and their country with his personality.

# CHAPTER 10

# THE MAKING
# OF JOHN BULL

I t is the end of July 1940. The British position is absolutely desperate. The last of the British Expeditionary Force has long since scuttled from France. The Germans are in the process of trying to destroy the RAF. Churchill is up inspecting the defences of Hartlepool—a town that had famously been shelled by German ships in the Great War.

He stops in front of a British soldier equipped with an American-made weapon—a 1928 Thompson SMG, or submachine gun. Churchill plucks it out of the soldier's hands, barrel first. He holds the gun, muzzle thrust down and forward, as if he is on patrol on the British coast. He turns to face the camera—and the resulting picture becomes one of the great images of his will to resist.

In fact, the photograph is so strong and arresting that it becomes a propaganda hit for both sides. Goebbels immediately reprinted Churchill and the tommy gun in leaflets that accused him of being a war criminal and gangster—a man who loved personally to flourish the very same killing machine as Al Capone.

The British used it, too, though with the tin-hatted soldiers cropped out—and in the British case the propaganda message was rather different. Yes, says the picture (which can be bought on all sorts of mugs and tea towels and posters to this day): our war effort is indeed being led by a civilian of advancing years, a man who is so outlandish in his garb that he is still wearing a tall 'Cambridge' bowler hat, a titfer he bought at Lock's of St James's in 1919—they still have the record—and which went out of fashion years ago.

Yes, he has the same taste in headgear as Stan Laurel, and yes he wears spotty bow ties and pinstriped suits and looks like a country solicitor. But I tell you what—that poster informs the viewer—this man Churchill has fired a gun many times. He knows how to cock it and load it.

He knows the business end of a tommy gun, and he knows how to shoot. To use an overused word, there is something iconic about that shot, because in 1940 Churchill was in the process of becoming an icon—almost literally.

He was transmogrifying himself into the spirit of the nation, the very emblem of defiance. Consider those round-cheeked features, the hint of merriment in the upturned lip, the frank gaze of the eyes. He has channelled that portly gentleman who for two centuries or more has embodied the truculent-but-jovial response of the British to any great continental combination. He has become John Bull, and he shares many obvious qualities with that eighteenth-century per-sonification of England—most familiar from prints and propaganda of the Napoleonic era.

He is fat, jolly, high-living, rumbustious—and patriotic to a de-gree that many have always considered hyperbolical and unneces-sary, but which now, in the present crisis, seems utterly right. It is impossible to imagine any of his rivals achieving this feat—not Hali-fax, Chamberlain, Stafford Cripps, Eden, Attlee—none of them.

No other leading British politician of the day could have toted that tommy gun and got away with it (and indeed, it is still a golden rule of all political photo-opportunities: 'don't touch the gun!' the image-makers hiss). None of them had the requisite swagger, and none of them had the colour, the contour, the charisma, the cut-through of the Churchillian personality.

To lead the country in time of war, to keep people together at a moment of profound anxiety, you need to 'connect' with them—to use more modern political jargon—in a deep and emotional way. It was not enough to appeal to the logic of defiance. He couldn't just exhort them to be brave.

He needed to engage their attention, to cheer them, to boost them; if necessary even to make them laugh and, better still, to laugh at their enemies. To move the British people, he needed at some level to identify with them—with those aspects of their character that he, and they, conceived to be elemental to the national psyche.

What are the key attributes of the Brits—at least in our own not-quite-so-humble opinion? Well, we think we have a great sense of humour, unlike some other countries we could mention. Ever since Shakespeare put that chauvinistic drinking-song into the mouth of Iago and Cassio, we have fancied our ability to drink your Hollander under the table, your Dane dead drunk, and so on. The British tend to be a bit suspicious of people who are inordinately thin (and we are now the second-fattest nation on earth); and in general we think of Britain as the natural homeland of the eccentric, the oddball and the individualist.

All four of these traits Churchill covered under the capacious bowler hat of his own personality. The interesting question, when we consider his role in 1940, was how far he confected that identity. Did it all just happen with complete and unconscious spontaneity? Or was he really the most brilliant self-image-maker and spin-doctor of them all?

There have been many who have argued that Churchill's effulgent public personality was the product of a certain amount of myth-making—by both himself and others. One of the things we believe about Churchill today was that he was John Bull-ish in his irreverence, in his deployment of wit—often barbed wit.

There are any number of anecdotes that appear to illustrate his bluff, hilarious and mordant manner. They cling to him like burrs. Many of them, alas, are not provably true—or certainly not true of Winston Churchill.

Take the one about the time he was sitting next to a clean-living Methodist bishop—at a reception, allegedly, in Canada—when a good-looking young waitress came up and offered them both a glass of sherry from a tray. Churchill took one. But the bishop said, 'Young lady, I would rather commit adultery than take an intoxicating beverage.'

At which point Churchill beckoned the girl, and said, 'Come back, lassie, I didn't know we had a choice.' Perhaps I am wrong, but that feels to me less like a true story about Churchill, and more like some after-dinner anecdote from the pages of *The Funster's Friend*—pinned on Churchill in the hope of making it more amusing.

Such accounts are mainly of interest because of the light they cast on his image—on the fact that people have thought Churchill the right sort of person to fit the story. Some of them could only be about Churchill, but are still dubious—like the yarn about the special sheaths that had to be fitted to the muzzles of the rifles of British troops about to be sent to the Arctic. These were made by a condom manufacturer, and were 10½ inches long. Churchill is said to have inspected the consignment and called for fresh labels. 'I want every box, every carton, every packet saying, British. Size: medium. That will show the Nazis, if ever they recover them, who is the master race.'

I apologise for retailing this sort of stuff—but there are many more out there in the same vein.

Sometimes modern scholarship has been able to dismiss claims of Churchillian paternity, even of the ones that have long been thought to bear his stamp. For years I have treasured that one about Nancy Astor, a Virginia-born lady of pronounced views who became Britain's first female MP and spent much of the 1930s saying that Hitler was an all-round stand-up guy.

'Winston,' she is supposed to have said to him, 'if I were your wife I would put poison in your coffee.' 'Nancy,' Churchill is alleged to have replied to her, 'if I were your husband I would drink it.' Alas, Churchill almost certainly never made this brilliant remark, or if he did, he had swiped it from someone else.

Martin Gilbert attributed the gag not to Churchill but to his great friend F. E. Smith—and then further researches spoilt the thing entirely by tracking it down to a 1900 edition of the *Chicago Tribune*, where it appeared in a joke-of-the-day column. Did the young Churchill somehow spot it that year, on his trip to America, and squirrel it away for use on Nancy Astor? I doubt it. Did someone simply recycle the joke, and decide that to be properly funny it needed to be put plausibly in the mouths of some famous people? Much more likely.

Again, I always believed—in fact, I think I heard it from my parents—that Churchill had once ticked off a pompous civil servant who objected to the use of prepositions at the end of sentences. 'This is the kind of English up with which I will not put,' Churchill is meant to have said.

Except that he didn't. It turns out to have been a joke that was published in the *Strand* magazine, ascribed to no one in particular—but was thought so good that it should be put in the mouth of Churchill. Nor did he say that 'In the future, the fascists will call themselves anti-fascists'. Doubtless a profound remark, depending on your view of politics—but it is not one of Churchill's.

Nor—and I almost cried when I discovered that this one wasn't true—did he ever say, of his relations with the exhausting and almost intolerable de Gaulle, 'The hardest cross I have had to bear has been the Cross of Lorraine.' It was actually said by General Spears, Churchill's envoy to France. But who ever remembers General Spears?

Then there is the beautiful put-down of G. B. Shaw, who sent him two tickets for a first night of one of his plays with the message that he should 'bring a friend, if you have one'. Churchill got the ball back over the net by saying that he couldn't make the first night, but would come to the second 'if there is one'.

Except that he didn't, because the omniscient Allen Packwood of Cambridge has found letters from both Shaw and Churchill—unanimously denying it.

Like some hyper-gravitational astral body, it is Churchill who magically claims the joke—when it turns out he never cracked it at all. Which has led some to wonder—mistakenly, in my view—whether he was really as fertile in humour as all that.

You could develop this line of thought, if you chose, and observe that his habits were not completely Falstaffian. He did indeed drink whisky and water from very early in the morning—but his daughter once pointed out that it was a very weak whisky indeed; just a splash of Johnnie Walker at the bottom of the glass, more of a 'mouthwash', as he said, than a proper drink.

As for his cigars, his valet and many others testify that he very rarely smoked them all the way through—generally leaving at least a third or a half in the ashtray. He understood perfectly well that they were not just tobacco; they were part of his brand. On the way to make his speech at Fulton, Missouri, in 1946, he called for the car to stop as they neared their destination. He patted his pockets, pulled out a cigar and popped it, unlit, into his mouth.

'Never forget your trademark,' he growled in his trademark growl. Far from being a dissolute Toby Belch, he showed—in his own way—remarkable personal discipline. He worked out with dumb-bells. In the dispatching of business he was more phenomenally industrious than anyone you have ever known. All of which suggests again, perhaps, that the more exuberant sides of his personality contained an element of calculated exaggeration—something a little bit borrowed, like the V for Victory sign that he took from occupied Europe, where it was scrawled by anti-Nazis on buildings and stood for '*vrijheid*' or freedom.

Was Churchill a poseur? No, though everybody to some extent acts out the identity they have assigned themselves. The extraordinary thing is that Churchill's public persona—his image—was overwhelmingly congruent with reality.

He might have nicked the V-sign from the Continent—but it was pure Churchill to turn it mischievously round, as he often did, so that it could be read to mean not just victory but 'fuck off'. And yes, whichever way you look at it, his potations were epic. He drank about a pint of Pol Roger champagne a day, together with white wine at lunch, red wine at dinner and port or brandy thereafter. He did once give up spirits (but not if diluted) for a year in 1936, for the sake of a wager; but that did not impede his consumption of other forms of alcohol on a scale that—in the words of his Private Secretary—would have felled a lesser human being.

Nor did he just wave his cigars around for effect, like some vain and Freudian accoutrement of masculine power. According to his secretary, he smoked between eight and ten large Cuban cigars a day. Even if he left a few inches unburned—and the ends were generally collected and stuffed in the pipe of the gardener at Chartwell—that is still a lot of cigars: about three thousand a year, it has been estimated, or 250,000 over his lifetime.

In spite of all this he managed to get into his eighties with a blood pressure of 140/80. It is as if his body was itself a physical symbol of the nation's ability to soak up punishment. Talk about Falstaffian behaviour: there is a gripping description of what it was like to watch Churchill eating in his own home, by a man who came to interview him at Chartwell. He wanted everything at once, in no particular order. He would eat a forkful of steak and kidney pie, then puff on a cigar, then gobble a chocolate, then gulp some brandy, then have another forkful of meat—and talking all the while.

As for his sense of humour, and his witticisms, well, the wonder of it really is how many of the stories turn out to be completely true. That is why so many apocryphal stories have been ascribed to Churchill—because the pearl of ornament has formed about the grit of truth; more than a grit—a boulder.

There are so many true stories about Churchill's behaviour that the false ones have been opportunistically added, by skilled forgers, in the knowledge that it can be hard sometimes to tell which is which. It really is true that in 1946 he met Bessie Braddock—a staunch Labour MP of ample proportions, who once called for some Tory councillors to be machine-gunned—when he was a little bit, as they say, 'tired and emotional'.

'Winston,' she bristled, 'you are drunk.' 'Madam,' he replied, 'you are ugly, and I will be sober in the morning.' That seems to our taste almost unforgivably brutal; but serve her right for being so personal. Anyway, he wasn't completely sloshed, said his bodyguard, Ron Golding, who confirmed the story; just a bit 'wobbly'. And it is all the better for being an instant reply.

F. E. Smith once said: 'Churchill has spent the best years of his life preparing his impromptu remarks.' This one just popped out, and has earned its place, I see, at number one in a *Daily Express* survey of the greatest insults in history.

It seems to be genuinely the case that he made the famous crack about the Lord Privy Seal, who had come to see him when he was in the toilet. 'Tell the Lord Privy Seal that I am sealed in the privy, and can only deal with one shit at a time,' he roared. Even if he didn't say all of it, he made the essential gag—Privy Seal/sealed in privy.

Again, we see his love of chiasmus—or reversing the word order in an unexpected way: like 'beginning of the end/end of the beginning', or 'I am ready to meet my maker; whether my maker is ready for the great ordeal of meeting me is another question'; 'we shape our buildings and afterwards our buildings shape us'; 'I have taken more out of alcohol than alcohol has taken out of me'; and there are many others.

Sometimes I have been tempted to dismiss a story as being surely apocryphal—only to discover that it really is true. He *did* say that. Take the yarn about the time he was on a lecture tour in America, and was served a buffet lunch of cold fried chicken.

'May I have some breast?' he is supposed to have asked his hostess. 'Mr Churchill,' the hostess replied, 'in this country we ask for white meat or dark meat.' The following day the lady received a magnificent orchid from her guest of honour. The accompanying card read, 'I would be obliged if you would pin this on your white meat'.

I had this one firmly on my list of forgeries—and then I had it authenticated by his granddaughter Celia Sandys. 'Where did you hear it?' I asked.

'Horse's mouth,' she said. You can't argue with that.

Churchill's humour is both conceptual and verbal. He not only used his colossal English vocabulary, but is also responsible for some of the greatest Franglais of all time. He has been credited with issuing this superb threat to de Gaulle: '*Et marquez mes mots, mon ami, si vous me double-crosserez, je vous liquiderai.*' ('And mark my words, my friend, if you double-cross me, I will liquidate you.')

Even if the whole thing isn't from him, he certainly said '*je vous liquiderai*'. All these remarks have in common not just that they are funny, but that they are staggeringly rude. Ramsay MacDonald, the Labour leader, was not just a 'sheep in sheep's clothing'. One day he went farther, with an attack that ranks in the great tradition of parliamentary invective, an insult of which his father Randolph would have been proud.

I remember when I was a child, being taken to the celebrated Barnum's Circus, which contained an exhibition of freaks and monstrosities, but the exhibit on the program which I most desired to see was the one described as 'The Boneless Wonder'. My parents judged that the spectacle would be too demoraliz- ing and revolting for my youthful eye and I have waited fifty years, to see The Boneless Wonder sitting on the Treasury Bench.

When he saw Stafford Cripps—the austere Labour figure who had briefly and incredibly been touted as his wartime rival—he said, 'There but for the grace of God, goes God.' He could be rough with colleagues, too. He said that the new Tory MPs around Rab Butler in 1945 were 'no more than a set of pink pansies', and when he was told by his Private Secretary that Butler and Eden were waiting outside to see him, he told Anthony Montague Browne: 'Tell them to go and bugger themselves.'

Since this was clearly audible to the waiting pair, he shouted out after the departing Browne: 'There is no need for them to carry out that instruction literally.' These are just a handful of the hundreds of glossy old Churchillian chestnuts, and they illustrate a key point about his political identity: that he had all the unruly combativeness of a bulldog, or of John Bull himself. It wasn't always to everyone's tastes; but in time of war you wanted someone so incorrigibly cheerful and verbally inventive that he could really stick it to the Nazis—or rather, to Corporal Schickelgruber and the Narzis.

To mobilise a democracy to war you must be demotic, and Churchill could do demotic better than any of his contemporaries. He loved puns, and wordplay, in the way that *Sun* headline writers love them. A socialist utopia was 'queuetopia'; he built a shed for his chickens called 'Chickenham Palace', and on the subject of chickens he went to Ottawa in December 1941 and told them how he had stuck it to Pétain and the vacillating French. 'When I warned them that Britain would fight on alone whatever they did, their generals told their Prime Minister and his divided Cabinet, "In three weeks England will have her neck wrung like a chicken." Some chicken! Some neck!'

They laughed because he was not only cunningly tailoring his language for a North American audience ('some chicken', rather than the more usual British English 'what a chicken'); he was punning on neck, which also means brazenness or cheek.

There is a final sense in which Churchill incarnated something essential about the British character—and that was his continual and unselfconscious eccentricity, verbal and otherwise. He invented words to suit himself. Mountbatten was a 'triphibian', which meant that he was capable of deployment on land, sea and air. The Lend-Lease deal was 'unsordid'—a word not found before or since. He had an aversion to staples and paper clips and therefore preferred documents to be joined by a treasury tag, or, as he put it, 'klopped'.

'Gimme klop,' he would bark. 'When I say klop, Miss Shearburn, that's what I want, klop.' One new secretary, Kathleen Hill, famously tried to fulfil this request by producing the fifteen volumes of *Der Fall des Hauses Stuart* by the German historian Onno Klopp (1822–1903). 'Christ almighty,' said Churchill.

He not only wore Laurel and Hardy hats of a kind that had been abandoned by everyone else; he startled people by designing and appearing in his own clothes—those blue velvet or sometimes cerise romper suits that made him look like an overgrown toddler.

There is a wonderful picture of him appearing before the Washington media in one of these bizarre outfits, with a smirk on his face reminiscent of Hugh Hefner about to attend a slumber party. When he wasn't wearing his bowler, he would wear an extraordinary variety of headgear. It has been said that Churchill never saw a hat he didn't like. That wasn't quite true: he'd put on a Glengarry, the traditional Scots cap, in the trenches, looked at himself in the mirror and said 'Christ!' before taking it off again.

But he wore top hats, yachting caps, fireman's hats, giant white astrakhan hats, kepis, solar topis, builder's helmets, fedoras, sombreros. He was the Imelda Marcos of hats. In fact we need only find a picture of Churchill in a Native American headdress and he could pose as the entire cast of Village People. All his life he had been a showman, an extrovert, theatrical, comical: there is a photo of him dressed for a fancy-dress ball at Sandhurst—meticulously made up, with carefully applied white face paint, as Pierrot the Clown.

He knew how to project his personality, and the war called for someone who could create an image of himself—decisive, combative, but also cheery and encouraging—in the minds of the people. Churchill alone was able to do that, because to a great extent he really was that character.

There is a sense in which eccentricity and humour helped to express what Britain was fighting for—what it was all about. With his ludicrous hats and rompers and cigars and excess alcohol, he contrived physically to represent the central idea of his own political philosophy: the inalienable right of British people to live their lives in freedom, to do their own thing.

You only had to look at Churchill, and see the vital difference between his way of life and the ghastly seriousness and uniformity and pomposity of the Nazis. Never forget: Hitler was a teetotaller, a deformity that accounts for much misery.

In his personal individualism and bullish eccentricity, Churchill helped define the fight. It was an idea that was to lead him badly astray in the 1945 election, when he made the mistake of comparing Labour government bureaucrats to the Gestapo. But it was absolutely what was needed for the war.

In late March 1944 you will find him again pictured with a tommy gun, inspecting the D-Day troops with Eisenhower. This time he is actually aiming the gun. He has it up to his shoulder and is pointing towards France. He is wearing the same pinstripe suit, the same bowler hat. I can hardly believe it is a coincidence. It is almost as if he is referring to that photo-opportunity of almost four years previously, and saying, 'I told you we could do it.'

Churchill's qualities allowed him to stand for the nation. It was also essential to the Churchill Factor that he was seen, more than any other politician, to be his own man: someone whose protean political identity enabled him to explode out of the straitjacket of party politics.

One of the reasons he was able to appeal both to right and left was that he had begun his career as a social reformer, a politician who could certainly claim to have done great things for working people.

# CHAPTER 11

# 'THE MOST ADVANCED POLITICIAN OF THE TIME'

Adolf Hitler was so impressed by photographs of the Midland Hotel, Manchester, that he decided it would be the perfect Nazi headquarters in Britain—once Britain had been brought to her knees, and the ruling classes either shot or led off in chains. It is indeed a very fine establishment: a vast ruddy brick fantasy of Edwardian Gothic, with 312 rooms and en suite bathrooms and Michelin-starred restaurants and health suites and Teasmades. I have stayed there several times myself, and used the excellent room service in the small hours. The full English breakfast will keep you going all day.

The hotel was also, once, the temporary address of Winston Churchill. It was here that he came in 1906, when he was fighting for the constituency of Manchester North-West, and here that he hung his hat. Those were the days, you see, when there was no moral pressure on MPs to have a 'home' in the constituency; and even in those days—perhaps particularly in those days—the Midland Hotel was the *ne plus ultra* of luxury. It was just three years old, and had cost £1 million to build; it had its own auditorium, and it made a hell of a contrast with some of the areas of Manchester that the thirty-one-year-old Churchill proposed to represent.

One cold winter evening he sauntered out in the company of his faithful secretary, Eddie Marsh. They found themselves in a slum, not far from the Midland, and Churchill discharged himself of the following aperçu: 'Fancy living in one of these streets,' he said, looking around him, 'never seeing anything beautiful, never eating anything savoury . . . never saying anything clever!'

A lot of people have taken exception to this remark. They say it shows condescension to the poor. He seems to reveal himself as a man so out of touch with the real world that he can't imagine people on low incomes ever saying anything worth hearing; and so ignorant of their lives that he can't believe they have anything worth eating.

We don't know whether these were his exact words, though Marsh is unlikely to have made it up; but there is no doubt that this quotation has helped build the case that Churchill was always a bit of a reactionary old elitist.

This is the man, after all, who believed in eugenics; a social Darwinist who at various times wanted penal colonies for vagrants and sterilisation of the unfit. He certainly spoke of humanity being divided into qualitatively different 'races'—in a way that we find intellectually very dodgy today—and used vocabulary to describe foreigners that was standard for the time, but these days is taboo.

He wrote to Clementine boasting that the children were working 'like blacks' to get Chartwell ready for her return; he ignored the Sino-Japanese war of the 1930s, saying he had 'no interest in the quarrels of the yellow peoples'.

He wanted to 'bomb or machine-gun' Sinn Fein, whose representatives are now feted at banquets at Windsor Castle. He said the Bolsheviks were 'baboons', and that communism was a 'horrible form of mental and moral disease'. Indeed, he once said that 'one might as well legalise sodomy as recognise the Bolsheviks'; an observation that looks a bit topsy-turvy today.

No one would appoint Churchill to any public office in modern Britain, not unless he toned it down a good deal. He said that making concessions to Mahatma Gandhi—now venerated as the father of modern India—was like 'feeding cat's meat to a tiger' (especially inapposite, given that Gandhi-ji was a devout veggie).

How much more right-wing can you get? Well, try this: as Home Secretary in 1910 he was alleged by the Labour Party to have sent armed troops against striking miners at Tonypandy in Wales; and in 1911 he certainly did authorise the troops to fire on striking dockers in Liverpool. During the General Strike of 1926 he used a scab battalion of printers and journalists to produce a work of stirring government propaganda called *The British Gazette*; he proposed that the BBC be closed down for the duration, said that 'a bit of bloodshed would not go amiss' and that he wanted to get the transport workers 'by the throat'. His 'whiff of grapeshot' approach was condemned by Labour and the unions, and by his fellow Liberals.

Now take all this together and ask yourself—does this man sound like a lefty-liberal milquetoast? Banning the BBC? Shooting at striking dockers, just for rioting and smashing things? There are aspects of Churchill that make him sound like a chap who has had a few too many at a golf club bar. And yet this is the same Churchill who was the begetter of some of the most progressive legislation for the last 200 years. Together with Lloyd George, he deserves the title of Founder of the Welfare State.

His achievements in the Second World War are so famous that

they have all but eclipsed his record as a social reformer: a record that deserves to be burnished and celebrated today. Churchill was heavily influenced by Lloyd George—indeed, the Welsh solicitor was one of the very few human beings to whom he deferred—but the measures he produced were his own, and driven by his own frantic energy.

He began in 1908 with a Trades Board Bill, designed to help low-paid workers—mainly female—who were engaged in 'sweated labour'. They were working making garments in the East End of London, in Leeds, and in Manchester. Their wages were being undercut by immigrants, notably from eastern Europe (*plus ça change*); and the Trades Boards were there to set legally enforceable minimum wages for certain jobs. It was a concept that was alien to the theories of the classical Liberals—the Gladstonians who were still to be found in the cabinet. But Churchill and Lloyd George were New Liberals—or Radicals.

Explaining why the measure was necessary, Churchill said:

It is a national evil that any class of her Majesty's subjects should receive less than a living wage in return for their utmost exertions. Where you have what we call sweated trades, you have no organisation, no parity of bargaining, the good employer is undercut by the bad and the bad by the worst; the worker, whose whole livelihood depends upon the industry, is undersold by the worker who only takes up the trade as a second string . . . where these conditions prevail you have not a condition of progress, but a condition of progressive degeneration.

Those are some of the arguments still made for the living wage today. To help combat unemployment (then running at about 8 per cent—and with virtually no benefits to support the victims), he was instrumental in setting up the first Labour Exchanges; and by early 1910 he and Clementine were able to tour seventeen of them. Just think, next time you look at a Jobcentre Plus: Winston Churchill started those.

He was the man who first hired William Beveridge—who was to go on and build the post-war welfare state in the 1940s; and Beveridge paid tribute to the force with which Churchill drove things through in that early epoch of reform. Writing of the first Labour Exchanges, Beveridge said they were 'a striking illustration of how much the personality of the minister in a few critical months may change the course of social legislation'.

Next, Churchill was the progenitor of unemployment insurance—the precursor of the dole. It was a contributory scheme, whereby the worker put in 2.5p a week, the employer put in 2.5p a week and the taxpayer put in 3p a week. It meant that if you were unemployed, or you fell ill, and provided you had made your contribution—then you were entitled to a payment that in today's money would be about £20 a week—not much, but a start. 'Insurance brings the miracle of averages to the rescue of the masses,' he said.

In the long run, of course, these averages provided no such miracle. The taxpayer now coughs up for the dole. The contributory principle has been more or less forgotten; but today's Jobseeker's Allowance is the direct descendant of Churchill's scheme.

All this was controversial stuff, and got the Tories hot under the collar—but it was nothing compared to his role in the Great Budget War of 1909 and 1910. The People's Budget of David Lloyd George was one of the decisive events of modern British history. It was a naked attempt at redistribution of wealth. It was an attack on inequality; and it was seen, inevitably, as an attack on the dukes and the very landed class from which Churchill emerged. Lloyd George wanted to pay for the various Liberal social protection schemes by whacking up taxes on the very rich, and above all by taxing land. He wanted a 20 per cent tax on the gain in value when land was sold.

The Tories were deeply hostile; the Tory peers threatened to block the budget. Churchill was all for it—and he and Lloyd George teamed up, criss-crossing the country like a vaudeville double act.

We find Churchill in 1909 lamenting the unfairness of the division of land in Britain. Of course there should be land taxes, he says. He has recently been to Germany (to see the German army on manoeuvres and to meet the Kaiser). It strikes him that class inequalities are nothing like as pronounced as they are in Britain: he sees countless small German farms—and no walls around the estates of the nobs. He contrasts it with Britain. 'All this picture makes one feel what a dreadful blight and burden our poor people have to put up with—with parks and palaces of country families almost touching one another and smothering the villages and the industry . . .'

Huge parks, crushing the villages of the poor! Huge palaces! Isn't this all a bit rich from the scion of Blenheim? A lot of people thought so, and when Churchill warned that inequalities would lead to class warfare, the King caused his Private Secretary to write to *The Times* to protest. Churchill bashed on. When the Lords tried to throw out the budget, he directed his fire at an institution that contained a fair few of his relatives. By January 1910 the budget crisis was still not over—and he described the Lords as a 'survival of a feudal arrangement utterly passed out of its original meaning, a force long since passed away, which only now requires a smashing blow from the electors to finish it off forever'.

It is now more than a century since Churchill denounced this infamy—of men sitting in Parliament by right of heredity—and there still are hereditary peers in the House of Lords. That shows he was either monstrously radical or far ahead of his time.

In the end the budget passed, after a gripping constitutional showdown. The King agreed that he would if necessary create enough Liberal peers to ram the benches of the House of Lords and outvote the Tory reactionaries; the landowning peers backed down. Lloyd George and Churchill got their way. Britain embarked on a century of redistribution of wealth.

He was no less of a lefty—at least in Tory eyes—when he got to the Home Office. He shortened prison sentences, when most holders of that office find themselves trying to lengthen them. He reduced the use of solitary confinement. He created a distinction, in British jails, between political prisoners and ordinary criminals—a distinction that still sticks in the craw of many right-wingers today. He may have been rhetorically tough on both Bolshevism and sodomy, but when it came to the application of the law itself, he was mercy personified. Throughout his life Churchill showed a benign indifference to people's sexual preferences (indeed, Eddie Marsh was himself gay, as Churchill surely knew), and he tried to limit sentences for acts that were then criminalised. On being told that a man had been sentenced to ten years' penal servitude for sodomy, he wrote to his officials: 'The prisoner has already received two frightful sentences of seven years' penal servitude, one for stealing lime juice and one for stealing apples. It is not impossible that he contracted his unnatural habits in prison.' That minute shows his natural instinct for clemency—and the barbaric nature of justice in Edwardian England.

When the Tories said he was being soft on young criminals, he would even play the class card. A right-wing Tory called Lord Winterton was assailing him in the Commons for refusing to incarcerate some young offenders, and Churchill replied: 'I wanted to draw the attention of the country . . . to the evil by which 7000 lads of the poorer classes are sent to gaol every year for offences which, if the noble Lord had committed them at College, he would not have been subjected to the slightest degree of inconvenience.' You can imagine some MPs seething at the idea that their champagne-fuelled university high jinks were being bracketed with mere criminality—and this from a fellow who hadn't even been to university. Most sensible people, of course, would have completely agreed with Churchill.

As for his handling of the strikes and riots that preceded the First World War, he has been grossly traduced by the modern Labour Party. In 1978 the Labour Prime Minister, Jim Callaghan, said the Churchill family had a 'vendetta' against the Tonypandy miners. As recently as 2010 a South Wales council tried to stop a local military camp being named after him; and there are still Labour MPs who will tell you that in 1910 Churchill brutally sent the army against defenceless working people. This is all tripe.

The record clearly shows that the troops at Tonypandy behaved with restraint. Indeed, Churchill was actually attacked by the Tories for being too soft, and holding the troops in reserve. It was true that he sent troops to try to contain the dockers rampaging through Liverpool in 1911, and true that they fired. But the destruction being caused was immense; the situation had to be brought under control and Churchill's own personal sympathies were with the strikers—as they had been with the miners at Tonypandy. 'They are very poor, miserably paid, and now nearly starving,' he said. Of dockers striking in London, he told the King they 'had a real grievance, and the large addition to their wages which they have secured must promote the health and contentment of an unduly strained class of workers, charged as has been realised with vital functions in our civilisation'.

Time and again we find him impatient with the boss class and siding with the unions. When he was Minister for Munitions in 1917 he faced a strike by armaments workers on the Clyde—and got them in for tea and cake at his ministry. He sorted it out by bunging them 12 per cent. He presented a Munitions Bill to allay some of the workers' grievances, and said 'no worker would be penalised for belonging to a trade union or taking part in a trade dispute'.

As for the General Strike of 1926, he certainly worked hard to bring the crisis to an end—but if anything he was on the conciliatory wing in his approach to the detail of the disputes. Throughout the summer and autumn he tried to bring the mine owners to accept that their impoverished workforce deserved a minimum wage, and declared that the capitalists were being 'recalcitrant' and 'unreasonable'. Once again he earned the scorn of the Tories, who felt he was trying to interfere with the right of management to manage.

There is plenty more. If we wanted to justify Churchill's entry in the great pantheon of lefty legislators, we could add reducing the pension age from seventy to sixty-five (we have just had to reverse this excessive generosity), or his repeated calls for the nationalisation of the railways, his call for a windfall tax on war profiteers and his introduction to British industry of that favourite of bolshy 1970s shop stewards—the tea break.

So which is it? It is time for the real Winston Churchill to stand forward in his true colours. There is a line in Gilbert and Sullivan to the effect that 'Every boy and every gal/ That's born into the world alive/ Is either a little Liberal/ Or a little Conservative'.

The Fabians Sidney and Beatrice Webb hailed him, along with Lloyd George, as 'the most advanced politicians of the time.' At almost the same time his fellow Liberal MP Charles Masterman proclaimed him an 'aboriginal and unchanging Tory'. One or other view was misguided, surely?

Of course there are and were plenty of people who explain the mystery simply: that he was a weathervane, who said so many different things at different times that, in the words of Beaverbrook, he ended up holding all views on all questions. Or, as Asquith put it, 'Winston has no convictions'.

I am not sure I attach much weight to criticism from ineffectual mutton-like Asquith—a man who repeatedly shafted Churchill, and who spent cabinet meetings writing pathetic love letters to Venetia Stanley, and who was so drunk that he often had to get Churchill to take over for him. Churchill's career covered a huge chunk of British history. He held high office more or less continuously from 1905 to 1922—a seventeen-year stretch that comfortably eclipses most modern politicians: and yet that was only his first period—before he had even become Chancellor, let alone Prime Minister.

Of course he sometimes said things that seemed to sit oddly with something he had said in response to another problem in another age. But those who accuse him of political inconsistency have underestimated the depth and subtlety of his political thought. My own view is that Churchill had a very clear political identity, and an unvarying set of principles.

He was both a reactionary and a liberal because he was essentially a buccaneering Victorian Whig. He believed in the greatness of Britain, in the empire, and the preservation of roughly the established order of the country in which he grew up. He also believed in science and technological progress and that government could and should intervene to help improve the condition of the people.

Above all he believed that there was a connection between those two objectives—the promotion and protection of Britain and the empire, and the promotion and protection of the welfare of the people—and that the second would help advance the first. That was the essence of his Whiggish Toryism.

Think of the kind of lives he would have seen when he walked out that night in wintry Manchester. In 1902 he had read Seebohm Rowntree, on the fate of the poor in York, and he said it had 'made his hair stand on end'. By 1906 the population boom meant that the squalor in the Manchester slums, if anything, was even worse.

He and Marsh saw houses with no running water, with no sewerage system, and with families living ten to a room. Here your baby had no more than a one in four chance of living to see its first birthday. In these slums Churchill saw people who were not just relatively poor—enduring poverty in the sense that we understand it; but absolutely poor: crushingly, grindingly, hopelessly poor in the sense that they were deprived of whole categories of things that most poor people these days would take for granted.

Seebohm Rowntree was very strict in deciding who could fairly be called poor. You could only be classed as poor, he said, if you couldn't afford any kind of transport at all, and if you had to walk if you wanted to visit relations or go to the countryside. To be poor, you had to be unable to buy postage stamps to write letters; you had to be unable to buy any tobacco or alcohol whatever; you had no money to buy dolls or marbles or sweets for your children, and no money to buy any clothes except the barest essentials. To be classed as poor, you had to be unable to afford to miss a single day's work. Those were the urban poor when Churchill began his political career—living in filth and destitution that would be unimaginable today. They made up fully 25 per cent of the population.

When Churchill made that remark about their lives, he was actually reflecting his own shock at the immensity of the gulf between their lives and his, and trying—as far as he could—to put himself in their broken shoes.

He had all sorts of reasons for caring about them, and wanting to help. Some of those reasons were selfish, some of them less obviously so. The beauty and riddle in studying the motives of any politician is in trying to decide what is idealism and what is self-interest; and often we are left to conclude that the answer is a mixture of the two.

He wanted to do something about the condition of the poor because, as I say, he believed in Britain and in the empire. He had seen

Winston Churchill in 1892, aged 18.

His father, Randolph.

His mother, Jennie Jerome.

Winston (right) and Jack, aged 14 and 9, with their mother in 1889.

The happy couple:
Churchill and Clemmie
during the first year of
their marriage.

On the election campaign trail, Chigwell, May 1945.

This photo appeared in Churchill's book *My African Journey*, published by Hodder and Stoughton in 1908.

Bathing at Deauville, 1922.

Prisoner of the Boers, Pretoria, November 1899.

With T. E. Lawrence (fourth from left), 'who is not in complete harmony with the normal', Gertrude Bell (third from left), and Clemmie (left), March 1921.

With Field Marshal Sir William Robertson inspecting the Tank Corps in 1915.

With General Pershing at a ceremony in London, July 1919.

Touring Bristol after German bombers had raided the city in April 1941.
With him are Clemmie and the US ambassador, John Gilbert Winant.

Accepting a cigar from a London factory worker during a morale-raising visit with the Australian Minister for External Affairs, Dr Evatt, in 1942.

8 June 1943: Allied Forces headquarters in North Africa, (left to right) Foreign Secretary Anthony Eden, Lord Alanbrooke, Air Chief Marshal Tedder, Admiral Sir Andrew Cunningham, General Alexander, General Marshall, General Eisenhower and General Montgomery.

LEFT: Trying out a Thompson 'Tommy' submachine gun in southern England, three months before D-Day.

BELOW: With General de Gaulle, 'the last survivor of a warrior race', whom he also called 'the monster of Hampstead' in Paris, 11 November 1944.

With General Montgomery (wearing a beret),
crossing the Rhine with American and Allied troops, 25 March 1945.

Waving to the crowds in
Whitehall on 8 May 1945,
the day he broadcast to
the nation that the
war with Germany
had been won.

With Lloyd George in 1934.

With Lord Halifax in Whitehall on 29 March 1938, shortly after Hitler's annexation of Austria.

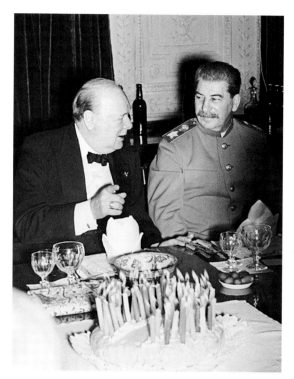

LEFT: With Stalin, 'The Old Bear', on Churchill's sixty-ninth birthday in Tehran, November 1943.

With Sir Anthony Eden at Chartwell in the late 1940s.

May 1943, with
Roosevelt near the
president's country
retreat, Shangri-La.

ABOVE: Speaking at an American Thanksgiving celebration
at the Royal Albert Hall in London, November 1944.

With President Truman en route to Fulton, Missouri,
for his famous 'Iron Curtain' speech, March 1946.

In full flow at the 1948
Conservative Party Conference.

7 May 1948, after his speech to the Congress of Europe at the Hague, overwhelmed
by the response. From left to right are leaders of the European movement:
Kerstens, Ramadier, Retinger and de Rougemont.

Winston Churchill, bricklayer, building a wall at Chartwell in 1928.

On holiday in Marrakesh, February 1959.

Churchill, early pioneer of air flight.

how German systems of *paritatisch*—cooperation between bosses and workers—were delivering results, and like all members of the British ruling class he could see Germany's growing industrial strength. He could see that the British economy would need a workforce that was fit and healthy and motivated, if the country as a whole was to compete.

He had fought in the Boer War, and he knew that in 1899 the army's recruiting officers had been stunned to find that 50 per cent of working-class volunteers had been simply unfit—through childhood disease or malnourishment—to be soldiers. Churchill wanted an army physically able to run an empire.

What is more, he wanted to improve the condition of the poor as a political precaution, because he could see that if poor people continued to be so humiliated, they would refuse to take it any longer. The early years of the twentieth century were a period of alarming political instability. There were great numbers of strikes, many of them violent, and with running battles between working men and the police.

Lenin said that in 1910–14 the spirit of revolution stalked England. Lenin was right; and Churchill was the very opposite of a revolutionary. He knew how precarious was the position of the minority to which he belonged. 'It was the world of the few,' he said of the society he grew up in, 'and they were very few.' Or, as he might have put it, never in the field of social conflict was so much owed to so many by so few.

He was radical precisely because he was conservative. He knew what all sensible Tories know—that the only way to keep things the same is to make sure you change them; or as Burke puts it, a state without the means of some change is without the means of its conservation. He grasped that. He saw that the only way to be successfully and effectively reactionary was to be more than a little bit liberal. As

Charles Masterman said: 'he desired in Britain a state of affairs where a benign upper class dispensed benefits to a bien pensant and grateful working class'. Which, by the way, is still the unspoken position of quite a few good-hearted metropolitan liberals today.

And then there is the final reason why Churchill championed social reform. He didn't just do it because it was in the interests of the economy and the army and the empire and, of course, in the interests of the poor themselves. He did it because it was in the interests of Winston Leonard Spencer-Churchill. From the very beginning of his political career we find him 'triangulating'—developing a centrist position that enables him to call on the broadest possible support. In 1902 he wrote that the answer to the country's political problems was a great central party, 'free at once from the sordid selfishness and callousness of Toryism on the one hand, and the blind appetites of the radical masses on the other'. On another occasion he said the key thing was to be 'Conservative in principle but Liberal in sympathy'.

This is partly how he felt about the world, and partly positioning. He saw how he could himself incarnate this coalition, how he could be the giant straddler, the colossus with one foot on either side of the entrance to the harbour. He dreamed of that role from the beginning. The Second World War gave him his cue.

It is unfair on Churchill to say he swung around with the wind. If anything, he showed more consistency than the Tory Party itself. When he wrote to Hugh Cecil in his famous and unsent letter of 1904, saying that he hated the Tory Party, their men and their methods, it was largely because they were abandoning the cause of free trade—which was then seen as essential for providing cheap food for the urban poor. The Tories were ditching his father Randolph's concept of 'Tory Democracy', which, if it meant anything, meant stitching together a coalition between the moneyed classes and the working people.

He was a free trader more or less without deviation (apart from a wobble in 1931, and some insignificant protectionist flourishes such as a duty on imported American films), and only returned to the Tory Party once the Tories had themselves returned to free trade. He was not just a free trader; he was a capitalist. As he said in 1924, 'the existing capitalist system is the foundation of civilisation and the only means by which a great modern population can be supplied with vital necessities'. He spoke out repeatedly against the pointless persecution of the rich. But he believed in capitalism with a human face, or compassionate conservatism.

At the very beginning of his career he emerges as a man determined to palliate the suffering that free markets and capitalism can cause. Yes, he was a tough antagonist of rioters and strikers, but he was also a noted conciliator, using his charm and grasp of detail to get a deal.

By the 1950s that suppleness had become perhaps less desirable. The country was richer than it had been when Churchill began in politics; the gap between rich and poor had been greatly reduced. It has been argued that Churchill's second premiership was too relaxed about union dominance, and therefore helped create the sclerosis of the 1960s and 1970s.

But if we think back to the state of the country in the years before the First World War, we can see that his instincts were right for the time. Look at the shambles in Europe in the 1920s and 1930s: a murderous communist revolution in Russia, and other communist uprisings in eastern Europe, and then a great rash of fascist dictators across the continent.

There was hardly a country that did not suffer some major

upheaval or constitutional abomination. Italy had Mussolini, Portugal had Salazar, Poland had Piłsudski, Austria had Dollfuss, Croatia had some Ustasha creep or other, Germany had Hitler—and Britain had good old avuncular Stanley Baldwin, with his air of a small-town bank manager.

All sorts of factors prevented Britain from suffering the fate of its continental counterparts. The country had not been invaded for almost a millennium. Its institutions had deeper roots. Parliamentary democracy was longer established. The English invented cricket, and so on. But surely in the mix we must add the wisdom and foresight of the young Winston Churchill and his friend Lloyd George; in seeing that it was time to allay discontent; to abate the anger of the dispossessed; to help stave off revolt by providing the first state-financed response to the manifest social injustice that he saw.

In that sense, you could argue that he helped save Britain from fascism not once, but twice. It was important, that walk around the slums of Manchester in 1906. Go there today and you see chic little bars and trendy young people in cool gear who look as though they must be something to do with the city's burgeoning tech sector. Ask them what they believe in, politically, and I expect it will be some variant of capitalism with a human face.

Churchill adopted this strategy not just because it was right for the empire or the economy or for himself as a politician, but because he was genuinely compassionate. He was never a brute, whatever Labour myth may say.

Then there is a further point we must now settle about the psyche of the man; a question that goes to the heart of the whole debate about Churchill that sputters on to this day. We need to be absolutely sure of the purity of his motives, as he prepared to steer the country in 1940.

I mean we need to know what he thought and felt about that primal act in which our species was probably born—and yet which seems so alien to most of my mollycoddled generation. There are some (perhaps many) who say that a crucial part of the Churchill Factor was his sheer willingness to make war.

# CHAPTER 12

# NO GLORY
# IN SLAUGHTER

War is the father of all things, said Heracleitus. War certainly fathered Churchill the hero. But was Churchill himself the father of wars? And was he as rampantly and gleefully philoprogenitive as some have suggested?

Let us go back to the end of the war to end wars. It was 9 August 1918, and though no one could quite see it at the time, the most shameful war yet recorded was about to enter the last convulsions of slaughter. With the help of 600 tanks the British Expeditionary Force had made dazzling gains at Amiens, surging through the barbed wire and grinding over the mud and the mangled corpses for a distance of, wait for it, eight whole miles in a single day. Thousands of Germans had been killed, thousands captured.

As so often in those days, we find Churchill in France, staying at the Château Verchocq. Ostensibly this was so he could observe the distribution of munitions—his job as Minister for Munitions—at first hand. In reality, one suspects, it was because he could not bear to be far from the centre of the action. He was driving towards the headquarters of the Fourth Army, and he passed some five thousand captured Germans: their eyes vacant with shock, their heads down, their skin still blackened with explosive. As he went by, Churchill noted that he 'could not help feeling sorry for them in their miserable plight and having marched all those miles through the battlefield without food or rest, and having been through the horrors of the fight before that'.

This was perhaps a bit odd. The British successes had been remarkable—but there was no reason, as far as he could tell in August 1918, to think that they would be decisive. He had been gloomy about the prospects of the war, and had predicted that it wouldn't end before 1919 at the earliest. The Germans were capable of inflicting continued mayhem on the British. Indeed, they would do so until the final whistle.

The sight of so many defeated and captured enemy soldiers should therefore have filled him with exhilaration, a fierce pleasure that the Boche was finally on the run. Instead—he felt for their misery. It became ever clearer that this was no false dawn. Germany was really losing the war, had all but lost; and Churchill was unlike many other lesser politicians.

He was radiantly unvindictive. Where they were petty, he was great hearted; where they proposed retaliation, he was eirenic. By November 1918, on the eleventh day of the eleventh month, the Germans had signed the armistice. The country was in chaos. The Kaiser had fled; influenza raged; communist insurrections were paralysing the cities—and partly as a result of the British blockade on German ports, there were huge numbers on the verge of starvation.

One November night Churchill found himself at dinner in London with his chums—F. E. Smith, the Attorney General, and Lloyd George, the Prime Minister. News was brought to them of the German hunger. Lloyd George wanted to leave the former enemy to suffer; Churchill said twelve ships full of food should be sent over immediately.

Lloyd George said they should shoot the Kaiser. Churchill said no. Four months later, in 1919, the German position was worse—and we find Churchill complaining in the Commons that it was repugnant to use starvation as a weapon against women, children and the elderly. He wanted the blockade lifted as soon as possible, and a peace deal done with Germany.

Finally they agreed the terms at Versailles—with their demands for vast and unpayable reparations from Germany. Churchill was at odds with Lloyd George and Woodrow Wilson, the US President, in seeing the essential folly of what had been done. The terms were too harsh. 'The economic clauses of the Treaty of Versailles were malignant and silly to an extent that made them obviously futile,' he said later. This is not only prescient; it tells us something about character and instinct.

In the preface to his history of the Second World War, Churchill gives us his famous maxim that a nation should show 'in war, resolution; in defeat, defiance; in victory, magnanimity; in peace, goodwill'. This is not just cant. It is really how he was. One of the biggest calumnies that has been directed at Churchill is that he was too warlike, bellicose, *va t'en guerre*, that he almost literally snorted and snuffed and stamped the ground and rolled his eyes like a mettlesome steed at the very thought that there might be the chance of a dust-up.

It is quite easy to see why people make this charge. Scrunch up your eyes and look back at the really big events of the first half of the twentieth century—what might be called the Churchillian epoch. It is dominated by the First and Second World Wars, the two most disgraceful and destructive conflicts humanity has ever engaged in. The First World War left a total of 37 million people dead across the world, including about a million British. A generation of talented young men was liquidated in the fields of Flanders—many of them pulverised or left in gigantic anonymous ossuaries like the one at Verdun.

The Second World War killed even more—60 million dead, and half a million British. Britain had been physically and emotionally pounded. The nation had lost a quarter of its wealth. When you look at the scale of those catastrophes, you have to ask yourself who was at the wheel at the time. To an extent that we have half forgotten these days, Churchill was integral not just to the management of one conflict, but both of them. Indeed, as they recede from us in time, they look more and more like a single event; fought over the same ground, with the same patterns, the same sorts of causes, and at least in one giant case the same personality at the top. Throughout those eleven years of butchery he was the shaping political and military intellect of the nation that began the century as the greatest military power on earth; and which ended the Second War with just about everything cruelly reduced except the reputation of the Prime Minister. He was the man who got the fleet ready for the First World War, and who conceived and promoted Britain's only original strategic contribution (which ended in further catastrophe). He personally directed the action in the Second World War, in a way that seems bonkers to us today.

He was a warlord, and the suggestion is that he was also therefore a warmonger—someone who so relished war that he actually helped to provoke the conflict that made him famous. That was the suspicion of that Tory wife, who wrote that he was another Goering, pumped up with bloodlust. That was the fear of a Conservative MP who wrote in 1934 that he was an extraordinary personality—'a man with such power that he constitutes a definite menace to the peaceful solutions of the many problems with which this country is confronted'.

Today we think of him as the incarnation of moral rectitude—a man who had the courage to stand up to tyranny and yet to remain good natured, humane, democratic, rubicund, fundamentally benign and English in his moderation. That is broadly right; but in the run-up to the war he exuded for many people a dark charisma, a satanic optimism about the possibilities of violence; and even today there are those who believe that beneath the jovial image is more than a touch of Darth Vader—or possibly even the Emperor Palpatine.

It is not so long ago that the *New York Times* best-seller list featured a curious diatribe by Pat Buchanan, in which he accused Churchill of a 'lust for war' in 1914, and argued—if argued is the word—that Britain should simply have stood by in 1939 and watched the Nazis enslave the rest of Europe. Buchanan said that Churchill was far more militaristic than the Kaiser or any of his heel-clicking *Junkers*, adding (perhaps correctly) that by 1914 'Churchill had seen more war than any soldier in the German army'.

Or take the views of another palaeo-conservative, Sir Peregrine Worsthorne, a former editor of the *Sunday Telegraph*, who recently wrote: 'seldom has there been a statesman as good at glorifying war, and as indecently eager to wage war, as Winston Churchill. All his works demonstrate his love of war, glamorise its glories and minimise its horrors.' Sir Peregrine is entitled to respect; he actually fought in the Second World War. But I am afraid his views just do not square with reality, or with the complexity of Churchill's nature.

Agreed: he was excited by war. He had a naturally emotional and romantic reaction to the drama, the scale of the event. When Sir Edward Grey made his speech to the Commons on 3 August 1914—on the eve of the First World War, when the lamps went out across Europe—Churchill wept. Asquith the Prime Minister noted his mood, and with some disapproval. 'Winston has got all his war paint on and is longing for a sea fight . . . the whole thing fills me with sadness.' Slightly more indulgently, Asquith's wife Margot said, 'Winston is longing to be in the trenches—dreaming of war, big, buoyant, happy even. He is a born soldier.' Churchill even blurted to Margot that he found war 'delicious'—instantly pleading with her not to repeat the remark—and was heard to say that peace was the last thing we should pray for. Many others noted his energy, his bounce, and the gleam of purpose in his eye.

It is unquestionably true that Churchill loved war in this obvious sense, that without war he knew there could be no glory—no real chance to emulate Napoleon, Nelson or his ancestor Marlborough himself. He knew how war and its risks had lifted men and painted everyday deeds with fame. That was why, as a young man, he had plunged himself so headlong into battle—while watching the newspaper accounts out of the corner of his eye. War sent the adrenalin spurting from his glands, and of course when he was fighting—when his blood was up—he wanted to hit the enemy as hard as he possibly could. At Harrow the fencing judges had noted his lunging attacks. Churchill believed, correctly, that if you get into a fight, you have got to let your enemy know that they are losing, and you have got to make the point with whatever tools you have available. He was ruthless in the application of violence.

We have just had a high-minded international debate about modern Syria's use of chemical weapons, a practice that everyone has rightly abominated. During the course of this debate hardly anyone sought to mention the role of our national hero in encouraging the use of gas in the First World War. He wanted to gas the Turks at Gallipoli, and one of his biggest contributions as Minister for Munitions was to ensure—within the space of a month in 1918—that a third of the shells fired by British guns contained mustard gas. He was so keen on mustard gas, in fact, that his generals positively had to restrain him from using it in the Second World War as well.

Churchill not only sent thousands to die at Gallipoli ('your father killed mine at the Dardanelles', as one Eton boy said to his son Randolph when he arrived at the school). He ordered the destruction of the French fleet in 1940, he unleashed area bombing on Germany—he took decisions that a modern politician would find unthinkable, and he did it all with brio and self-confidence. And yet it is surely obvious that there is still an overwhelming difference between a person fighting hard when he comes under attack, and a person being so belligerent that he is himself the cause of conflict. There is a difference between aggression and resistance; or at least, between attack and counter-attack.

Of course he wanted personal kudos in the late Victorian imperial wars. That doesn't mean he approved of the causes in which he enlisted. Remember his disgust at Kitchener's treatment of the Mahdi's tomb, or his attack on the 'criminal and cowardly' war on the North-West Frontier. He detested unprovoked imperialist aggression and jingo. He didn't believe in war for the sake of mere colonial expansion. He took these liberal views from the Victorian battlefield into Edwardian government.

One morning in February 1906 he was at work as a junior minister in the Colonial Office when he was interrupted. A visitor was outside. Eddie Marsh had tried to give her the brush-off, but she was having none of it. She was a tall, rather handsome woman called Flora Lugard, and she was a kind of Boadicea of the British Empire. A former Colonial Editor of *The Times*, she had actually coined the name 'Nigeria', so baptising that vast country, and was known to be as hard as nails. She was lately married to a noted slaughterer of the natives by the name of Sir Frederick Lugard, and her mission was to tell the young 'boy' (as she described Churchill) how he should damn well run West Africa. Her answer was that he should give it as a satrapy to her husband and herself, so that they could run it the way they wanted: sometimes from London, sometimes on the spot, and always with lavish use of the best and most well-oiled modern weapons.

She found that the 'boy' knew exactly who she was, and he knew all about her husband. He had already noted the way the walrus-moustached Sir Frederick conducted himself—the grass huts torched, the thousands of defenceless tribespeople he had killed with shells and bullets. Churchill had written that the 'chronic bloodshed' was 'ridiculous and disquieting'. 'The whole enterprise is likely to be misrepresented by persons unacquainted with imperial terminology as the murdering of natives and the stealing of their land,' he said. He told Flora Lugard—fairly politely—that he did not approve of her approach. So began an ideological feud. He quashed the Lugards' plan to be the tsar and tsarina of a 'sultry Russia' in West Africa. Lugard was sent packing to Hong Kong. Flora Lugard protested, to anyone who would listen, that Churchill was wrong; that power flowed from the barrel of a gun, and that hers was the only way you could run a place like Africa.

Churchill said that there was no point in holding on to large chunks of Nigeria, and that he was all in favour of pulling out. Churchill certainly believed in the empire—and annexed a bit of Kenya when he was there in 1907. But he did that with a pencil, rather than a Maxim gun. He did not hold with wars of conquest, or wars of aggression—and no such aim can possibly be ascribed to the British in either 1914 or 1939.

He was indeed responsible for the build-up of the navy in the years immediately preceding the Great War; and quite right. But he didn't go into politics as a militarist. In 1901 his maiden speech caused a good deal of Tory tut-tutting, because it seemed to be so oddly pro-Boer. 'If I were a Boer, fighting in the field,' he said, 'and if I were a Boer, I hope I should be fighting in the field . . .' I say, said the Tory benches, rolling their eyes. He wishes he were fighting against us, does he?

From the outset he was sniffy about excessive military expenditure—just like his father before him—and by 1908 he was campaigning against more spending on Dreadnoughts—so as to be able to spend more on social programmes. When he got to the Admiralty he certainly changed his tune on defence spending: like all ministers, he was captured by the need to boost his department; and by then the problem of German expansion was obvious. But it was Churchill who tried to slow down the race to war. He was the one who proposed naval 'holidays'—a moratorium on both sides in the building of battleships.

Even on the brink of war, it was he who tried to go over and persuade the German naval supremo, Admiral von Tirpitz, to cool it. The Foreign Office wouldn't let him go. On the very eve of catastrophe he was to be found arguing for a meeting of European leaders—what he would later call a summit—to sort things out.

Churchill neither yearned for war, nor gloried in slaughter. When he came back from the trenches in 1916—having seen unimaginable horrors—he spoke to the Commons with the ashen disgust of a Wilfred Owen or a Siegfried Sassoon. He had seen the squalor and the graves dotted higgledy-piggledy in the trenches. It had been his task to write to the widows of those who were killed. He had seen the metronomic rhythm of killing. 'What is going on, while we go away to dinner or home or bed?' he asked his fellow MPs. 'Nearly 1000 men—Englishmen, Britishers, men of our race—are knocked into bundles of bloody rags.'

Churchill never wanted another war; he had seen enough. In 1919, as Secretary of State for War, he tried to trim military budgets by instituting the ten-year rule: that the British government would act on the assumption that there would not be another war in Europe for ten years. When he was Chancellor, in the 1920s, he again campaigned against spending on defence; and this time he had the direct authority to make the cuts. Indeed, by the late 1930s the Chamberlainites were still (unfairly) trying to blame him for the country's lack of readiness.

By the late 1930s he was of course urging his colleagues to spend more on defence, to match the expansion of the Luftwaffe. But you could not conceivably describe his attitude as bellicose, or lip-smacking, or warmongering. He spoke as a Cassandra, as one who had glimpsed a charnel-house of the future. In the Czech crisis of 1938, after Eden had resigned, he spent a night unable to sleep. 'I saw the daylight slowly creep in through the windows, and saw before me in mental gaze the vision of death.'

Historians will continue to debate the causes of the First World War, and the truth is that no European power emerges well from that catastrophic episode. What we can safely say is that Winston Churchill was not one of the culprits, and that the blame lies substantially—though of course by no means entirely—with Germany, and with German militarism and expansionism. Whatever happened at Sarajevo in 1914 was no excuse for an attack by the Kaiser on Belgium and France. Britain had absolutely no choice but to follow the rules of 500 years of foreign policy—and try to prevent a single power from dominating the continent.

The Second World War was caused almost exclusively by a maniacal German leader, and a paranoid desire for revenge. They are flying in the face of the evidence, those polemicists who posit some moral equivalence between Churchill and the Kaiser, or Churchill and Hitler. Churchill tried to avert war. He fought against it.

One of the most interesting and attractive features of his mind is that he spent much energy not only trying to avoid war, but in producing innovations—technical and scientific—to try to minimise its impact on the human frame.

War is the father of many things, but in Churchill's case, compassion was the mother of invention.

# CHAPTER 13

# THE SHIPS THAT WALKED

I t feels weird walking through the wood this afternoon—and in a way that is because it is so easy. There is nothing to stop me. I just lift the wire loop on a makeshift gate and I am strolling through the haunted grove.

The birds are in good voice, the trees are pushing out their tender leaves. There isn't a soul in sight. I am here at Ploegsteert wood in southern Belgium, not far from the French border; and as I meander over the mossy forest floor I think of how things might have looked a hundred years ago.

This wood was once famous in Britain. Almost every newspaper reader would have known the name—or rather the name the soldiers gave it. This was Plugstreet, on the Western Front. A century ago the trees were shot to stumps, the branches shredded, the birds silent, the soil contaminated with explosive and other toxins. This was where Lieutenant Colonel Churchill came out on his nocturnal prowlings, terrifying the rest of the patrol by making a noise like a 'baby elephant'. I can see the remains of the trenches they might have snuck through on their way to the front, now full of black and slimy water. They would have tiptoed to the edge of the mutilated wood, and then on some nights their commanding officer would have gone on—sometimes alone—to no man's land, and the very edge of the German lines.

That's no man's land, there. I can work out from my map where it was—an absurdly narrow strip running north–south through the fields. On one side there are some of those famous Belgian Blanc Bleu cows, with the *dikbil*, the double buttock that makes for the finest steaks. The far field is ploughed, a heavy brown corduroy that has been sown with whatever Brussels has decided pays the most this year. Between them is a little metalled track that leads—according to my map—to the German lines. I decide to get back in the old Toyota.

It is time to perform a military manoeuvre, a feat that it took Churchill and the British army five terrible years to achieve. I am going to do it in not much more than a minute. I fire up the people carrier. I engage drive. A quick swig of Stella for the nerves—and we're trundling slowly forward.

First I am bouncing over some ruts; now we're on the tarmac. I must be doing 15 miles an hour, now 20, 25. I am going over the trenches and the craters; I am passing irresistibly through the barbed wire. The shells, the bullets—nothing can stop the lunging Toyota and its 2.49-litre power plant.

On either side of the lines, weary and broken men are peering from their muddy foxholes and staring at each other with a wild surmise, then breaking into whoops. And then we have done it, almost before you can register the achievement. I have reached the German lines; and as they struggle to react I am through them—slicing effortlessly past the reserve lines and the hospital tents, and the terrified Germans are grabbing their rifles in panic and stampeding from the latrines.

I give a little toot of triumph, and quite unmolested I execute a U-turn. I leave the Kaiser's army and drive back from east to west, the same 500 pathetic yards, towards Ploegsteert wood. On the way back I stop somewhere in the middle. I park on the verge and go out into the ploughed field. This is the bit where no human being could venture and survive.

Here's why. There's one here, and here, and here. Every ploughing season thousands of fragments of ancient and rusty metal make their way to the surface from the past.

This one looks like a bit of fuse, a large knob that is corroded into a cancer of iron and rust and still amazingly heavy. This could be some shell casing, and some more here. I don't know what they are but they eloquently explain why neither side could win. There is no cover beyond the wood, just these wide fields under open Flemish sky.

No matter how much pluck or spunk or 'gallantry' they showed, the young men were cut to pieces every time. They happened to be here at a moment of asymmetry in the evolution of warfare, when mankind had lately invented metal projectiles that could penetrate human flesh, from a distance, with huge velocity and explosive power. No one had yet come up with a defence. For three awful years the position was unchanged.

You can imagine Churchill's frustration as he saw his men dying—with not an inch of territory to show for it. As soon as he got here he tried to find out what had happened to his plan.

In November 1915 he wrote a long memo to the Commander-in-Chief, Sir John French, in which he unburdened himself of all sorts of tactical proposals. Some of his ideas sound frankly a bit whacko. He wanted men to be issued with special shields, made of steel or composite, that reached from the helmet to the hips. He proposed that they should form up on the edge of the trench, lock shields, and march forwards, fifteen abreast. He seemed unaware that he was asking twentieth-century soldiers to advance towards machine guns in a defensive posture that was well known to Greek hoplites.

He suggested that soldiers be equipped with oxyacetylene torches—of a kind he had seen cutting through sheet metal in the docks—in order to make their way through the barbed wire. It was not clear what he thought would happen if the gas tank was hit by a bullet. But his main interest was in what he described as a new type of vehicle. He said they were 'moveable machine gun cupolas as well as wire smashers', and that they were capable of 'traversing any ordinary obstacle, ditch, breastwork or trench'. There were about seventy of such experimental vehicles already being built, he informed General French.

Sir John should go and see them, he urged. 'The spectacle of such a machine cutting wire entanglements has only to be witnessed to carry conviction. It resembles the reaping operations of a self-binder'—by which he means a primitive version of what we would now call a combine harvester.

Alas, Sir John never had the chance to inspect this mutant farm machinery. He was sacked by Asquith, who was beginning to panic, not surprisingly, at the lack of progress being made under his leadership. So in January 1916 Churchill tried again.

He took his paper—with its proposal for a new type of armoured combine harvester—to French's successor, Douglas Haig—a man who is traditionally blamed for much of the paralysis in British strategy. Haig seemed interested. A little later Churchill was asked to go to the British Operational Division at St Omer, to explain his ideas. The general there said he had heard from Haig that there were some new contraptions being devised by the Admiralty, for use in trench warfare.

Did Churchill know anything about it? He certainly did. Indeed, he could have been forgiven for being stupefied and appalled by the continued slowness of the army top brass to pick up his idea. It was over a year earlier, in December 1914—when he was still at the Admiralty—that he had first grasped the nightmare of the stalemate, with trenches and barbed wire stretching intermittently from Switzerland to the Channel.

Churchill had been partly inspired by the science fiction of H. G. Wells, and his description of ironclad 'landships'. On 5 January 1915 he wrote to Asquith, suggesting that it was time for some kind of technological breakthrough. We needed a machine that could deal with the trenches, he said; and if we didn't develop one, the Germans certainly would. Asquith responded quite quickly, for him, and asked the War Office to look into it.

The army formed a committee to investigate the matter, and decided that any such machine would just sink under the weight of its own armour. Too impractical; dismissed.

There matters might well have rested, with unthinkable consequences. But Churchill did not let it drop. He was at the Admiralty, remember. He was in charge of ships, not the tactics of the army. This was theoretically none of his business. But on 18 January 1915 he wrote to his colleagues at the Admiralty with what sounded like a bizarre request. He wanted an experiment performed.

Someone—he did not specify who—was to take two steam rollers and yoke them together with long steel rods, 'so that they are to all intents and purposes one roller covering a breadth of at least 12 to 14 feet'. Then he wanted his officials to go and find a 'handy' site, near London, and dig about a hundred yards of trenches, as they did in

France. The ultimate objective, he said, was to allow the monster machine to run along the length of the trenches: actually on top of them, with a giant wheel on either lip. The objective would be to 'crush them all flat and bury the people in them'.

This is Churchill at his dizzying best. There are flaws in his idea. What if the two rollers are running at different speeds, or in different gears? Surely the rods would just snap or shear? He hasn't worked out that the machine will need a single engine. But you can almost hear the crunching of his giant mental cogs as he grips the problem; and the problem of grip.

The mud, he is thinking now. The hellish seas of mud. The machine will slip and slide unless . . . aha . . .

'The rollers of these machines will be furnished with wedge-shaped ribs or studs, which can be advanced beyond the ordinary surface of the wheel when required, in order to break the soil on each side of the trench and accentuate the rolling process.' It's like peering through a telescope at some distant nebula, and seeing the clouds of interstellar gas as they resolve and harden into a planet.

An idea was being born. Perhaps without even knowing it, he was describing caterpillar tracks. All it needed, he concluded, 'was a big enough pair of steam rollers and an unscaleable bullet-proof house for the crew'. He signed off with a superbly peremptory order that the whole thing should be achieved within two weeks: 'WSC'.

You can imagine the reaction of the naval engineers. He wants us to bolt or solder some steam rollers together? And he wants us to muck up some park with a load of experimental trenches? But they did it.

So began what came to be known as the Landships Committee, and you can see why it was convenient for Churchill to adopt the H. G. Wells terminology. There was no particular reason why this project should be led from the Admiralty, unless they pretended they were discussing a form of ship. On 22 February 1915 this small group met for the first time, under the direction of one of several heroes of the story, Mr Eustace Tennyson d'Eyncourt, the Director of Naval Construction. He reported to Churchill.

The first discussion was mainly about the very point that the First Lord of the Admiralty had raised: how to make sure that the great beast did not just skid in the mud. They discussed the potential of cleated wheels, and also of 'pedrails', a peculiar device by which lots of little feet were fixed to the rim of the wheel, each gripping the ground in turn as the wheel turned. Two days later, Tennyson d'Eyncourt wrote to Churchill with news. They had made cracking progress.

They were proposing to make a 25-tonne model that would be 'a tractor of real military value carrying 50 men with machine guns and capable of negotiating enemy trenches'. They were getting closer. Churchill wrote back tersely, and on the same day: 'As proposed and with all despatch. WSC.'

By 3 March they had two designs—one with a big wheel at the back, and one with a caterpillar track. It was time to spend money. With no authorisation from the War Office, and certainly without consulting his cabinet colleagues, Churchill placed an order for the prototypes. He hadn't a clue which would be more effective: so he ordered both—a dozen caterpillars and half a dozen big wheels. In the hope of encouraging a spirit of competition, the Admiralty engaged two contractors. They were called Foster and Foden, and they were given a 10 per cent profit margin. The overall cost was £70,000—£5 million today, which strikes me as being pretty cheap by the standards of modern defence procurement, and when you think of the military history that was being made.

While the men continued to be massacred in Flanders, Tennyson d'Eyncourt and his team beavered away at the problem. Which was better? The cleats or the pedrail? And how could they overcome this basic problem: making the occupants of the vehicle safe, but without encumbering it with so much armour that it would sink in the mud? From his vantage point at the Admiralty, Churchill continued to chivvy and encourage; and then, in May 1915—disaster.

His own career went off course. He ended up in the ditch with all his wheels in the air, and no hope of getting him out. He lost office over Gallipoli, hounded out, effectively, by Tories who wouldn't work with him in government. He tried, rather tragically, to keep a role in the Landships project. He asked Balfour, who succeeded him at the Admiralty, whether he could continue to chair a small joint committee between the Admiralty and the War Office. Nothing came of it.

He took his mentor, Lloyd George, who had become Minister for Munitions, to see the muddy open-air laboratory at Wormwood Scrubs, where belching, roaring iron scarabs were being hurled at ramparts and ditches, with mixed results. Alas, the project was no longer his baby: he had no role, formal or informal. Without his creative drive, the Frankentractor languished. On the Western Front, men continued to go over the top, with hideous consequences. As far as the military top brass were concerned the plans for a new machine were all but buried.

By the autumn of the year Churchill was himself at the Western Front, performing his unique act of penitential soldiering, and the following year he took over as lieutenant-colonel in command of the 6th Battalion of the Royal Scots Fusiliers. He saw the horror and the pity at first hand. He wrote his long memo; and it was only after he had been to see Sir Douglas Haig—and found Haig so worryingly vague—that the project seemed to come to life.

On 14 February 1916 Tennyson d'Eyncourt wrote him a joyful letter. He was sorry it had all taken so long. The whole enterprise had become bogged down, metaphorically as well as physically. 'After los-

ing the great advantage of your influence I had considerable difficulty in steering the scheme past the rocks of opposition and the
more insidious shoals of apathy.'

But he was thrilled with the result, he told Churchill. The latest
war-hog was positively athletic. It would easily clear a 4 foot 6 perpen-
dicular parapet and then cross a 9-foot gap. It had 6-pounder guns
in 'sponsons'—bulges on the side—like a battleship; and it could fire
broadsides as well as forwards. It went through wire entanglements,
he boasted, 'like a rhinoceros through a field of corn . . . It looks like
a great antediluvian monster, especially when it comes out of boggy
ground. I hope it will scare the Bosches.'

He ended with an awkward but heartfelt tribute to the humiliated
Churchill. 'Allow me to offer you my congratulations on the success
of your original project, and wish you all good luck in your work at
the front.'

Production of the Landship began. In the interests of secrecy the
factory workers were told to call them 'water tanks', with the vague
suggestion that they were gigantic bowsers, destined for the thirsty
battlefields of Mesopotamia. Tanks they became, for short, and tanks
they still are, even in Russian.

In the history of British breakthroughs, the tank is unusual. It is
not just that some of the key ideas were British—that is quite common. The development was British and the practical application was
British, in the sense that by 1917 Britain was producing hundreds of
them—more than any other belligerent nation.

By now Churchill himself was once again responsible for their
production—because in July of that year Lloyd George had him back
in the cabinet, as Minister for Munitions. The press freaked out. The
*Sunday Times* said any such appointment would be 'a grave danger
to the administration and to the empire as a whole'. The *Morning
Post* warned, 'That dangerous and uncertain quantity, Mr Winston

Churchill—a floating kidney in the body politic—is back again at Whitehall.'

They could not have been more wrong. Churchill was indispensable to success. Frantically he worked to equip the forces with the devices—planes, gas shells and tanks—that he believed were essential to break the deadlock; and still the slaughter intensified. That autumn the Haig strategy of head-on assault plumbed new depths of madness. In spite of the anxieties of both Churchill and Lloyd George, the general launched the Ypres offensive—in which almost 850,000 men were to die, including 350,000 British soldiers. It was carnage on a scale never yet seen by men—an industrialised version of Cannae.

And then, at last, the tanks were ready—and in numbers. There were 400 of them in action at Cambrai on 20 November 1917, where they made significant gains. Now Churchill went into over-drive. He set up a Tank Board, with a target to deliver 4,459 by April 1919. When tank factory workers got uppity, he threatened to send them to the front. That sorted them out. Then came the great psychological moment: it was at that Battle of Amiens, on 8 August 1918, when the armoured leviathans really rattled the Germans.

Six hundred British tanks burst through German lines, grinding over the trenches, gripping the mud with their tracks and with the enemy's bullets flattening themselves on their hard metal hides—just as Churchill had imagined. It is true that the Germans learned quite fast not to be so scared—just as the Romans overcame their terror of Hannibal's elephants. In the following weeks they were to become efficient at taking out the tanks. But the damage to German morale had already taken place. General Erich Ludendorff called day one of the Battle of Amiens a 'black day' for the German army; and it can be seen as the beginning of the end.

It was the tank which was decisive on that day. Think of all those disconsolate captured soldiers Churchill saw on the 9th. They had been routed with the help of machines that he co-invented. Everywhere he went, he reported, he saw the tracks of the beasts.

Let us be clear about the exact nature of his role. It is true that he had, personally, a great natural flair for invention and improvisation—and he loved thinking about things in a practical and mechanical way: from the 'bellybando', a brown paper tube he devised to stop his cigars disintegrating, to the question of how to stop the bobbing of the prefabricated ports of Mulberry Harbours on D-Day. As a small child he loved building forts, and he and his brother Jack made a trebuchet with which they successfully fired apples at a cow.

He loved painting and bricklaying, and creating ponds and earthworks. He was not only one of the first of his generation to fly a plane; he was one of the first to drive a car (so scarily that his fellow Hughligans refused to be his passengers); and, indeed, to imagine the possibility of the atomic bomb; and to wonder what would happen if you fitted a torpedo to a plane. His enthusiasm for technological innovation—and its potential to advance the human race—was of a piece with his Whiggish personality. He had a marvellous ability to visualise, to articulate, and to fire the imagination and confidence of others.

He was certainly no scientist, but his endlessly fertile and playful intelligence legitimised the boffins in their desire to experiment, and to please him. Some of the resulting wartime ideas were brilliant but barmy, like the plan to create gigantic floating aircraft carriers by mixing ice with sawdust. This substance was known as 'pykrete', after its inventor, Geoffrey Pyke of the Royal Navy, and there is a story of how Mountbatten demonstrated its astonishing rigidity to Churchill and Roosevelt.

Mountbatten brought a great block of frozen pykrete to the Quebec conference in 1943, and shot it with his service pistol. The guards outside the room rushed in, thinking there had been an assassination, while the bullet whanged off the pykrete and almost killed the British Air Marshal Charles Portal.

That is the way of scientific experiment. Pykrete might have been a triumph, but wasn't. The tank might have been a flop, but worked to devastating effect. And it might have been a flop had it not been for Churchill's imaginative drive: his ability to hold an idea in the forefront of his mind and then work away at it—like the process of getting his mental vision to appear in oils on a canvas—until he had made the idea a reality.

His interest in machines was of course partly aggressive: he wanted planes, tanks, gas and bombs because he wanted to win, and as fast as possible. But again the underlying motive was compassion, to reduce the mayhem and misery that he saw. 'Machines save life,' he said at the beginning of 1917, before the tank had yet proved its worth. 'Machine-power is a great substitute for manpower. Brains will save blood. Manoeuvre is a great diluting agent to slaughter.'

That was why he went for the great flanking operation at Gallipoli; that was why he pioneered area bombing even in the First War, and that was why he personally oversaw the production of huge quantities of mustard gas. That was why he wanted the tank—to reduce the mortality rate of men who were asked to walk or run into a hail of metal projectiles.

Dotted in the fields and lanes around Ploegsteert are the cemeteries with their rows and rows of white stone crosses—witness to the criminal waste and stupidity of those tactics. For his role in pioneering the tank, Churchill surely deserves credit not just for saving lives but for shortening—and, arguably, helping to win—the First World War.

And not just with the tank, of course. When Germany eventually capitulated, it was very largely thanks to the slow boa-constrictor-like strangulation of the Royal Navy blockade, protracted over five years, and which by 1918 had brought the Germans to the brink of starvation. It was thanks to Churchill, as pre-war First Lord of the Admiralty, that the oil-fuelled fleet was ready in 1914 to do the job. We owe him, then, for ships on land and sea.

I WANDER BACK to the wood he used to frequent, and I stand there with my almost empty beer can and a cigar, communing in a kind of daze with the shades of those who died. My meditation is shattered. A Belgian farmer has seen the car parked by the wood, and he is advancing towards me with the air of one who wants me off his land.

I almost point out that a lot of British soldiers died terrible deaths to defend the title of Belgian farmers to these very woods; but I think better of it. Has he heard of Winston Churchill? I ask him. He looks thoughtful. Did Churchill fight in the war? he asks. I confirm this.

'One must always respect those who fought in the war,' says the farmer. Well, I will drink to that. I drain the Stella and leave the ghostly wood. No one else in the First World War had anything like Churchill's record, of risking his life at the front, and simultaneously originating and promoting wholly new directions in the grand strategy of the conflict. How did he do it?

There is a reason why Churchill drove forward so much new technology, why they didn't just remain in some naval designer's sketchbook. I have by now read a large number of his memos and notes, and I have been amazed not just by his bureaucratic stamina but by his phenomenal attention to detail.

Of all the politicians of his generation, Churchill was not just the best speaker, the best writer, the best joke-maker, the bravest, the boldest and the most original. It was crucial to the Churchill Factor that he was also the biggest policy wonk you ever saw.

That was an essential feature of his handling of the war effort in 1940. Of course he could do the big picture, and the great sweep of history; none better. But there was one aspect of Churchill's character that consistently surprised his biographer Roy Jenkins, and that was his work rate.

# CHAPTER 14

# THE
# 100-HORSEPOWER
# MENTAL ENGINE

Come on, girl,' says Inches the butler. 'He's asked for you and he doesn't like to be asked twice.' He points up the stairs and you feel your heart thud.

Let's say you are in your early twenties. You are a pretty Home Counties sort of girl in flattish shoes with a sensible skirt and nothing too fussy about your jewellery or make-up. You haven't been to university, but you have good shorthand and can type like the wind.

You could be any one of the dozens of secretaries or literary assistants—of both sexes—that have stood trembling at the bottom of these stairs, over the decades. But let's say you've found a position in the great man's entourage some time in the 1920s or 1930s; it doesn't really matter when.

The big red-brick house is always a scene of immense activity when Churchill is there, and the grounds look a bit like a zoo—or a zoo under construction. There are pigs and goats and dogs and cats and mandarin ducks and black and white swans and geese and fishponds, with giant ornamental goldfish, and men with diggers at work on what looks like a hydroelectric project, with a series of dams being constructed down the slope of the hill.

When you get inside, it is like the opening scene of *The Marriage of Figaro*. There are people rushing everywhere: maids and chauffeurs and footmen and cooks, and smooth young men with an air of scholarship who are carrying sheaves of paper, and a lovely little child with golden hair who seems to be the youngest of the family.

Now you have to go upstairs and attend to the needs of the mind that somehow powers all this motion, and without which it subsides as though turned off by a switch.

'Hurry up,' says Inches, and you go up the blue lino stairs with rubber nosing and you knock on the door of what you have been told is the study. There is a muffled shout from somewhere within, as though from a prisoner in a cupboard.

You enter a large high-beamed room, with a black and empty fireplace at one end, beneath a rather gloomy picture of Blenheim Palace. There's a stand-up desk against one wall, and a sit-down desk against another, and an old pinkish carpet on the floor. There's a faint smell of cigar—but of Winston Churchill there is no sign.

'Sir?' you quaver.

'Here!' comes a shout, and then you see a little door in the far corner, which looks as though it might be the entrance to an airing cupboard, or a large drinks cabinet. You go through. You can't quite believe that these are the sleeping arrangements of one of the most powerful men in Britain.

Someone has whispered that Mrs Churchill likes to spend the night elsewhere, because the couple have radically different biorhythms. This is certainly no bedroom for a lady. It is more like a monk's cell.

There is a sepia picture of Lord Randolph Churchill on the wall, and a tiny bathroom off to one side; and there in the low bed is a terrifying sight. He is surrounded by books and papers and dispatch boxes strewn all over the place; and by him a big chromium-plated cuspidor, with something nasty at the bottom of it, because a cuspidor is a glorified bowl for spitting into.

There is a glass of what looks like a weak whisky and soda on the bedside table, a marmalade cat on the coverlet, and he is sitting up in bed wearing a red silk kimono and a fierce expression, with his greying strands of hair askew. He champs his cigar and you realise he is saying something to you.

'I beg your pardon, sir,' you say.

'Get it down,' he snaps, and you twig that he has already begun dictating.

Quickly you compose yourself, and whip out your notebook or letter-paper, and start recording his words. He breaks off. A terrible scowl comes over his face, like that of a bull meditating whether to charge a rambler in a fluorescent cagoule.

His toes twitch under the bedclothes, and he is making little sibilant noises like a kettle or a saucepan of porridge.

You keep your pen poised above your work, your head down. Then he speaks again, and his tone is startlingly seductive, even lubricious.

'Daarling . . .' he says.

You look up in alarm to see that it's OK: he's talking to the cat. He goes on, switching from Tango the marmalade cat back to you, and you realise you're having a slight problem.

Owing to the cigar, and the way he says 'sh' instead of 's', you find yourself asking him to repeat things.

'God's teeth, girl!' he exclaims, and you find yourself overcome. It's all too much. You can't help it.

The tears begin, and instantly he is transformed. All his attention is focused on you, and he smiles and fixes you with his merry blue eyes. 'Don't mind me when I snap,' he says, and explains that he is not cross with you, not at all; he is just trying to think of what to say, and hates having his flow disrupted.

Now he is off again. The toes are twitching as he crafts every sentence so as to find the natural cadence of the language, rhythmical, musical; and now it is over. He brings his hand crashing down, like a conductor signalling the end of a Beethoven symphony.

'Gimme!' he says—and you hand over the memo or letter.

He reads it, and then takes out a fountain pen and—holding it quite high on the barrel—he initials it; and that's it. You are gone, dismissed—until half an hour later you are mysteriously summoned again. It seems he has thought of something else.

This time both the study and the bedroom are empty, and there is a sploshing from the little bathroom. Golly, you think. In between his spongeing and sluicing he instructs you to draw up a little chair next to the door and begins dictating another letter, and then you muffle a shriek as he emerges, with a tiny towel around his waist that seems to fall off him as you close your horrified eyes . . .

When you open them, he's half decent, and dictating again. 'KBO', he concludes this letter—which you later discover means 'Keep Buggering On', an injunction he often uses to his colleagues.

So it goes on throughout the day, with Churchill dictating streams of material to his helpers of both sexes. He seems to be working on several books at once, not to mention newspaper articles, speeches and further memoranda.

He has a generous booze-fuelled lunch, and then a nap, and then he is either painting or doing a spot of bricklaying with his bricklaying tutor, Mr Kurn, or even playing bezique, a card game with which he has become almost obsessed. Then it is announced that he has to go to London, and you sit crushed in the back of the brown Daimler, with your noiseless typewriter on your lap, and on one side the dispatch boxes, on the other a large tan-coloured poodle called Rufus, with his tongue in your ear, and the cigar sending gusts of smoke backwards in your direction.

For the next two hours he proses away, and you marvel at the lushness of his vocabulary, the endless synonyms, the tautologies, the pleonasms. He goes to Parliament, he goes to the Treasury; he deals in the course of the afternoon and evening with huge quantities of text and produces thousands more words of every kind and every one of them minutely conserved by his helpers, as if they were worker bees collecting royal jelly from the queen.

By now you are beginning to flag. He is not. He is still at it after dinner—though you have gone to bed, relieved by another secretary. He whirrs on into the night as though his battery is made of some superior mixture of chemicals, unknown to other men. By the time he finally gets his head down in his London flat, it is as late as 3 a.m. And he is going to repeat the whole thing the following day; and by then you realise what they say about him is true: that the closer you get to Winston Churchill, the more convinced you become of his genius.

PERHAPS THE BIGGEST mistake you can make about Churchill is to think that he is some kind of orotund frontman, a mere impresario of ideas—a Ronald Reagan with a cigar. Reagan once famously joked of his own approach to life, 'They say hard work can't kill you—but I figure, why take the chance?'

That was emphatically not Churchill's maxim. It is not just the books—he produced thirty-one of them and of those fourteen were 'proper' or original publications, rather than compilations of material already published. Try counting his innumerable entries in the parliamentary record: dozens of speeches and interventions and questions every month, in a career that lasted almost uninterrupted for sixty-four years. His published speeches alone run to eighteen volumes and 8,700 pages; his memoranda and letters comprise a million documents in 2,500 boxes.

He presented five budgets as Chancellor, and would speak for three or four hours (modern Chancellors do no more than an hour). *And he had no speech writer.* He did it all himself; and when he wasn't dictating, or writing, or dominating some conversation, or painting, or laying bricks, he was putting on more intellectual weight.

He had read at least five thousand books, and had committed so much poetry to his elephantine memory that people took him to be a kind of jukebox. You just pushed his button and out it came. When he was staying with Franklin and Eleanor Roosevelt at Shangri-La, he impressed the US President by being able to give him the nonsense rhymes of Edward Lear.

Then Roosevelt quoted some famous lines from the patriotic American poem 'Barbara Frietchie' by John Greenleaf Whittier: 'shoot if you must this old grey head/ But spare your country's flag, she said'.

Churchill stunned the presidential couple by giving them the whole darn thing—astonishing, since it is a conspicuously American poem, and hardly the kind of poem he would have learned at Harrow; and masterfully diplomatic it was of Churchill to pull it out of his hat. 'My husband and I looked at each other,' said Eleanor Roosevelt, 'for each of us could have quoted a few lines, but the whole thing was quite beyond us.'

The Aga Khan had the same sort of floaty feeling when Churchill began quoting huge chunks of Omar Khayyam. Had this man learned it to impress him? No, he just happened to have it in his head. He kept and stored these literary delicacies for years, perfectly pickled in the alcohol-washed runnels of his brain. He could pull them out at any moment: the *Lays of Ancient Rome* for the cabinet, Shakespeare for his children. Even in his eighties he was able suddenly to summon obscure lines of Aristophanes for Sir John Colville.

If you have a spare fifteen minutes, go on YouTube, and look at the sublime out-takes of Churchill's only televised party political broadcast, from 1951. He sits there gazing at the camera with utter savagery, while they make him repeat his script over and over again. Finally, he breaks off from being tormented by the producers and gives them what for by reciting a long section from Gibbon about the spread of Christianity.

This is important, this gift of memory, because it meant that he could hold the data in his head that enabled him to win arguments and dominate his colleagues. In 1913 Asquith complained to his love-object Venetia that they had just had a three-hour cabinet, two and a quarter hours of which were occupied by the remarks of Churchill. He became the natural go-to man for a complex negotiation, partly because of his charm and friendliness but mainly because he grasped the subject so deeply that he was fertile in expedients and compromises. He handled the negotiations on everything from the partition of Ireland to the creation of Israel to the General Strike; and the reason he was so central to these formative twentieth-century events was not so much that he muscled his way to centre stage, but that his colleagues simply recognised that he was the man with the wattage to do it.

His wasn't a notably mathematical or financial brain. As he admitted during the controversy over whether or not to go back on the Gold Standard, he had 'limited comprehension of these extremely technical matters' (like his father, also Chancellor, who complained about all these 'damned dots'); and after a session with a load of bankers he complained that they were all 'speaking Persian'. For this he can surely be forgiven. The history of the last 100 years is full of occasions when it is perfectly obvious that the bankers themselves haven't the faintest understanding of what they are trying to say.

What he had was stamina, power, sheer mental grunt. 'There comes Winston Churchill, with his hundred horsepower mind,' said someone before the First World War, when 100 horsepower was a lot.

Some people have very quick analytic brains, but no particular energy or appetite for work. Some people have loads of drive, but limited talent—and most of us, clearly, have our own moderate portions of each. Churchill had the lot: phenomenal energy, a prodigious memory, a keen analytic mind and a ruthless journalistic ability to sort his material so as to put the most important point first. He also had the zigzag streak of lightning in the brain that makes for creativity.

His psychological make-up (need to prove himself to father, partial megalomania, etc.) meant that he *had* to work; he was incapable of idleness. Much has been made of his so-called depression or 'black dog', as he called it—using an expression that already existed at the time. Others think this has been overdone, and I am inclined to agree.

He certainly got a bit blue in the 1930s, when he was out of office, but in general he was well used to managing what is for many people the creative cycle: depression—exertion—creativity—alcoholically enhanced elation—depression and so on. He just spanned the cycle faster than anyone else, as though he had a higher RPM, and his output was consequently enormous. He was like Dr Johnson, in that he made tremendous demands of himself, with his superego flagellating him onwards. He explained what it was like: 'You know, I hate to go to bed at night feeling I have done nothing useful in the day. It is the same feeling as if you had gone to bed without brushing your teeth.'

He was in one way archaic in his attitudes—driven by a lust for glory and praise, and a fear of public shame. But there was also plenty of post-Christian guilt in the mix. Whatever the exact composition of the fuel, the Churchill engine was perfectly suited to the complexities of government. He was a Whitehall warrior, and he was a details man, sometimes maddeningly so.

At the Treasury he would busy himself with such minutiae as the cost of Foreign Office telegrams. When he arrived back at the Admiralty in 1939 he was making inquiries about the number of duffel coats issued to individual ships. He took it into his head to order that backgammon, not cards, should be played on Royal Navy vessels.

If you want an example of his love of 'minutes'—dictated messages on government, of which he would produce dozens a day—look at this amazing document that is framed on the wall at Chartwell. It is a testy response to what seems to have been a very moderate Foreign Office suggestion, about respecting the names people give their own cities.

*Prime Minister's*
*Personal Minute:*

*Serial No: M 387/5 A*

**FOREIGN OFFICE**

*1. The principle at 'A' is entirely disagreeable to me. I do not consider that names that have been familiar for generations in*

*England should be altered to study the whims of foreigners
living in those parts.*

*Where the name has no particular significance, the local
custom should be followed. However, Constantinople should
never be abandoned, though for stupid people Istanbul may be
written in brackets after it. As for Angora, long familiar with
us through the Angora Cats, I will resist to the utmost of my
power its degradation to Ankara.*

*2. You should note, by the way, the bad luck which
always pursue peoples who change the names of their
cities. Fortune is rightly malignant to those who break
with the traditions and customs of the past. As long as I
have a word to say in the matter Ankara is banned,
unless in brackets afterwards. If we do not make a stand
we shall in a few weeks be asked to call Leghorn Livorno,
and the B.B.C. will be pronouncing Paris Paree.
Foreign names were made for Englishmen, not
Englishmen for foreign names. I date this minute from
St George's Day.*

*WSC*

*23.4.45*

And look at the date: the Germans are still fighting, British troops
are still dying—and he finds time to dictate a humorous minute
about place names.

Sometimes, though, his colleagues were grateful for that eagle
eye. Shown some pictures of dummy British battleships at Scapa
Flow, he noticed something odd. There weren't any seagulls around

the funnels. The Germans might rumble the deception. So they put enough food around the funnels to bring the birds—and the Germans, presumably, were fooled.

This indefatigability was absolutely essential from 1940 on. He had chosen the nation's fate. By sheer charisma and force of personality, he had determined that Britain should fight on. But he still had to keep hauling the machine in the direction he wanted; he was the strongman pulling the 747 across the runway; the tug changing the course of the supertanker. As one aide put it: 'the ferment of ideas, the persistence in flogging proposals, the goading of commanders to attack—these were all expressions of that blazing explosive energy without which the vast war machine, civilian as well as military, could not have been moved forward so steadily or steered through so many set-backs and difficulties'.

OF COURSE, he couldn't have done it without you—I mean you, the young secretary, now back on duty, and taking more dictation. It was part of Churchill's triumph that he was able to turn the people around him into his personal hive, his 'factory', as he called it; and on the whole it was a wonderful factory to work in. If he could be occasionally snappish and impatient he could also be kind and loving to those who helped him, paying for their medical treatment and their time off work for sickness.

He needed the factory to help him process the quantity of data he deployed, and to give him that grasp of detail. And it was the grasp of detail, of course, which enabled him also to be a big-picture man. The reason he was so formidable, in that long and wretched slide to war, is that he had the facts; he knew the reality about Germany and he intuitively understood the threat the Nazis posed to the world.

It is regularly said that his views were discounted at the time, because he had been wrong so often before; and it strikes me that this is an assertion that needs to be challenged. He made terrible mistakes, of course; but even before the Second World War, there is a case for saying that he had been much more right than wrong.

# CHAPTER 15

# PLAYING ROULETTE
# WITH HISTORY

It hardly bears thinking about, really. Winston Churchill had plenty of narrow squeaks—but when he agreed to loiter in the tearoom of a Munich hotel, he had no idea of the risk he was running. He was almost caught in the photo-opportunity from hell: the one handshake that was likely to prove most damaging to his long-term reputation.

It was July 1932, and he had come to Germany to research the battlefield of Blenheim, with a view to adding some colour to his life of Marlborough. He was staying at one of the swishest hotels in the city, the Regina Palast—the same place, incidentally, that was to accommodate Neville Chamberlain and his wretched delegation when they came to the summit of 1938.

Already there were parades of fascist youths down the streets of Munich—right outside the hotel. Conjure up in your mind brown leather shorts and rippling thighs; oom-pa-pa marching bands and red and black swastika bunting floating in the breeze. Think beaming girls in dirndl serving foaming steins in the hotel *biergarten*, their blond hair whorled in strange pastry shapes around their ears.

Then add Churchill with his lively eyes and puckish curiosity, watching it all from an open window, drinking it in, working it out. His journalist son Randolph was with him on the trip, keen to find out about the Nazis; and he introduced his father to a curious geezer by the name of Ernst 'Putzi' Hanfstaengl. This Putzi was a tall, gangling German-American businessman in his mid-forties. He had been educated at Harvard—so he spoke excellent English. Like Franklin D. Roosevelt he had been a member of the Hasty Pudding club, where he had developed his talent for the piano. Indeed, he was the author of some of the famous Harvard songs.

He was talkative, jokey, sardonic, with tweeds and a kipper tie that came, in the fashion of the day, only halfway down his shirt front. He was also a leading Nazi and intimate of Hitler, for whom he acted as a kind of international spin-doctor.

One night Winston, Randolph and Putzi Hanfstaengl stayed up round the piano; and though it is not clear whether Churchill followed his normal practice of singing lustily and tunelessly along, he was certainly pleased to find that Putzi knew many of his favourite tunes. At the end of this enjoyable recital, Putzi started rhapsodising about Hitler, and his successes in revitalising Germany.

Churchill immediately asked about Hitler's anti-Semitism. Putzi tried to allay his fears. As Hanfstaengl later wrote: 'I tried to give as mild an account as I could, saying that the problem was the influx of eastern European Jews and the excessive representation of their co-religionists in the professions.'

Hmmm, said Churchill: 'Tell your boss from me that anti-semitism may be a good starter, but it is a bad sticker.' This is a racing expression. It is a polite, upper-class English way of saying that in bashing the Jews, Hitler was backing the wrong horse.

I tell you what, Putzi told Churchill. He should meet Hitler. It would be a piece of cake, perhaps literally. It seemed that Hitler came to this very hotel, every afternoon at 5 p.m. They could bond over a couple of slices of Black Forest gateau. Putzi was sure that the Führer would be 'very glad' to meet the English party.

Churchill's natural journalistic curiosity was aroused—and indeed Randolph was almost certainly angling for just such a meeting. As Churchill said later in his memoirs: 'I had no national prejudices against Hitler at this time. I knew little of his doctrine or record and nothing of his character.'

For two days Churchill and Randolph waited; sometimes in the American bar, sometimes in the sunny *biergarten* outside. It is eerie to think of our hero, kicking his heels like a stringer correspondent in some Munich hotel, and waiting to be favoured with an audience by a man fourteen years his junior who was to go on to become his bitterest enemy.

Imagine if they had met. Churchill would have joined the embarrassing roll-call of British MPs and aristocrats to be pictured with a leader who was to become a universal by-word for evil. Halifax; Chamberlain; Lloyd George; Edward VIII; they all made that goof.

(The only man to come through it with colours flying was Churchill's parliamentary aide Bob Boothby, MP, who famously replied to Hitler's megalomaniacal greeting of 'Heil Hitler!' with the only logical response: 'Heil Boothby!' said Boothby.)

If Hitler had come into that hotel tearoom or bar, Churchill would have been forced at the least to be courteous, if not cordial—and that would not have looked good in 1940.

The interesting question is why Hitler chose not to come. He met plenty of other people in Munich. He dazzled Unity Mitford, for instance, and even bought her tea. Why shouldn't he have seen a man who was famous throughout England, had held most of the great offices of state, and who had a formidable reputation for foreign affairs?

Before Putzi went off to fix the momentous encounter, he asked Churchill to give him something to go on. Were there any questions that the Englishman wanted to ask, so as to serve as the basis for their discussions? Yes, said Churchill. He returned to the point that exercised him.

'Why is your chief so violent about the Jews?' Churchill asked Putzi Hanfstaengl. 'I can quite understand being angry with the Jews who have done wrong or are against the country, and I can understand resisting them if they try to monopolise power in any walk of life; but what is the sense of being against a man simply because of his birth? How can any man help how he is born?'

With these unimpeachably liberal, humane and Churchillian sentiments in his ears, Putzi returned to the Führer; and got nowhere.

'What part does Churchill play?' sneered the Nazi leader. 'He is in opposition and no one pays any attention to him.'

To which Hanfstaengl replied: 'People say the same about you.'

I reckon Hitler decided to swerve Churchill not just because he thought he was washed up, kaput, finito. It was because he didn't like the sound of this boisterous and opinionated English fellow, who was so fervent about democracy and so mysteriously squeamish about anti-Semitism.

He avoided the Regina Palast hotel until the Churchill party was gone; and for the second time in history—they were apparently only a few hundred yards from each other in the trenches in 1916—the two men came close, but never met. Later, of course, Hitler was to issue plenty of invitations to meet Churchill in public, when such a meeting would have been obviously to the Nazis' advantage; and Churchill always declined.

Right at the beginning of Germany's nightmare, before Hitler had even become Chancellor, Churchill spotted the evil at the heart of Nazi ideology. There is something innocent in the way he phrases the question to Putzi: 'what is the sense of being against a man simply because of his birth?' In the months and years that followed, Churchill's puzzlement was to turn to outrage.

While Nazism remained obdurately fashionable in some parts of British society, Churchill campaigned with growing vehemence against Hitler's mistreatment of minorities. It helped that he had been to Germany. He had drunk in the atmosphere: he had actually seen the files of young men and women, fit, tanned, full of revanchist excitement.

On 23 November 1932 he made a prescient speech to Parliament. He observed that 'all these bands of sturdy Teutonic youths, marching through the streets and roads of Germany, with the light of desire in their eyes to suffer for the Fatherland, are not looking for status. They are looking for weapons.' When they had the weapons, he prophesied, they would use them to ask for the return of their lost territories. France, Belgium, Poland, Romania, Czechoslovakia, Yugoslavia—they were all in peril, said Churchill. A 'war mentality' was springing up across Europe. It was time to tell the British people the truth about the danger, he said. They were a tough people, a robust people, the British: they could take it, he said. Others, of course, said he was being alarmist: a warmonger.

Six years later he was to be proved crushingly and overwhelmingly correct in his analysis. That was the basis of much of his prestige in 1940—that he had made the right call about Hitler, almost from the start. He put his shirt on a horse called anti-Nazism, and he did it early, at a time when no one much fancied the nag, and his bet came off in spectacular fashion.

To some extent all politicians are gamblers with events. They try to anticipate what will happen, to put themselves 'on the right side of history', to show off their judgement to best advantage. In 1902 Churchill observed that a politician needs 'the ability to foretell what is going to happen tomorrow, next week, next month and next year. And to have the ability to explain afterward why it didn't happen.'

He loved staking his reputation in the way that he loved all risky activities—flying a plane, riding along the front at Malakand, crawling around no man's land. It gave him the chance to test his egocentric thesis that he was special, that somehow the bullets would whistle past him; that a guardian angel or daemon hovered over him, that Lady Luck was on his side and really rather doted on him. He gambled for money, at the tables of Deauville or Le Touquet, and one of his secretaries describes him leaping out of a taxi and rushing into the casino at Monte Carlo—shirt-tails flapping—and returning a short time later with enough to buy their rail fare home.

No other politician had taken so many apparently risky positions; no other politician had been involved in so many cock-ups—not only living to tell the tale, but flourishing in spite of them. The surprising thing, by the time he lounged in that Munich hotel in 1932, was that he had any reputation left to wager.

Now is the moment to look in a bit more detail at the lurid series of disasters that traditionally landmark accounts of his pre-1940 career. We need to consider the interaction between Churchill and these events: the extent to which he was responsible—and, indeed, the extent to which they were really disasters. Let us begin with:

# The Antwerp Blunder.

Sometimes posterity can be kinder than your contemporaries. In October 1914 the German armies were devouring the Low Countries. Churchill took it upon himself personally to mastermind the defence of Antwerp—a port so strategically important that Napoleon once called it 'a pistol pointing at the heart of England'. Afterwards, the media was withering. The *Morning Post* said it was a 'costly blunder, for which Mr W Churchill must be held responsible'. The *Daily Mail* said it was a 'gross example of mal-administration which has cost valuable lives'. It seemed to his cabinet colleagues that the First Lord of the Admiralty had gone nuts—shooting off to Antwerp, prancing around in a cape and a yachting cap while the Germans bombarded him.

At one stage he asked for the right to resign from the cabinet and take up a military command. He wanted to be General Churchill, he told Asquith—a suggestion, Asquith said, that made his colleagues rock with unquenchable laughter.

In the end Antwerp surrendered, and thousands of British troops were captured; Churchill vamoosed to London, where he got a pretty frosty reception from Clementine—since he had missed the birth of Sarah, their third baby. But was it so mad an idea?

Remember what was happening in the autumn of 1914. The Germans were racing towards the Channel ports. The loss of Ostend and Dunkirk would have been disastrous, since it would have been much more difficult to reinforce the troops in Flanders. The point of the Antwerp mission was to persuade the Belgians to hold out for ten days or so—to win a breathing-space and protect the other ports.

As it was, Churchill was able to hang on for six days. But it was enough. The other ports were saved. So let us rate the Antwerp Blunder out of 10. I would say it had a **FIASCO FACTOR** of 2, since it was really a success; and that it had a **CHURCHILL FACTOR** of 9 out of 10, since it is almost impossible to imagine that the Belgians would have stuck it out if he had not been there.

It has always been harder to make any kind of case for:

# The Gallipoli Catastrophe.

On the face of things, this was one of the biggest military disasters in a war that had many disasters. By late 1914 the trenches stretched from Switzerland to the English Channel. Churchill was casting around for ways both to use the fleet, otherwise relatively underemployed, and to get round the abbatoir of the Western Front. Where could they go? First they thought of the Baltic, but the Germans were in charge there. Then he hit on the concept that often commended itself to him: the 'soft under-belly'. He wanted to attack Germany's ally, Turkey.

He would use the fleet to ram the Dardanelles—a narrow strait between the Mediterranean and the Black Sea; capture Constantinople; take the Ottomans out of the war; relieve the pressure on Russia; bring in Greece, Bulgaria and Romania on the Allied side—and bingo! (we may imagine Churchill jabbing triumphantly at the map) the way would be clear to attack the Germans from both sides. Things did not go well.

The whole operation was finally wound up in 1916, by which time there had been about 180,000 Allied casualties, most of whom died of disease on the beaches and the promontories of the Gallipoli peninsula, without getting anywhere near Constantinople.

So many Australians and New Zealanders were sacrificed that Gallipoli became a cause of deep and folkloric bitterness and estrangement from the imperial power. The Irish regiments were so mauled that the episode is said to have encouraged the fight for independence. Churchill was effectively sacked by Asquith in May 1915, and went into a complete decline.

'I thought he would die of grief,' said Clementine. 'I am finished,' he groaned. Is there nothing to be said for the Dardanelles?

Well, it was at least an attempt to break the stalemate on the Western Front. Someone had to come up with an alternative to 'chewing barbed wire in Flanders', said Churchill—and he was surely right.

He was unlucky in his admirals, one of whom had a nervous breakdown; he was unlucky in his colleagues—notably Lord Fisher, the aged and frog-faced First Sea Lord, who blew endlessly hot and cold and then threw a colossal strop, flouncing out of office at the crucial moment. He was unlucky not to be able to control the timing of the operation, or to launch it with the *élan* it required.

But even if you make allowances for bad luck, we must accept that the whole concept was probably flawed. It seems to rely on a series of heroic assumptions about what would happen if Constantinople was eventually captured; and the surely imponderable outcome of a Balkan campaign. For his wild overoptimism, Churchill must take the blame.

As it was, ships were sunk, admirals dithered, men were machine-gunned on beaches or died of dysentery, and Mustafa Kemal emerged as a hero of the Turkish nation for his role in seeing off the British Empire. We have no alternative but to give the Dardanelles a **FIASCO FACTOR** of 10 and a **CHURCHILL FACTOR** of 10, since it would certainly not have happened without him. It could have worked—if a long series of cards had fallen the right way—but the mesmerising disaster convinced many people that Churchill not only possessed bad judgement, but that he was positively unstable in his vanity: in his desire somehow to engage personally in the conflict.

It says something about his bomb-proof ego that by the end of 1919 he was at it again, in an episode that has become known as:

tafa Kemal (Atatürk) were threatening the British and French gar-
risons on the Gallipoli peninsula. These were stationed at Chanak,
or Canakkale—the town nearest to the ancient site of Troy. Prime
Minister Lloyd George was very anti-Turk and pro-Greek, and was
keen to launch a kind of Christian war against the Mohammedans.
He thought Chanak would be an excellent pretext to biff Johnny
Turk.

For reasons that are not entirely clear, Churchill decided to do a
U-turn and announce that Lloyd George was right. This was odd,
since Churchill was generally rather pro-Turk, like his father. And in
foreign policy, as in life, it would be fair to say that he was not motivated by religious considerations of any kind. I am afraid it looks as
though his only real reason for wanting a fight with the Turks at
Chanak was to avenge the Dardanelles, to erase his personal psychic
scar—not a good motive.

Thankfully, both Lloyd George and Churchill managed completely to muff their moment. Churchill issued a portentous press
release on 15 September 1922 in which he announced that military
action had the support of Canada, Australia and New Zealand—
without breaking the news to the governments of those countries.
They were not pleased, having no particular zeal to send more men
to further Churchill-inspired massacres in the Dardanelles.

The press and public were alarmed. The headline of the *Daily
Mail* was 'Stop This New War!', which more or less summed up the
mood. The Conservatives decided that they had run out of patience
with Lloyd George and Churchill. They met at the Carlton Club to
pull the rug out from under the Coalition (and gave birth to the
1922 Conservative Private Members' Committee). Andrew Bonar
Law said Britain could not be the policeman of the world; Baldwin
put the boot in.

The Chanak crisis was solved by diplomacy, but the British government fell, and Churchill was out. We must give Chanak a modest **FIASCO FACTOR** of 4, and a **CHURCHILL FACTOR** of 5, since he shared authorship with Lloyd George. But the political consequences were pretty seismic.

And his recovery was therefore doubly remarkable. When you look at this period—from 1922 to 1924—you really feel that he is an elemental force in British politics, too big to be sunk by the destruction of his Liberal Party, too big to ignore. Soon he was having chats with Baldwin about rejoining the Tories, twenty years after he had deserted them. In November 1924—even though he had just won a large majority—Baldwin reached out to the forty-nine-year-old renegade and made him Chancellor of the Exchequer. Dumbfounded, he accepted. 'I had the greatest difficulty convincing my wife that I was not merely teasing her,' he said.

It is widely agreed that Churchill's Chancellorship—whatever its merits—was blighted by wrongly

# Going Back on Gold.

. . . and at the wrong rate. Everyone now accepts that this was a catastrophic error. The value of sterling was pegged back at its pre-war rate of $4.87—which meant the pound was overvalued, with fatal consequences for British industry. Exports became too expensive to compete on world markets. Businesses tried to cut costs by laying off staff or cutting wages. There were strikes, unemployment, chaos— and then the crash of 1929, and still no escape from the punishing regime of the Gold Standard.

In the end the pound was forced off gold in 1931 by a series of speculative attacks on the foreign exchange markets—just as it was prised out of the Exchange Rate Mechanism in 1992. Churchill carried the can for the whole disaster, and John Maynard Keynes wrote a denunciation called *The Economic Consequences of Mr Churchill*. It was indeed his decision, and as Chancellor, he cannot escape the blame.

All we can do is enter some crucial mitigating points. First, he was himself instinctively against it. He could see the problem a strong pound would pose for British business and industry. In February 1925 he objected to the plan: 'I would rather see Finance less proud and Industry more content.' Before he took the decision, he wrote long memos to his officials asking them if they could explain their support for the Gold Standard; and was much displeased by their woolly answers.

The officials talked vaguely of 'stability'. But how did that help British manufacturers, if their goods were being priced out of the market? He took to quoting, with approval, William Jennings Bryan's impassioned 1896 criticism of the Gold Standard: 'You shall not press down upon the brow of labour this crown of thorns; you shall not crucify mankind upon a cross of gold.'

He was absolutely right. The trouble was that he was surrounded by a lot of clever people who thought they knew about economics; and they thought the Gold Standard was a frightfully good idea. The most ineffably self-confident of them all was the Governor of the Bank of England, the nattily dressed Montagu Norman. 'I will make you the golden Chancellor,' he told Churchill. But Norman was not alone in his delusions.

The City was for it; the Labour Party was for it; Stanley Baldwin himself thought it would be easier just to get on and do it. In the end Churchill held a famous dinner party at Number 11 Downing Street, on 17 March 1925, and invited Keynes to come and put the contrary point of view. Alas, Keynes had a cold and was off form. Churchill the gold-o-sceptic found himself outnumbered, and reluctantly conceded.

The point is that he went back on gold in spite of his better judgement—and his judgement was better than that of a whole host of supposed financial experts. For those who remember recent British monetary history, he was in exactly the same position as Mrs Thatcher when she was bamboozled (by Nigel Lawson and Geoffrey Howe) into joining the disastrous European Exchange Rate Mechanism in 1989.

Both Churchill and Thatcher had the right instincts about the monetary straitjacket of a fixed exchange rate; both, after long resistance, submitted to the view of the 'experts'. Going back on gold gets a **FIASCO FACTOR** of 10, in view of the economic mayhem that ensued, but we should surely rate it no higher than **CHURCHILL FACTOR** 2, since any other minister would have done it without a second thought—and he certainly gave it a second thought.

Partly as a result of the economic mess that he helped to create, Churchill and the Tories were kicked out again in 1929; Labour overtook the Tories for the first time in parliamentary seats; and he now spent more than ten years 'in the wilderness'. He needed a new political fox to chase, a new cause to fight. He soon found a way of infuriating just about everyone, including the Tory Party leadership under Stanley Baldwin. Of all his misjudgements, the one that still looks the worst today is his

# Misjudgement Over India.

He decided that it was his mission to resist any move towards Indian self-government—and he did so in a style that to us looks patronising and blimpish almost beyond belief.

In 1931 he memorably denounced Gandhi as a semi-naked fakir. He said it was 'nauseating' that this pioneer of non-violent resistance should be simultaneously engaged in organising civil disobedience while engaged in talks with 'the representative of the King-Emperor'—i.e. Lord Irwin (later to become the Hitler-appeasing Halifax); as if Gandhi were some kind of terrorist. It was an absurd remark from a man who himself had no scruple about negotiating with gun-bearing Irish nationalists.

He prophesied bloodshed. He spoke in apocalyptic terms of the inability of the Indians to engage in self-rule, of the misery of the Untouchables and the inevitability of intercommunal violence. He put himself at the head of a movement of irreconcilable imperialist romantics—die-hard defenders of the Raj and of the God-given right of every pink-jowled Englishman to sit on his veranda and sip his chota peg and glory in the possession of India.

Polite opinion held that he had slightly lost the plot. All parties were in favour of greater Indian independence—even most Tories. What was he up to? I am afraid his motives were not exactly pure. He was certainly outraged by the prospect of losing India, and the blow to the 'prestige' of the British Empire, not to mention the loss of export markets for Lancashire cotton. In that sense, he seemed selfish and chauvinistic in his objectives.

He wasn't really a passionate lover of India—he hadn't been there since 1899, when as a young subaltern he had spent most of his time tending his roses, collecting butterflies, playing polo and reading Gibbon. He wasn't even particularly expert in the subject. Appearing before one House of Commons committee he seemed—most unusually—to restrict himself to rhetorical generalities. The awful truth is that he was engaged in political positioning.

He wanted to succeed Stanley Baldwin as leader of the Tories; he needed to curry favour with the right wing of the party—who did not think much of this floor-crossing ex-Liberal. India was the perfect issue on which to demonstrate his reactionary credentials. He gave long and florid speeches to rallies at which—like the Ukippers of today—he revelled in the way that he and his supporters were treated as fruitcakes and loonies. 'We are a sort of inferior race, mentally deficient and composed principally of colonels and other undesirables who have fought for Britain,' he boasted.

The strategy failed. The India Bill was passed. The Labour government got its way, with Tory agreement, in giving greater self-government to what is now the world's largest democracy and an economic powerhouse. He was marginalised—proved wrong by events. The best that can be said is that he showed characteristic grace in defeat: in 1935 he sent a message to Gandhi, wishing him well. 'Make a success and if you do I will advocate your getting much more.' It is also worth bearing in mind that he was not wholly wrong in his prophecies: the end of British rule, when it finally came in 1948, was indeed accompanied by appalling intercommunal violence in which about a million people died; and the problems of the caste system persist to this day.

But that is not a good enough defence of a policy that now looks quixotically retrograde. Let's give the Indian misjudgement a **FIASCO FACTOR** of 5 and a **CHURCHILL FACTOR** of 10.

By 1935 Baldwin was back as Prime Minister—but this time Churchill had gone too far in his rebelliousness, not least over India, and there was no place for him in the cabinet. Clearly there was scope for him to make mischief again. Could he find another campaign, another cause by which he could thrust himself to centre stage? Could he manage another cock-up? He sure could!

# The Abdication Crisis.

In the late autumn of 1936 it became widely known that the King, Edward VIII, was having an affair with an American divorcee by the name of Wallis Simpson. Peculiar as it may seem to us today, this was thought to be a quite indefensible way to behave. Churchy, pipe-puffing Stanley Baldwin was quietly horrified. He decided that the King could indeed marry a divorcee—but that he would have to abdicate.

The young King's plight was desperate. He could feel the ice floes shifting under him. He knew that his time on the throne could be running out. He needed someone to guide him, someone with experience, someone with weight in public affairs. He went—where else—to Churchill. The two men knew each other already: the King had been to stay at Blenheim; Churchill had got on well with him, and had even written a couple of speeches for him.

He had dinner with the King at Windsor, and then wrote a hilarious (and probably drunken) letter explaining how to survive, including the sensible observation that now was not the time to leave the country. Churchill became the unofficial leader of the 'King's Party', and on 8 December, after a jolly good lunch at some Anglo-French binge, he decided to give the House of Commons a piece of his mind.

The heart of the matter, in his view, was that this was a matter of the heart, and the King was the King; and that if ministers had a problem with Mrs Simpson, then they, not the monarch, should step down. Alas, he completely misread the mood of the Commons. He was howled down by MPs, most of whom had spent the last few days listening to the peevish and puritanical mutterings of their constituents.

The yammering grew so loud that eventually he had to sit down, without finishing what he was going to say. Harold Nicolson said: 'Winston collapsed utterly in the House yesterday . . . He has undone in five minutes the patient reconstruction works of two years.' Many people—even friends of his—concluded that this time he really was finished. Let's give the Abdication crisis a **FIASCO FACTOR** of

6 and a **CHURCHILL FACTOR** of 10, even if modern taste would award the argument to Churchill, of course.

Today's electorate wouldn't give a hoot if their monarch decided to marry a divorcee (come to think of it, the heir to the throne and his wife have both been married before). But that is emphatically not how it was seen at the time. Yet again, Churchill was written off: a progressive and compassionate instinct was seen as somehow ultra-monarchist and toadying.

He was by now sixty-one, and he looked obsolete, washed up, a great Edwardian sea creature flapping helplessly on the shingle and spouting empty nothings from his blowhole. Hardly anyone would have believed, at that point, that within three and a half years he would be Prime Minister.

LET US REVIEW this list of debacles—the richest and most jaw-dropping to be borne on the battle honours of any politician. What do they tell us about the character of Winston Churchill? Most obviously, we see that he had just that—what they used to call character. Any one of these fiascos, on its own, would have permanently disabled a normal politician. That Churchill kept going at all is tribute to his bounce-back-ability, to some Kevlar substance with which he insulated his ego and his morale.

It helped that he was so extrovert, so naturally self-expressive. He did not internalise his defeats, and with the exception of Gallipoli he did not gnaw his innards with self-reproach. He did not allow these abundant and picturesque prangs to change his fundamental view of himself; and it is a comment on the natural laziness of human beings that other people tend to judge you mainly according to your own judgement of yourself.

He bounced back so often because he had so much to believe in.

Many people have observed glibly and slightly infuriatingly that if Churchill had missed his moment in 1940, he would have gone down as a 'failure', a man who never achieved very much. That is absurd.

No modern politician can hold a candle to his efforts: founding the welfare state, reforming prisons, building the navy, helping to win the First World War, becoming Chancellor, etc., etc.—and we are speaking of the period in which he is said to have been a 'failure', *before* the Second World War. He had so many enterprises and initiatives that it is no surprise he had setbacks, and he bounced back from these fiascos because people could instinctively recognise something in the way he conducted himself.

It wasn't just that you could often make a very good case that he had been right: Gallipoli contained the germ of a sound strategy; Soviet communism was indeed barbaric; the Gold Standard was foisted on him; and so on. What do you notice about the classic Churchillian debacle, the key thing that distinguishes it from the fiascos that finish the careers of lesser men?

Did you spot it? Never did anyone draw the conclusion—as Churchill crawled from the smoking ruins of his detonated position—that he had been in any way personally corrupt.

Never was there the faintest whiff of scandal. None of his disasters came close to touching his integrity. It wasn't just that he was a pretty safe pair of trousers (though there seems to be some recent doubt about that). That wasn't the point.

He never seems to have lied, or cheated, or been underhand, let alone been motivated by financial gain. He took his positions because (a) they seemed to him to be right and (b) because he conceived that they would serve to advance his career; and there was no disgrace in making both calculations at once, after all: he thought they would be politically useful because they were right.

He arrived at his decisions not casually, but after massive research and cogitation—and it was this sheer volume of information flowing over his gills which helped him instinctively to point his nose up-stream. In 1911, three years before the outbreak of war, he wrote a long memorandum for the Committee of Imperial Defence, predicting the exact course of the first forty days of the conflict—where and how the French would fall back, where the Germans would come to a halt.

General Henry Wilson said the paper was 'ridiculous and fantastic—a silly memorandum'. Every word of it came true, to the very day. Germany lost the Battle of the Marne on the forty-first day, and the stalemate began. This wasn't science fiction he was writing; he wasn't just staring out of the window and chewing his pencil.

He said the war would last four years, when others said it would be over by Christmas. He saw the failings of Versailles. He got things right because he was better informed than almost every other politician. By the mid-1930s he was getting secret briefings from men in Whitehall and the military who were appalled by appeasement—Ralph Wigram and others—and who were desperate for someone to raise the alarm about Germany.

Sometimes he knew more than Baldwin himself, and on one occasion he publicly humiliated the Prime Minister by his superior knowledge of the strength of the Luftwaffe (the Nazis had a lot more planes than Baldwin claimed). He followed intently what was happening in Germany; he constantly called the attention of Parliament to the persecution of the Jews—from 1932 onwards—and warned of Nazi ideology. When Hitler got 95 per cent of the vote in November 1933, he said that the Nazis 'declare war is glorious', and that they 'inculcate a form of bloodlust in their children without parallel as an education since Barbarian and Pagan times'.

Louder and louder he rang his alarm bell, because he could see with terrible clarity what was going to happen. He saw the truth

213

about Hitler more clearly even than poor old Putzi Hanfstaengl, with whom he had caroused in Munich.

The ivory-tinkling spin-doctor eventually fell foul of Goebbels, and was denounced by Unity Mitford to Hitler—apparently for making unpatriotic remarks. In 1937 Putzi received some terrifying orders: he was to get in a plane, with a parachute, and jump out over war-torn Spain—to go behind the republican lines and work undercover to help the fascist forces of General Franco.

It didn't sound like a mission from which he was expected to return. He did as he was told, mainly because he assumed he would be shot if he didn't. The plane took off and headed for Spain, chugging hour after hour through the sky, with Hanfstaengl sitting in the back with his parachute on and in a state of gibbering fear.

It wasn't just the prospect of the jump. Even if he survived, he was sure the Spanish republicans would capture him—and probably tear him to pieces. Eventually the plane landed with an engine malfunction, and he found that they were still in Germany. They had been going in circles.

The whole thing was a ghastly practical joke by Hitler and Goebbels. Putzi decided understandably that he was giving up Nazism for good, and fled to England and then America. Churchill saw what Hitler's own spin-doctor had tried to conceal from himself—the fundamental savagery of the regime.

The difference between Churchill and others was that he acted on his insights. He not only meditated on what was happening; he tried to change it. Most politicians go with the flow of events. They see what seems inevitable, and then try to align themselves with destiny— and then (usually) try to present matters as well as they can and try in some feeble way to claim credit for whatever has occurred.

Churchill had a few fixed ideas about what *should* happen: the preservation of the British Empire, the encouragement of democracy, the boosting of British 'prestige'—and then he used his Herculean strength to bend the course of events so as to conform to those ideals. Think of him dredging and damming a river so as to find his father's watch.

That was why he was associated with so many epic cock-ups—because he dared to try to change the entire shape of history. He was the man who burst the cabin door and tried to wrestle the controls of the stricken plane. He was the large protruding nail on which destiny snagged her coat.

The last thing Britain or the world needed in 1940 was someone who was going to sit back and let things unfold. It needed someone with almost superhuman will and courage, to interpose themselves between the world and disaster. He spoke of his relief when he took office in 1940, because this time—unlike with Gallipoli or the Russian bungle—he had full authority to direct events; which is why he chose to be both Prime Minister and Minister of Defence.

Our argument so far has been that Churchill, in comparison to his rivals at home and abroad, was like some unbeatable card in a game of Star Wars Top Trumps. He was the best for work rate, for rhetorical skills, for humour, for insight. He beat his rivals for technical originality and sheer blind bravery. If you have ever played that excellent game, you will know what I mean when I say that he was also the character with the greatest 'Force Factor'. It is time to see how he played that card in the Second World War.

# CHAPTER 16

# AN ICY
# RUTHLESSNESS

The French sailors had no time to get angry and barely a moment to prepare their souls for the end. When the bombardment began at 5.54 p.m. on 3 July 1940 the dominant feeling was surely one of total disbelief. Those were British ships—the very ones they had cheered when they arrived in the morning. They were British sailors; allies—the same people they had been out with on shore leave in Gibraltar, painting the town red.

They were meant to be friends, for God's sake—and yet for ten minutes those friends sent down a rain of death: a shelling that is still recognised as one of the most concentrated big-gun naval barrages in history. Out of the 15-inch muzzles of HMS *Hood*—then the largest battleship ever built—came the first salvo, and at 2,500 mph those three-quarter-ton projectiles described their elegant arcs across the azure sky.

The light was ideal. The targets were motionless. The conditions were altogether perfect. Then the other British ships joined in, and the explosions became so loud that the Frenchmen who survived reported a bleeding from their ears. HMS *Valiant* fired her guns, along with HMS *Resolution*.

The gunners toiled in the heat, sweat running down their half-naked forms, firing and firing until the colossal steel tubes were red hot. Soon they were getting their range, starting to find the French ships nicely. Since the mouth of the harbour had just been mined by British planes, there was nothing the French could do. As one British sailor said many years later, it was like 'shooting fish in a barrel'.

On the French side, witnesses spoke of sheets of flame, and balls of fire landing in the sea; of men with their heads missing, and men so badly burned or maimed that they called to their colleagues with the terrifying plea of '*achève-moi!*': finish me off! Then a British shell hit the magazine of France's most advanced warship, the *Bretagne*— and the noise was like the death of Krakatoa.

A mushroom cloud rose over the harbour and within minutes the *Bretagne* had capsized. Some of her crew leapt into the evil black sea, bubbling like chip fat, where they held their breath and swam underwater to escape the burning oil. Most of the complement was drowned.

Altogether the British shot 150 shells into the fortified harbour at Mers-el-Kébir, near the Algerian town of Oran, on that cloudless day in 1940. By the time their guns fell silent, five French ships were crippled and one destroyed; and 1,297 French seamen had been killed. A massacre had taken place; and there were plenty who were willing to call it a war crime.

Across France there was a sense of indignation, a hatred that the Nazi propaganda machine scarcely needed to fan. For the first time since the Battle of Waterloo in 1815, the British had fired on the French and with murderous intent. Posters were circulated everywhere of a French sailor drowning amid the inferno, or of the British war leader as a bloodthirsty Moloch. Relations between London and the new Vichy regime were ended, and to this day the memory of Mers-el-Kébir is so toxic as to be taboo in discussions between Britain and France.

If it had been left to him, said Admiral James Somerville, he would never have given the order. The British sailors were sick at heart as they saw what they had done; incredulous that these were really their instructions. Generations of French schoolchildren have been taught that there was one man who decreed that massacre and whose busy fingers wrote out that murderous ultimatum. Those teachers are right.

When Churchill rose to explain his actions the next day in the House of Commons, he expected to be assailed on every side. He had unleashed the most lethal modern weaponry on effectively defenceless targets—and on sailors with whom Britain was not at war.

As he later admitted, he felt 'ashamed' as he stood up to speak, before a packed Chamber. His typed notes trembled in his hands. He gave a full account of the events that led up to the disaster. He wound up by saying that he would leave the judgement of his actions to Parliament. 'I leave it also to the nation, and to the United States. I leave it to the world and to history.'

With this he sat down; and something peculiar happened. To his surprise, there was no disapproving silence. On the contrary, they were cheering. They were on their feet and waving their Order Papers in scenes of jubilation such as the Commons had not seen for years. His cabinet colleagues were clustering around and clapping him on the back—in what seems to us a bizarre and tasteless response to the deaths of almost 1,300 Frenchmen.

Amid the rejoicing sat Churchill, a hunched figure in his black jacket and striped grey trousers, with his chin in his hands and tears flowing down his cheeks.

To understand this tragedy, you must appreciate how much Churchill loved France. As his doctor Charles Moran once observed, 'France is civilization.'

He had grown up in France's belle époque; Paris was the city where his parents chose to get married, the city of lights and infinite diversions, the place he went to spend his gambling winnings—on books and 'in other directions'. Even for an Englishman as patriotic as Winston Churchill there was no shame in acknowledging the superiority of the French quality of life: the wine, the food, the cheese; the elegance of the chateaux; the fun and style of the casinos; the pleasure of bathing on the Côte d'Azur, and of trying to capture its outstanding natural beauty in paint. French was the only foreign language in which he even attempted to make himself understood. But it went deeper than that.

Churchill believed in the greatness of France, and it came as a terrible shock, in the opening weeks of his premiership, to see the humiliation of the army that had once been led by Napoleon, the man whose bust reposed on his desk. He had done everything in his power to keep France in the war, to put some lead in the pencil of the French politicians and generals. As the news got worse and worse, he flew out to France himself—on four occasions—where he tried to revivify the despondent French leadership with his manful Franglais. He risked his life just to get there.

On one occasion he was flying back in his Flamingo when the pilot had to dive suddenly to avoid two German planes that were strafing fishing boats near Le Havre. That was on 12 June—and thirty-six hours later the French telephoned again, this time to demand an urgent meeting at Tours. He turned up at Hendon to find that the weather was too bad for take-off.

'To hell with that,' said the sixty-five-year-old aviator. 'I'm going, whatever happens. This is too serious a situation to bother about the weather.' They duly arrived at Tours in a thunderstorm—a pretty hairy experience even today, and which must have been unnerving for Beaverbrook and Halifax, who had come with him on the mission.

The runway had been freshly cratered by the Germans, and there were some French ground crew lounging around who had no idea who they were. Churchill had to explain that he was the Prime Minister of the United Kingdom and that he needed a '*voiture*'.

When they got to the prefecture they found that there still didn't seem to be a welcoming party; still no one recognised them. They wandered around the corridors until eventually the British delegation were taken to a nearby restaurant for cold chicken and cheese. Poor old Halifax: I don't suppose it was his style of diplomacy.

At last the French Prime Minister, Paul Reynaud, turned up, and asked miserably whether Britain would release France from her obligations, and allow her to surrender. Churchill tried one last time to apply his patent morale-boosting electro-convulsive Franglais therapy to the recumbent French. There was no response.

The patient had expired; and on 14 June the Germans were goose-stepping down the Champs-Élysées. Marshal Pétain—hollow eyed, snaggle toothed and utterly defeatist—was in charge. The capitulation was complete; the French had passed up the chance to fight on from North Africa, and the British were now alarmed about what they would do next, and in particular about what would happen to the French fleet.

This was the second biggest in Europe after the Royal Navy, bigger than the German Kriegsmarine. Some of the French ships were state-of-the-art, better equipped even than the British vessels. If they fell into German hands they could be lethal to British interests. And what, frankly, could stop them falling into German hands? Everyone had seen the speed with which the Germans had overwhelmed the Maginot Line. Nowhere was safe from the panzers.

If Britain was to fight on, Churchill had to eliminate the risk those French ships embodied. And there was a further consideration. If Britain was credibly to fight on he had to show to the world that the country he led was truly made of fighting stuff; that Britain would do whatever it took to win. This was crucial, because there were sceptics at home and abroad.

Remember how frail his position still was, how distrusted he was by the Tory Party. The Leader of the Labour Opposition, George Lansbury, had resigned because he objected to war, and there were plenty of others who took the same view on both sides of the House. The Lords was full of Stilton-eating surrender monkeys—arch-appeasers such as Lord Brocket, the Earl of Londonderry, Lord Ponsonby, the Earl of Danby, as well as Bendor, the Duke of Westminster, a flamboyant and charming personality who said that 'the war was part of a Jewish and Masonic plot'. Those were the days when Tory prime ministers had to pay more attention to the views of dukes and earls.

These would-be quislings were not alone. Rab Butler, then a junior Foreign Office minister, was caught telling a Swedish diplomat that he thought Britain should do a deal—if Hitler offered the right terms. Even Churchill's buddy and supposed ally Beaverbrook was in favour of a negotiated peace. The city was full—as it always is—of people who preferred to make money than go to war.

There were sceptics in the ranks of his own closest officials; perhaps not surprisingly, since they had all until recently been serving Neville Chamberlain. His Private Secretary, Eric Seal, muttered about his boss and his 'blasted rhetoric', and indeed he was among the few who remained immune to the new Prime Minister's charm ('fetch Seal from his ice floes', Churchill would say).

Worse still, there were doubters among the most important audience of all—in the White House and on Capitol Hill. The American electorate opposed involvement in the war by a huge majority—thirteen to one, according to one poll. President Roosevelt had promised that he would not 'entangle' America in any European conflict, and he knew that if he broke that promise he would be punished at the presidential elections in November that year.

These days there are many conservative American politicians who ritually denounce Neville Chamberlain, and his spaghetti-like refusal to stand up to Hitler. The whole notion of appeasement has become a kind of cuss-word in American politics—and reasonably so. But it is worth remembering that in May and June of 1940, when Britain stood alone against what was by then well known to be a racist and anti-Semitic tyranny, there were some senators of the United States who did not exactly bust a gut to help; and certainly not immediately.

The US Secretary for War was an ardent isolationist called Harry Woodring, who spent the days between 23 May and 3 June deliberately delaying the shipment to Britain of war material that had already been condemned as surplus. He insisted that the goods must be properly advertised, so that anyone could buy them before they were sold to the British. This was while British soldiers were dying on the beaches of Dunkirk, in the biggest military disaster of the last 100 years.

The Senate Foreign Relations Committee blocked the sale of ships and planes; the War Department refused to hand over some bombs the poor French had already paid for; and a senator called David Walsh managed to scupper a deal by which Britain was to buy twenty motor torpedo boats: useful things to have, you might have thought, if you were facing the prospect of a seaborne invasion by the Nazis.

Other Americans, of course, were far more sympathetic. They included much of the media and the President himself. But Roosevelt was limited in what he could do by the terms of the Neutrality Act, and by the general climate of the times. He also hesitated by reason of simple prudence. On 15 May—barely a week after taking the reins—Churchill sent him a letter in which he requested military help, in the form of some antiquated American destroyers.

This appeal was not perhaps phrased as judiciously as it might have been. He begged, he pleaded for the destroyers, and he concluded with a veiled threat: that if Britain fell, then there would be nothing to stop Hitler expropriating the entire British navy, and using those ships against the United States herself. In this first substantive exchange of that pivotal relationship, Churchill failed to imagine how his correspondent might react.

Roosevelt took one look at this communication, and concluded from its note of wheedling and blustering desperation that perhaps Britain might indeed be about to go the way of every other European country; in which case what on earth was the point of sending some destroyers, whose guns could simply be turned back on the USA?

Churchill had inadvertently made a point against himself; he had excited and not allayed the anxiety in Washington about a British collapse. Then there was one other international observer who was known to have his doubts about Britain, and her ability to fight on: and that was Admiral François Darlan of the French fleet.

This Darlan was a prickly customer, who had become so enraged at what he saw as the inadequacies of Britain's assistance to France that he became positively Anglophobe. At one stage he had to be calmed down, and reminded that he was fighting the Boche and not the rosbifs. He had met Churchill during those ghastly funereal encounters in early June, and he had assured him that the French fleet would not fall into German hands. But what trust could possibly be placed in the word of Darlan?

He might well be an honourable man; he might believe it was unthinkable that his fleet should be used by the Germans—but then plenty of unthinkable things had already taken place. As long as the fleet was within German reach, there seemed little to stop those boats eventually flying a Nazi flag. That was not a risk that Churchill thought he could run.

Some historians have been strongly critical of Churchill's behaviour. In a fascinating study, Richard Lamb has argued that he was far too brutal and impetuous; that more time should have been given to his admirals to sort it out with the French; that Churchill sanitised the official history after the war—exploiting the fact that he was Prime Minister again in 1951—and effectively stifled criticism of his 'butchery'.

What is certainly true is that Churchill was in charge of the whole process, driving events like a bulldozer. As soon as France had fallen, he became obsessed with the risk posed by those sleek, fast, modern French ships. In the War Cabinet on 22 June he noted the qualities of the *Richelieu* and the *Jean Bart* and others. They should be bombed, he urged, or they must be penned in their harbours by British mines. Their captains should surrender or be treated as traitors.

Halifax led the rest of the cabinet in trying to cool him down. 'All efforts must be made to make the parleys a success,' he said; but two days later Churchill was at it again. The armistice had come into effect. France was out of the war. What were we going to do about those damn ships?

Now the naval chiefs joined the cabinet in opposing violence against the French. Even the First Sea Lord, Sir Dudley Pound, normally a Churchill yes-man, said he could not recommend an operation against them.

On Churchill bashed and butted like a bull at a barn door. In Gibraltar the British admirals held a conference, at which every flag officer was invited to give an opinion, as well as all the naval liaison officers from the French ports in North Africa. Was it a good idea to prepare some kind of action against the French fleet?

No, said the experts, the men on the spot; the very threat of force would be 'disastrous' and more likely to turn the French against the British. They protested in vain. Churchill trampled their hesitations with autocratic indifference. Lamb argues that at this stage in the war he was virtually a military dictator.

By 1 July the chiefs of staff and the cabinet had been bludgeoned into seeing things the Churchill way. Operation Catapult was launched, to neutralise and if necessary to sink the French fleet. It didn't matter to Churchill that the French were doing their best to honour what they thought were their commitments. They scuttled ships and submarines in French ports, and the remainder they indeed sailed away from German-occupied France. The *Richelieu* and twenty-four others sailed from Brest to Morocco; the *Jean Bart* sailed from St Nazaire; others left Lorient.

In fact the French left not a single vessel in the German-occupied zone—and yet Churchill still felt that 'at all costs, at all risks, in one way or another we must make sure that the Navy of France did not fall into the wrong hands and then perhaps bring us and others to ruin.'

Before the armistice the British had assured the French that it would be satisfactory if the French fleet were taken to North Africa, or to Toulon, outside the German zone. Now perfidious Albion was again going back on her word.

On 3 July the British task force under James Somerville arrived outside Mers-el-Kébir, and the French sailors were thrilled—thinking they would shortly be together on the high seas, taking the fight to the Germans. Then the British planes appeared in the sky, dropping mines in the harbour mouth. French suspicions grew.

A British envoy was sent to negotiate with the French admiral Marcel Gensoul. At first Gensoul refused to see him, thinking it was beneath his dignity to parley with a mere captain—but Captain 'Hookie' Holland managed to hand over the ultimatum from Churchill.

The French were told to scuttle their ships, or sail them either to British ports or to the West Indies; or face the consequences. The day wore on. The tension grew. Hookie Holland bobbed up and down in his lighter, surrounded by French vessels. Finally at 14.42 Gensoul signalled that he was ready to receive the British delegate for 'honourable discussions'. By 16.15 Holland was on board the French flagship, the *Dunkerque*, and they began to make progress.

Gensoul showed him orders from Darlan, making it clear that if Germany tried to seize the boats, he should sail to America or scuttle them. 'If we had known all this before, it would have made all the difference,' said Holland. Gensoul then went farther: he was willing to disarm all his ships, even though this meant exceeding his instructions. But by then it was too late.

Darlan had sent naval reinforcements; there was no saying when they would arrive. A full-scale battle between the British and the French fleet was in prospect. Churchill sent a short telegram: 'Settle matters quickly'. The fate of the sailors was sealed. The bombardment began.

As he said later, 'It was a terrible decision, like taking the life of one's own child to save the state.' In its icy logic, Churchill's decision was also 100 per cent correct.

Whichever way you cut it, the French should have recognised that their ships were now effectively forfeit to the Germans, or at best they were bargaining counters in negotiations with the Nazis. Lamb argues that the Germans merely wanted to 'control' the French fleet in the sense of 'check' or 'supervise'—'control' as in passport '*kontrol*'.

That is surely implausible. The Germans had captured Paris; they had their boot on the French neck. Ultimately they could have made the French do whatever they wanted with those ships. The French guarantees were worthless, and they should have recognised as much. Darlan and his admirals should have swallowed their pride and abandoned all pretence of autonomy and done what Churchill suggested: sailed to British ports, or to the Caribbean—and if he had done so, Darlan would have been a hero.

It was Churchill's duty as Prime Minister to remove any threat to his country's independence; and he was right to be ruthless at Mers-el-Kébir, because the following week there began the Battle of Britain.

THROUGHOUT THAT lovely summer the British craned their necks to watch one of the decisive battles of world history. They watched the destiny of the world written in the vapour trails of the planes that tussled in the skies above southern England. They saw blackened Germans tottering up their garden paths and they found bits of plane on suburban streets.

They watched their RAF protectors as they performed their astonishing aerobatics, sometimes bringing down the enemy, sometimes crashing in dreadful blazes or heaps of tangled metal. Week after week they had a clear sense of what was at stake: that this attack on the RAF was the prelude to a full-scale invasion of Britain. They had every reason to think that they were next on Hitler's itinerary of conquest.

It is sometimes said that Churchill exaggerated the threat of invasion, to promote national cohesion and get the country behind him. I am not sure that is so. He believed the threat was so imminent in June 1940 that he took to the firing range at Chequers, and began practising with his revolver and his Mannlicher rifle. Every day he would study the tides to work out when the Germans might come.

The *Deutsche Allgemeine Zeitung* prophesied on 14 July that London would follow Warsaw, and be reduced to ashes. On 19 July Hitler spoke to the Reichstag and offered Britain a choice between peace and 'unending suffering and misery'. He drew up the plans: Operation Sea Lion, he called it, a multi-pronged seaborne invasion of the south coast.

If Hitler had won control of the skies and the seas, there is little doubt that he would have gone for it. He had assembled 1,918 barges off the coast of Holland, and if he had been able to convey his force across the Channel, it is hard to see how Britain could have fought on for long. The army had been routed at Dunkirk; there were no fortifications or fall-back positions.

The country had not been successfully invaded for 900 years—and so London was not only the biggest and most sprawling city in Europe (a great fat cow, as Churchill called the capital). It was also the least defended: the only surviving walls and battlements were made by the Romans, and they weren't in great shape.

Hitler had a giant strategic imperative in attacking Britain: he had to knock out Britain before he went east, and took on Russia. Even in July 1940, the whole shape and dynamics of the war were clear to Winston Churchill—just as he had foreseen the shape of the First World War as well.

'Hitler must invade or fail. If he fails, he is bound to go east, and fail he will,' he said at Chequers on 14 July. He saw, with his unerring and pellucid understanding of the big picture, that if Britain could survive, if Britain could hang on—then Hitler would lose, because not even the Nazi war machine could fight on two fronts at once.

It was thanks to Churchill—and at crucial moments, thanks to him alone—that Britain did hang on. It is clear that there was some-

thing utterly magical about his leadership that summer. With his poetic and sometimes Shakespearean diction he made people feel
noble, exalted—that what they were doing was better and more important than anything they had done before.

He mentally elided ideas of Englishness and freedom, and it
helped that the weather was fine, because there is nowhere lovelier
than England in June; and perhaps that gentle beauty sharpened the
general sentiment he encouraged: that the threat must be repelled,
and that this was an island to fight and to die for. He gave the people
an image of themselves: as a tiny band of heroes—analogous to the
tiny band of RAF pilots—holding out against tyranny and against
the odds, the story from Thermopylae to the Defence of Rorke's Drift
in the Zulu war—the eternal and uplifting story of the few against
the many.

In this mood of adrenalin-fuelled exhilaration the British indeed
accomplished extraordinary things. There is only one period that I
can discover in the last 120 years when British manufacturing output
overtook Germany's—and that was the summer of 1940. Britain produced more planes than Germany; and by the autumn they had seen
off the Luftwaffe. Goering made the fatal mistake of turning the attention of his fighters and bombers to the towns of Britain, and giving up on Dowding's airfields.

The Germans might so easily have won. There were some evenings
when every plane available to Britain was up in the sky, desperate to
hold them off. And if Goering had controlled the skies, then that
invasion fleet could have made an untroubled crossing of the Channel; and that armada would have been all the more frightening and
lethal—and Hitler's confidence would have been all the greater—for
the addition of those French warships.

The German fleet had been badly knocked about in the Norwe-
gian campaign; with the addition of the French, they might have

been invincible. What Churchill did at Mers-el-Kébir was indeed butchery, but it was necessary. It was the chilling and calculated act of a skull-piling warlord from the steppes of central Asia.

But that is what he was: a warlord. He was leading and directing military action in a way that is unthinkable for a modern democratic politician. He had done his best for France, right up until the capitulation and beyond; he had made his generals commit men and material to the battle long after it was obvious that the game was up—indeed, he is blamed for needlessly throwing away the 51st Highland Division, many of whom were killed or captured, and for wasting time and energy by trying to create an Asterix-like redoubt against the Nazis in Brittany.

Now that France had fallen, he drew the only logical conclusion— and the real tragedy is surely that neither Admiral Gensoul nor Darlan could see how radically their world had changed. I think I can understand why the House of Commons was so elated by this depressing and in many ways disgusting massacre.

It was partly that Britain had finally done something warlike: after a year of dither, shambles and evacuations—from Norway to Dunkirk—the British armed forces had 'won' something, no matter how one-sided the contest or how hollow that victory.

More importantly the MPs could tell from the event that the man they had reluctantly commissioned to lead them had a streak of belligerent ruthlessness unlike anyone else. They knew that no other politician had the guts, the nerve, to do what he had just done. They could suddenly see how Britain might win.

That was why they waved their Order Papers. And that was the message that Churchill sent via Mers-el-Kébir to Washington, where they were still refusing to send the ancient destroyers: that Britain was not going to give in, but would do whatever it took.

Churchill ended that speech on Oran to the House of Commons by saying that he left the judgement of his actions 'to the nation and the United States'; and the second audience was crucial. The son of Jennie Jerome knew that he had no hope of eventual victory unless and until he could also embroil his motherland.

# CHAPTER 17

# THE WOOING
# OF AMERICA

From the very beginning of his premiership, he saw what he had to do. Randolph Churchill has recorded how on 18 May 1940 he went into his father's bedroom at Admiralty House. He found the Prime Minister standing in front of his basin and shaving with an old-fashioned Valet razor.

'Sit down, dear boy, and read the papers while I finish shaving.'
I did as I was told. After two or three minutes of hacking away, he half turned and said: 'I think I can see my way through.' I was astounded, and said: 'Do you mean that we can avoid defeat?' (which seemed credible) 'or beat the bastards?' (which seemed incredible).
He flung his Valet razor into the basin, swung around and said:—'Of course I mean we can beat them.'
Me: 'Well, I am all for it, but I don't see how you can do it.'
By this time he had dried and sponged his face and turning round to me, said with great intensity: 'I shall drag the United States in.'

Never mind the speeches, sublime though they were. Set to one side the strategic decisions, not all of which now look flawless. If you want to understand how he won the war, look at the way he wangled and wheedled his way to Washington, and his subtle but unmistakable manipulation of the priorities of the United States.

He used a tool of diplomacy that was as old-fashioned and erratic as the man himself. It was called charm. That was the secret of Churchill's success. It wasn't easy, and there were times when it didn't look as though it would work at all.


LET US GO forward more than a year: to his first wartime meeting with Roosevelt, at a remote and underpopulated harbour called Placentia Bay in Newfoundland. It is 10 August 1941. Two great gunboats are converging on this place of rock and mist and pine—a landscape unchanged since the first Europeans arrived in North America. Like some modern version of the Field of the Cloth of Gold, the potentates have come to parley.

In one ship there are admirals and generals led by the wheelchair-bound President of the United States. They have brought offerings of hams and lemons and other delicacies unobtainable in wartime London.

In the other ship is a nervous British posse led by Winston Churchill. They have brought ninety ripe grouse in the storerooms, and goodies from Fortnum and Mason. Churchill has spent the voyage reading three Hornblower novels in a row—as well he might, because his military options are running out.

The British get there too early. They have forgotten to turn their clocks back to American time—so they pull out and chug around for a bit, before returning for the rendezvous. A launch puts out from the British ship, the *Prince of Wales.*

If we consult contemporary footage, we see the Americans waiting on the deck of the *Augusta*. There is Roosevelt strapped into an upright position, in which he seems immensely tall.

There is movement below. The British have arrived. They are coming up the gangway; and here he is. As soon as Churchill is on the scene, it is impossible to keep your eyes off him.

He is wearing a short double-breasted coat and a yachting cap that has been pulled down over one eye, making him look a bit like a tipsy bus conductor. He is the only man champing a cigar, and conspicuously shorter than the others—all the rest of them stiff and erect in their braid; and he is somehow burlier in the shoulder.

He instantly presides over the choreography of events like a twinkle-toed boxer or ballroom dancer. He introduces one man to another; he salutes; he shakes hands; he salutes; he beams—and then comes the moment he has been waiting for during that emetic nine-day Atlantic crossing. It is his turn to shake hands with Franklin D. Roosevelt, the President of the United States; the first time they have met since 1918.

He knocks off another wristy salute and then—standing some distance away, so that Roosevelt will have to lean down and towards him to make contact—he holds out that surprisingly long arm. Churchill knows how much is at stake.

The war, to put it mildly, is not going well. For the British land forces, it has been a tale of one humiliation after another. They have been duffed up in Norway, kicked out of France, expelled from Greece—and in a particularly chastening episode they have managed to surrender Crete to a much smaller force of German paratroopers. The Blitz has already taken the lives of more than thirty thousand civilians. The U-boats are savaging British shipping—and even prowl the waters around them here on the coast of Canada.

Now Hitler has just broken his word—again—and launched himself upon Russia; and if Russia goes down, as seems likely, there is every prospect that the German dictator will be the unchallenged master of the continent from the Atlantic to the Urals. If that happens, Churchill knows that he will be forced from power, and that Britain—one way or another—will make an accommodation with fascism.

As he stretches out that elegant white hand he knows he is reaching for his only lifeline; and yet there is nothing about him to convey the gloom of his position. On the contrary, his face is suddenly wreathed in smiles, babyish, irresistible.

Roosevelt smiles back; they grip hands, for ages, each reluctant to be the first to let go, and for the next two days Churchill maintains his schmoozathon. We don't know exactly what they say to each other at the first such Atlantic conference—the direct ancestor of NATO; but we know that Churchill lays it on thick. His mission is to build up a sense of common destiny; to work with the grain of Roosevelt's natural instincts, and to turn the USA from distant sympathisers into full-blown allies in bloodshed.

On the way out to Canada, Churchill has already tried to create the mood. 'We are just off,' he has cabled Roosevelt cheerily. 'It is 27 years ago today that the Huns began their last war. We must make a good job of it this time. Twice ought to be enough.'

We, eh?

Twice, eh?

That must have seemed a bit presumptuous in the White House. No one in Washington has given any commitments to entering another world war, let alone to sending American troops.

Sedulously Churchill works on that idea: of the two nations, united in language, ideals, culture. Surely they should also be united in their foes? On the Sunday morning there is a divine service. The crews of the two ships are suggestively mingled together, and they sing hymns—chosen by Churchill—that express that single heritage: two broadly Protestant nations bound together against a vile and above all a pagan regime.

They sing 'Onward Christian Soldiers', and 'O God Our Help in Ages Past'. Finally they sing the traditional appeal for divine mercy on those who go down to the sea in ships: 'For Those in Peril on the Sea'. This complement of British sailors knows all about peril on the sea.

It is only a few months ago that the ship has been involved in the chase of the German battleships *Bismarck* and *Prinz Eugen*. The men singing today have seen their sister ship HMS *Hood* (she that opened fire at Oran) explode in a vast fireball. Indeed, they were so close that they had to steer straight through the wreckage of a disaster that cost the lives of 1,419 officers and crew. The *Prince of Wales* was also hit; she lost men, too. Her decks have lately been running with blood—and yet here she is, her tables laden with game birds.

That is the message from Britain to America: we are fighting, and we are dying, but we can take it; what about you?

In deference to Roosevelt's immobility, the two leaders sit side by side to sing and to pray, Churchill with his black horn-rims on to read the words. The men stand in hundreds under the vast 14-inch guns of that doomed vessel. There are lumps in throats, tears in eyes. The reporters tell each other they are witnessing history.

At length the summit is over. A communiqué is produced, grandly entitled the 'Atlantic Charter'. Churchill begins the turbulent crossing back to Britain—bearing . . . what?

The awful truth—and one he masterfully strove to conceal from Parliament and public—is that in spite of all his expert dramaturgy he had virtually nothing to show.

The British cabinet swiftly approved the 'Atlantic Charter'. The US Congress didn't even glance at the document, let alone ratify it.

Churchill's military attaché, Ian Jacob, summed up the quiet despondency of the British delegation as they heaved homewards over the grey Atlantic: 'Not a single American officer has shown the slightest keenness to be in the war on our side. They are a charming lot of individuals but they appear to be living in a different world from ourselves.'

Andrew Schivial, a British civil servant from Stockton, recorded that he felt 'left in the air when it was all over, with a vague feeling of dissatisfaction'. All the British got for their venture was 150,000 old rifles; no American troops—not even the whiff of a promise of American troops.

It seems incredible, looking back, that it took so long—two years and four months—before the USA joined Britain in the war against Hitler. Across the conquered continent, Jews, gypsies, homosexuals and other groups were already being rounded up and killed, if not yet systematically.

The Nazi policy of racially based murder was not quite as well publicised as it was to become, but it was not exactly secret. How could the Americans have stayed aloof, in all honour and conscience?

The answer to this question is to look at it the other way round. This was a war that did not yet threaten vital American interests, on a continent far away, where there had taken place in living memory a slaughter that had shamed mankind. How could any politician plausibly explain to the mothers of Kansas that it was their duty to send their sons to their deaths in Europe? And for the second time?

Since the injunctions of George Washington himself it had been the guiding principle of American policy that the republic should steer clear of foreign entanglements. Many Americans still resented Woodrow Wilson for getting them into the First World War; many Americans were sceptical about Britain; many were actively hostile.

Odd as it may seem today, there were many who regarded the

Brits as a bunch of arrogant imperialists who had burned the White House in 1814 and who had a talent for getting other people to do their fighting.

Who was there to put the opposite case? Not the poisonous Joseph Kennedy, who was recalled at the end of 1940, having done a lot of damage to Britain's standing; nor the British ambassador in Washington. This was none other than our old friend the Earl of Halifax: the beanpole-shaped appeaser—he who used to go hunting with Goering.

Halifax was the British envoy charged with appealing to the finer feelings of the United States—and he was having a terrible time. Shortly after arriving he is said to have sat down and wept—in despair at the culture clash. He couldn't understand the American informality, or their habit of talking on the telephone or popping round for unexpected meetings.

In May 1941 the aristocratic old Etonian endured fresh torment when he was taken to a Chicago White Sox baseball game and invited to eat a hotdog. He refused. Then he was pelted with eggs and tomatoes by a group called the Mothers of America. Even for an appeaser, it seems a hell of a punishment. There was no way Halifax was going to get the Americans to drop their isolationism.

It had to be Churchill. First, he was half American—and some of his English contemporaries thought that this contributed the zap to his personality, perhaps even an element of hucksterism. Beatrice Webb said he was more of an American speculator than an English aristocrat. Secondly, he had been there on four trips before the war, lasting for a total of five months. He knew the place and had come deeply to respect and admire the Americans.

He first went in 1895, when he stayed with a friend of his mother called Bourke Cockran—whose rhetorical style he claimed to have adopted. He went again in 1900, on his Boer War lecture tour; and had a slightly rough ride from Americans who thought he was an emanation of the colonialist mentality. His audiences were patchy, and after listening to his accounts of his heroism some of them tended to side with the Boers. This experience may have coloured his attitude in the 1920s, when he became positively exasperated by America's attempts to displace Britain's naval power, especially in the Caribbean. When Eddie Marsh reproached him for his imperialist attitude, saying that he should 'kiss Uncle Sam on both cheeks', Churchill replied, 'Yes, but not on all four.'

He became so anti-American—even at one stage suggesting that it might be necessary to go to war—that Clementine said he had disqualified himself from becoming Foreign Secretary. He went again in 1929, when he saw the Wall Street Crash (in which a man hurled himself from a skyscraper before his eyes) and was understandably appalled by Prohibition.

As one American temperance campaigner told him, 'Strong drink rageth and stingeth like a serpent'.

To which Churchill replied, 'I have been looking for a drink like that all my life.'

But the decisive trip was in 1931, after he had left office and begun perhaps the most right-wing period of his political life. He saw the American spirit of enterprise, the way their best people tended to go into business rather than politics. He saw that America was achieving *il sorpasso*—overtaking Britain and all other European powers to become by far the most powerful economy on earth. He recognised that the world's economic recovery depended on American expansion and growth.

Gone was Churchill the anti-American; gone was any idea of somehow fending off the challenge. Now he began to formulate a new doctrine—of two nations with a common past and a common tradition, joint trustees and patent-holders of Anglo-Saxon ideas of democracy, and freedom, and equal rights under the law.

So began his relentless advocacy of the 'English-speaking peoples', and with his Anglo-American self (naturally) as the incarnation of this union. He proposed a common citizenship. He even suggested that the pound and the dollar should be merged into a single currency, and designed a curious £$ symbol.

This was the Churchill that set out to woo America in 1940. He began in that position known to every love-struck member of the human race, and which we might call romantic asymmetry. That is to say, the relationship meant a lot more to him than it did to Washington.

As he later put it, no lover ever studied the whims of his mistress as carefully as he studied Franklin Roosevelt. Since the President had once served in the navy he wrote to him in ingratiating terms 'as one former naval person to another'. He took any opportunity to get the White House on the telephone. He started cultivating American journalists, and inviting them to Chequers.

He aimed his speeches squarely at the American audience who were listening to him in ever greater numbers on the radio. He ended the great 4 June 1940 speech with a direct appeal:

Even though large tracts of Europe and many old and famous States have fallen or may fall into the grip of the Gestapo and all the odious apparatus of Nazi rule, we shall not flag or fail. We shall go on to the end. We shall fight in France, we shall fight on the seas and oceans, we shall fight with growing confidence and growing strength in the air, we shall defend our island, whatever the cost may be. We shall fight on the beaches, we shall fight on the landing grounds, we shall fight in the fields and in the streets, we shall fight in the hills; we shall never surrender, and if, which I do not for a moment believe, this island or a large part of it were subjugated and starving, then our Empire beyond the seas, armed and guarded by the British Fleet, would carry on the struggle, until, in God's good time, the New World, with all its power and might, steps forth to the rescue and the liberation of the old.

Notice the invocation of the Almighty—then as now a considerably bigger player in American politics than He is in Britain. He uses the same formula in the climax of the Oran speech in July: he leaves the judgement on his actions to the United States.

Slowly he began to make progress—but it was hard going, and expensive. First there was the destroyers-for-bases deal. Britain handed over bases in Trinidad, Bermuda and Newfoundland in return for fifty mothballed destroyers. The old bathtubs barely floated—only nine of them were operational by the end of 1940.

Then the Americans agreed to sell some weapons; but the terms of the Neutrality Act meant that Britain had to pay in cash, on the nail. In March 1941 an American cruiser was sent to Cape Town to pick up the country's last remaining 50 tons of gold bullion, like bailiffs collecting the flat-screen TV. British businesses in America were sold at knock-down prices. When the British started protesting that they were broke, the American government took to querying Britain's real ability to pay, like a social services department accusing some elderly benefit recipient of concealing her assets.

As for Lend-Lease, by which supplies were continued on the strength of future payments, Churchill may have publicly called it 'the most unsordid act in history'. In private he said that Britain was being skinned and flayed to the bone. Under the terms of the agreement, the Americans insisted on interfering with Britain's overseas trade, and stopped the UK from importing much-needed corned beef from Argentina.

The Lend-Lease Act continued to muck up Britain's right to run its own commercial aviation policy, even after the war was over. It is startling to think that this supposedly unselfish and unsordid act of the US government entailed payments that ended only on—wait for it—31 December 2006, when Mr Ed Balls, then Economic Secretary to the Treasury, wrote a last cheque for $83.3 million or £42.5 million and a letter of thanks to the US government. Has any other country ever been so slavishly punctilious in honouring its war debts?

It has been argued that America took so much cash off Britain in the early stages of the Second World War that this liquidity finally lifted the USA out of depression. The first cranks of the US war machine were powered by UK gold—and yet in spite of the excellent terms they had secured, there were plenty of American politicians, in early 1941, who apparently thought the deal was too generous to the Brits. The Bill was passed in Congress by 260 votes to 165. What were they thinking of, those 165 senators who refused to throw Britain this highly expensive life-jacket? Did they want to watch the old place sink? Well, the truth is that possibly some of them did, just a little.

That was the audience Churchill had to win over. And yet by the end of that same year those same congressmen were eating out of his hand. On Boxing Day 1941 they packed into the chamber—senators and members of the House of Representatives, cheering and cheering Winston Churchill before he had even stood up to speak. What had changed their minds?

Well, there was the small matter of Pearl Harbor, and Japan's unprovoked aggression; and then there was Hitler's deranged decision, a few days later, to declare war on America. That may have helped, at last, to encourage the congressmen to identify more closely with Britain. The interesting question is why the Führer decided to make what looks like a colossal strategic mistake. Why did he declare war on America—when it was still perfectly conceivable that America could have stayed out of the European war?

The answer is that he had already concluded that America was effectively on Britain's side. By the autumn of 1941 the USA was helping escort convoys; they had troops in Iceland; they were helping with training and supplies of all kinds. Yes, Churchill had succeeded in that strategic mission he had explained so clearly to Randolph eighteen months previously. By the end of 1941 he had become one of the most popular performers on American radio, second only to the President himself. By guile and charm and downright flattery, America had been dragged in.

Three days after Pearl Harbor he received appalling news. The *Prince of Wales* had been sunk by Japanese torpedoes off the coast of Malaya, with the loss of 327 lives. Of the British sailors who had been at Placentia Bay, almost all were dead. The *Repulse*, too, was sunk.

It had been Churchill's decision—and his alone—to defy the scepticism of his naval chiefs and send those ships to the Far East. No one knew what the purpose of the mission was, what Churchill hoped to achieve with his 'castles of steel'; and perhaps the truth is that there was no real strategic logic.

Churchill wrote to Roosevelt as he dispatched the British flotilla, boasting of their firepower. 'There is nothing like having something that can catch and kill anything,' he said. They couldn't catch the Japanese torpedo planes, and they died for the sake of a Churchillian flourish. The purpose was surely political: to show the Americans, once again, the strength of British resolve and the reach of her power. Now that gesture was doubly pointless: the Americans were in.

Still—Churchill needed to make absolutely sure. As soon as he heard of Pearl Harbor, he rang Roosevelt; and then began making preparations to get over to Washington. After Placentia Bay Roosevelt had come to realise that Churchill had one of those bouncy-castle personalities that starts filling the room and pressing everyone else against the wall. He suggested Bermuda rather than the White House. Churchill was having none of it.

For three weeks he was the irrepressible house guest of the President and Mrs Roosevelt, in which time he contrived to exhibit himself naked to FDR ('The British Prime Minister has nothing to hide from the President of the United States'), to have a small heart attack and to put on a virtuoso performance of Anglo-American schmaltz, culminating in that speech to both houses of Congress.

It is tremendous stuff. He invokes the memory of his mother; he quotes the Psalms; he appeals to God; he parodies Mussolini; he hams himself up with glorious archaic phrasing. 'Sure I am . . .' he says, rather than 'I am sure', as if he were channelling Yoda. His arms go out, they go up. He hammers the air, he clasps his lapels, he glowers and scowls and clenches his jaw in exactly the manner they have been hoping for.

The Germans, the Japanese, the Italians, he asks his audience: 'What kind of a people do they think we are?' Notice that—a single people, the Americans and the British. 'Here we are together,' he says. 'Twice in our lifetime has the long arm of fate reached out across the Atlantic to pluck the United States into the forefront of the battle . . .' Except that in this case the long arm didn't belong to fate so much as to Churchill. He did the transatlantic plucking.

As Harold Macmillan later wrote, 'No one but he (and that only with extraordinary patience and skill) could have enticed the Americans into the European war at all.'

That does not strike me as being much of an exaggeration. The world may owe its prime debt to F. D. Roosevelt, who ultimately had to take the decision to commit American blood and treasure. But without Churchill, I really don't see how it could have happened. No other British leader would have set that strategic objective—to drag America in—and pursued it with such unremitting zeal.

Anyone who is still inclined to feel critical of the United States, for delaying so long before entering the war, should go to the American cemeteries at Omaha Beach. Walk among the thousands of white stone crosses (and the occasional Star of David) that are arranged with such perfect symmetry on the rolling green lawns; see the names and the states: Pennsylvania, Ohio, Tennessee, Kansas, Texas—every state in the union. I doubt very much you will keep back the tears.

It is seventy years, as I write these words, since those soldiers made that sacrifice, on a scale and with a bravery that my generation finds incomprehensible. They weren't wrong, those American congress-men, when they warned of the human consequences of engagement in another European war. Their doubts were reasonable; and it was Churchill who overcame them.

He later described how on the night of Pearl Harbor, 'saturated and satiated with emotion and sensation I went to bed and slept the sleep of the saved and thankful'.

He had succeeded in his key strategic purpose; but he had not yet won.

# CHAPTER 18

# THE GIANT
# OF THE
# SHRUNKEN ISLAND

The King was in a state of agitation, bordering on mild panic. It was 11 p.m. on a Friday night, and he still had not heard from his most important and in some ways his most insubordinate subject. He rang his Private Secretary. Any news from Churchill? There was no news.

The date was 3 June 1944, and in theory there were just two days to go until D-Day. The whole war depended on this operation, the largest and most complex military undertaking in history; the fate of the world seemed to hang in the balance—and Churchill was being utterly impossible.

The sixty-nine-year-old veteran of wars on four continents was insisting on one more hare-brained escapade. He was exercising his right, as Minister of Defence, to be conveyed on HMS *Belfast* to the coast of Normandy, where he would personally oversee the first bombardment of the German positions. He didn't want to go on D-Day plus one, or D-Day plus two: he planned to be there with the first wave of ships and men; to see the water roiling with machines and blood; to hear the crump of the shells.

The idea was nuts. That was certainly the view of the King's Private Secretary, Sir Alan or 'Tommy' Lascelles. The first he had heard of it was on 30 May, when the King emerged from a tête-à-tête lunch with Churchill at Buckingham Palace. Churchill had confided that he intended to go and watch events from the British battle-cruiser. The King had immediately said that he would go, too; a suggestion that Churchill did nothing to discourage.

'This will never do,' said Lascelles to himself. But at first he tried to be casual. Would it be quite fair to the Queen? he asked the King. It would be necessary to advise the young Princess Elizabeth on a choice of Prime Minister—in the perfectly conceivable event of both the heads of the British state and government ending up at the bottom of the Channel. And it was just unfair, added Lascelles, on the poor captain of the *Belfast*, who would have to worry about his sacred charges in what would almost certainly be an inferno of fire.

Hmm, said the King, who had no desire to be accused of such selfishness. He could see the point. Within a few minutes the courtier had talked down the Sovereign. But what about Churchill?

Quickly Lascelles drafted a letter for the King—which George VI wrote out obediently, in his own hand—and pelted round to Downing Street.

*My dear Winston [said the King (or Lascelles)], I have been thinking a great deal of our conversation yesterday and I have come to the conclusion that it would not be right for either you or I to be where we planned to be on D-Day. I don't think I need emphasise what it would mean to me personally, and to the whole allied cause, if at this juncture a chance bomb, torpedo or even a mine should remove you from the scene; equally a change of sovereign at this moment would be a serious matter for the country and Empire. We should both I know love to be there, but in all seriousness I would ask you to reconsider your plan. Our presence I feel would be an embarrassment to those fighting the ship or ships on which we were, despite anything we might say to them.*

*So as I said, I have very reluctantly come to the conclusion that the right thing to do is what normally falls to those at the top on such occasions, namely to remain at home and wait. I hope very much that you will see it in this light, too. The anxiety of these coming days would be very greatly increased for me if I thought that, in addition to everything else, there was a risk, however remote, of my losing your help and guidance. Believe me yours very sincerely George R I.*

This elegant royal veto achieved nothing. Churchill forged on. The next day there was a meeting in the Map Room in the Downing Street annexe in Storey's Gate. Admiral Sir Bertram Ramsay was called from his duties, and asked to explain to the King and Churchill how Churchill could be present at D-Day. He did his best to rubbish the idea. The ship would never be nearer than 14,000 yards from the French shore, he said. Churchill wouldn't be able to see a thing, and frankly he would know less about what was happening than those left behind in London.

Ramsay was then asked to leave the room. When he came back he was told that the plan had been changed. Operation 'WC' would go ahead—but with the King as well. Ramsay flipped; or, as Lascelles put it in his diary, 'To this the unfortunate man, naturally enough, reacted violently.'

By this stage Churchill could see that it was going to be difficult to get the King on board; so he cut his losses. He announced in 'his most oracular manner' that he would need cabinet approval to allow the King to come with him on the *Belfast*, and he would not be able to recommend that they give it. As he chuntered on, it became clear to Lascelles that Churchill still intended to go himself, and the courtier allowed his features to register his general horror and disapproval.

As the King put it, 'Tommy's face is getting longer and longer.' Churchill was oblivious, so—with some difficulty—Lascelles interrupted the conversation again, addressing the King.

'I was thinking, Sir, that it is not going to make things easier for you if you have to find a new Prime Minister in the middle of Overlord.'

'Oh,' said Churchill, 'that's all arranged for. Anyhow, I don't think the risk is 100–1.'

Next Lascelles tried to suggest that Churchill was being constitutionally improper: no minister of the Crown could leave the country without the Sovereign's consent. Churchill countered jesuitically that HMS *Belfast* didn't count as abroad, since it was a British man-of-war. Lascelles said it was a long way outside British territorial waters; but it was no use. It was like holding a bull elephant by the tail.

Lascelles left the meeting feeling that 'in this instance his naughtiness is sheer selfishness'. Everyone was against it: the staff at Downing Street, Pug Ismay, Clementine—but Churchill was absolutely determined: to smell the cordite, to see the plumes of salt water as the shells and bombs exploded around him in the sea. What was Lascelles going to do?

The only answer was another monarchical missive, he decided. He sat down and drafted a second and firmer reprimand, from the King to Churchill.

> *My dear Winston, I want to make one more appeal to you not to go to sea on D day. Please consider my own position. I am a*

249

*younger man than you, I am a sailor, and as King I am head*
*of all the services. There is nothing I would like better than to*
*go to sea but I have agreed to stay at home; is it fair that you*
*should then do exactly what I should have liked to do myself?*
*You said yesterday afternoon that it would be a fine thing for*
*the king to lead his troops into battle, as in old days; if the king*
*cannot do this, it does not seem right that his Prime Minister*
*should take his place. Then there is your own position. You will*
*see very little, you will run a considerable risk, you will be*
*inaccessible at a critical time when vital decisions may have to*
*be taken, and however unobtrusive you may be, your mere*
*presence on board is bound to be a very heavy additional*
*responsibility to the Admiral and Captain. As I said in my*
*previous letter, your being there would add immeasurably to my*
*anxieties, and your going without consulting your colleagues*
*in the Cabinet would put them in a difficult position which*
*they would justifiably resent.*

*I ask you most earnestly to consider the whole question*
*again, and not let your personal wishes, which I very well*
*understand, lead you to depart from your own high*
*standard of duty to the State. Believe me your very sincere*
*friend George R I.*

The dispute had now become a constitutional crisis. There was
only one man who could conceivably have stopped Churchill from
going, and that was the King; and in order to get his way George VI
was obliged to write twice, and finally to warn Churchill that he was
about to violate just about every code of loyalty he possessed: loyalty
to the Crown, loyalty to the cabinet, loyalty to the armed services and
loyalty to Britain herself. It was heavy stuff.

Finally, on Saturday, 3 June, Churchill climbed down—with much grumbling. He was entitled to go and watch any battle he saw fit, he protested. He was Minister of Defence. But he sulkily accepted the key point advanced by the King—that it was unfair to prevent the monarch from going to Normandy, and then to go himself and steal the King's thunder. 'That is certainly a strong argument,' he said.

The episode casts an interesting light on the edginess of the government on the eve of D-Day, and on the evolving relations between ministers and the Crown—it must be one of the few twentieth-century examples of a prime minister being specifically countermanded by the King. In Tommy Lascelles we see the role of 'them'—the shadowy mandarins and courtiers who take so many of the decisions the politicians are incapable of taking (and do so to this day).

But the really fascinating question is why Churchill cared so much; why he was so utterly determined to put himself again in the front line of battle. There are several obvious answers, and the first is surely that he was nervous about D-Day.

We have the advantage of knowing that the operation was going to be a success. That was far from clear at the time. Alan Brooke thought that it might be 'the most ghastly disaster of the whole war'. The weather could so easily have turned bad. Rommel might have suddenly reinforced the target zone. Eisenhower was all set to take responsibility for an evacuation, if things went against the Allies.

This was the amphibious operation for which the Allies had been building up for years; this was their shot at winning back the Continent. And Churchill had previous form when it came to risky amphibious operations. Churchill wanted to be there because burned in his psyche was the memory of Gallipoli—and of all the errors of the Dardanelles the one for which he felt the bitterest remorse, rightly or wrongly, was his failure to go there himself. Now was his chance to exorcise that disgrace, to emulate the practice of his illustrious antecedent in leading his troops personally into battle and to

251

show the world that he was truly a Marlborough, and not just a Marl-borough lite. He needed to be there to make sure that the troops did not just get bogged down, as they had at Gallipoli, and indeed as they had on the Western Front in the First World War.

And then there was another reason for getting in that ship—a motive that will come as no surprise to us by now, and which Las-celles certainly detected. As the royal Private Secretary wrote to sum up the whole affair, 'The King, in fact, was only trying to save Win-ston from himself, for the real motives inspiring him to go to sea in *Belfast* are his irrepressible, though now most untimely, love of adven-ture, and, I fear, his vain, though perhaps subconscious, predilection for making himself "front page stuff".'

There, I am sure, Lascelles has judged our man well. Churchill could see the headlines; he could see the photos—standing impervi-ous on the bridge, soggy cigar clamped to his lips, as he called the shots from the *Belfast*'s 12-inch guns; the conductor of the loudest and most explosive overture in the history of ballistics. He could see the way it would look—the man entrusted to give the roar of the British lion; and this time a roar of artillery and not just rhetoric.

That was why he at first endorsed the idea of the King coming too; because that would have been an even bigger story: Britain's mon-arch and Prime Minister, dauntless and unbowed by five years of war, directing the recapture of the mainland. That was the 'front page stuff' he was after; and in a way it wasn't just about him and his ego, and what he had achieved. It was about Britain, and her standing in the world.

IN MY INNOCENT youth I believed that Britain had 'won the war' not just through Russian sacrifice and American money, but thanks also to the heroism of the British fighting man. I read 'Commando' comics, in which men with woolly hats and supercolossal forearms would lunge at cringing Germans, with a cry of 'Take that, Fritz' from their huge jaws and with a candle-flame of bullets bursting from the muzzle of their guns.

I remember vividly being taught by a fine classicist who had himself been imprisoned by the Japanese; and I received the clear impression that the battle of El Alamein was the turning-point in the war. Monty hit Rommel for six, and then Jerry began to take a bit of a pasting, what? So it came as a bit of a shock to read, over the years, what really happened.

It appeared that the battle of El Alamein, at the end of October 1942, was not quite as pivotal to history as I had been led to suppose. Indeed, there were some British historians who were so ungracious as to call it the 'unnecessary battle'. Operation Torch was due to happen only a few weeks later—Allied landings to drive the Germans out of North Africa. It seemed that El Alamein wasn't so much a decisive military victory as a vital political figleaf.

By the autumn of 1942, Britain's military record was a virtually unbroken series of bungles, evacuations, catastrophes and all-round defeats, often at the hands of forces that were numerically vastly inferior. It was as though the country had entered the Premiership with the reputation of Manchester United and ended up playing like Tunstall Town FC. 'I can't get the victories,' complained Churchill. 'It's the victories that are so hard to get.'

It wasn't just at Norway, Dunkirk, Greece and Crete where British forces perfected the manoeuvre that might be known as the 'rabbit' or headlong scuttle. The year 1942 was even worse, with a dismal series of debacles that began in the Far East with the sinking of the *Prince of Wales* and the *Repulse*. Then there was the fall of Singapore, when Churchill wrote to his generals specifically instructing them to fight to the last man and to choose death before dishonour.

They decided, on the whole, to ignore his advice, and that dishonour was vastly preferable. Rangoon was abandoned. The raids on St
Nazaire and Dieppe were much trumpeted for propaganda purposes, but achieved little, for the cost of many lives. Then there was
the fall of Tobruk—news of which was handed to Churchill on a pink
slip while he was actually sitting with Roosevelt in the White House.
He was utterly mortified—especially since he had once again issued
his personal and express instructions that the troops should fight to
the bitter end.

Once again, British troops had been routed by a much smaller
German force. All sorts of possible explanations have been offered
for this relative underperformance of Britain—previously regarded
as one of the most ferocious and successful military powers the world
has ever seen. In his various brilliant meditations on this theme, Max
Hastings has been unsparing in his criticisms.

By Hastings' account, none of the generals appears to have been
much cop. Not even Monty deserves a place in the ranks of 'history's
great captains'. When they were not simply dim, they were too often
idle and complacent. They were also risk-averse and had a serious
dislike of bloodshed; perhaps understandable, given the memory of
the First War, but a disadvantage in a fighting force. The wider officer
class contained a large supply of duffers who had joined the military
on the grounds that it was a cushy billet and an easier way of living
than trying to run a business.

The equipment was substandard, or at least not as good as German equipment; and then there was the awful suspicion that man for
man the British just did not have the same kind of fire in their bellies
as their foes. As Max Hastings puts it, 'Many British officers per-
ceived their citizen soldiers as lacking the will and commitment routinely displayed by the Germans and Japanese.' Or as Randolph

Churchill shouted, rather unpleasantly, during a 1942 discussion in Downing Street, 'Father, the trouble is your soldiers won't fight.'

Whether this was true or not—and plainly it was a verdict that was at odds with the innumerable acts of individual bravery performed by British troops around the world—the important point was that people believed it to be true. British underperformance became the subject of embarrassment at home, and mockery abroad. In July 1942 a survey of American opinion asked which nation was doing the most to win the war: 37 per cent said the USA, 30 per cent Russia, 14 per cent China and only 6 per cent thought highly of the British and their exertions.

All this was of course gall and wormwood to Churchill, whose whole political *raison d'être* was to boost the prestige of Britain and the British Empire. After the fall of Singapore, Churchill was politically at his lowest point during the war, and may even have contemplated resignation. His frustration was obvious when, in the wake of Singapore, he declared, 'We had so many men, so many men. We should have done better.' When he heard of the fall of Tobruk, he said, 'Defeat is one thing; disgrace is another.'

His ego had become entirely engaged and identified with British military success—which made it easy for his rivals to torment him. 'He wins debate after debate but loses battle after battle,' said the Labour MP Aneurin Bevan, brutally, in the House of Commons; and indeed, public anxiety became so acute that Churchill's own domestic position actually became quite shaky.

When in August 1942 he went to Moscow to see Stalin, to explain that there would be no second front that year, the Soviet leader taunted him unmercifully. 'You British are afraid of fighting. You should not think the Germans are supermen. You will have to fight sooner or later. You cannot win a war without fighting.'

This was pretty nauseating coming from Stalin. The Russian leader was the man who enabled the whole Nazi aggression of 1940 to take place—by authorising the Molotov–Ribbentrop pact, and carving up Poland with Hitler. Stalin had been so shocked and terrified by Hitler's eventual betrayal, when the Führer turned on Russia and launched Barbarossa, that he went and hid himself for five days in a darkened hut. It goes without saying that Churchill was an infinitely better, braver and greater man. But it rankled to hear such stuff—and the insults were all the more wounding for containing an element of truth.

When it finally came, victory at El Alamein did much to redeem British prestige: the political threat to Churchill abated. He no longer had to worry—incredible as it may seem to us today—that his Labour rival Stafford Cripps could replace him as war premier. Aneurin Bevan's wounding sarcasm was stilled. The British public were given the victory they craved. But the truth was unmistakable: as the war wore on, Britain counted for less and less.

In 1940 the nation had stood alone—an embattled paladin with her banner raised for freedom. By 1944 Britain was contributing only a fraction of the Allied effort. The Americans were supplying the money, the Russians were getting on with the grisly business of killing the Germans—750,000 of them at the Battle of Stalingrad alone. And so it became Churchill's function to try physically and personally to assert Britain's right to respect, to be the lead-lined boxing glove that enabled the country to punch above her weight.

That explains his love of summits, his amazing itineraries during the Second World War. Sir Martin Gilbert has calculated that between September 1939 and November 1943 he travelled 111,000 miles, spending 792 hours at sea and 339 hours in the air—far exceeding the work rate of any other leader. We see his prodigious energy on these trips: a man of almost seventy sitting on his suitcase before dawn at a cold airfield in North Africa, while his staff try to work out where they are meant to be. We see him bouncing in the unpressurised cargo holds of bombers, his oxygen mask adapted so as to accommodate his cigar. Planes he had used were shot down later, flying the same routes.

On the morning of 26 January 1943 he arrived at the British embassy in Cairo, in time for breakfast. To the amazement of the ambassador's wife, he asked for a glass of cold white wine. Alan Brooke recorded that

> a tumbler was brought which he drained in one go, and then licked his lips, turned to Jacqueline and said, 'Ah, that is good, but you know, I have already had two whiskies and soda and two cigars this morning'!! It was then only shortly after 7.30 am. We had travelled all night in poor comfort, covering some 2300 miles in a flight of over 11 hours, a proportion of which was at over 11000 ft, and there he was, as fresh as paint, drinking wine on top of two previous whiskies and two cigars!!

While Hitler and Stalin stayed in their bunkers, Churchill would do anything to get to the action. That was why he was so keen to inveigle himself and the King on that boat: to show the world—and especially the Americans—that Britain and the British Empire still counted: because he and the King, the incarnations of that empire, were personally recapturing the Continent. And with the same motive he insisted that British and Canadian forces should have the glory of comprising half those vast invading forces—even if the operation was led by an American, and even though it was the Americans who did most of the eventual fighting.

When he finally got to go over to Normandy—on D-Day plus six, and with the consent of the King—he insisted that the ship he was on 'had a plug' at the Germans. The captain happily complied, and a volley was duly discharged in the general direction of the Nazis. It was a completely abstract exercise; but Churchill was thrilled. He had become First Lord of the Admiralty in 1911—and he had never yet fired a shot from ship.

It was as if he could somehow aggrandise Britain's military effort by taking part himself—inflating the British contribution with his own presence and prestige. In August 1944 he went to watch the landings at St Tropez; and in the same month he was to be found in Italy, personally firing a howitzer towards Pisa. He picnicked in an Italian castle, with the Germans firing towards him from a distance of 500 yards away.

In December 1944 he launched his entirely personal mission to rescue Greece from communism—in which he succeeded—and gave a press conference in Athens to the sound of shellfire outside. In the spring of the following year he was there in Germany, to see the Allied advance. In early March he came to the Siegfried Line—huge dragon's teeth of concrete that were meant to serve as an impenetrable frontier, sinister and symbolic guardians of the Fatherland. Churchill inspected these carefully—but somehow it wasn't enough. He needed to express the full ecstasy of his triumph.

He lined up the generals: Brooke, Montgomery, Simpson, about twenty of them—and one reporter from the *Stars and Stripes*. 'Let's do it on the Siegfried Line,' said Churchill, and then, to the photographers, 'This is one of the operations connected with this great war that must not be reproduced graphically.'

He then undid his flies and pissed on Hitler's defences, and so did his colleagues. As Alan Brooke later wrote, 'I shall never forget the childish grin of intense satisfaction that spread all over his face as he looked down at the critical moment.' To anyone who feels the smallest disapproval, think of what he had been through. If any dog had the right to mark his new territory, it was Churchill.

A few weeks later he insisted on walking on the German-held side of the Rhine, at a place called Buderich, and then came under fire, with shells exploding in the water about a hundred yards away. The American General Simpson came up to him and said, 'Prime Minister, there are snipers in front of you; they are shelling both sides of the bridge; and now they have started shelling the road behind you. I cannot accept responsibility for your being here and must ask you to come away.'

Alan Brooke watched as Churchill put his arms around a twisted girder of a bridge. 'The look on Winston's face was like that of a small boy being called from his sandcastles on the beach by his nurse.' Churchill was doing what we have seen him do all his life, from the first day he came under fire in Cuba. He was trying to insert himself into the military narrative; and this time his purpose was political.

In manpower and in fighting ability Britain was now dwarfed by Russia and America. As he put it, a small lion was walking between a huge Russian bear and a great American elephant. But he was still there; he was still one of the 'Big Three'. He was still fighting the war in a way that no other political leader would have dreamed of doing. No other wartime jefe—not Roosevelt, Hitler, Stalin, Mussolini—had his compulsive desire to interpolate himself in the battle and to become the story.

By sheer force of personality he asserted his right to equality in the conference chamber, as he struggled with Stalin over the fate of eastern Europe. As long as Churchill had to be given honour and respect, the same could be said for Britain and the empire; or so he imagined. In the end, of course, his priorities were not exactly shared by the British people, or indeed by the British army.

They weren't as interested as he was in concepts of 'glory' or 'prestige'—and that is perhaps not entirely a bad thing. All sorts of uncomplimentary things have been said about the fighting spirit of the British troops, but the key point is surely this: that they were citizen soldiers from a mature democracy with a long history of free speech. They knew not to have blind faith in the orders they were given; the First World War put paid to that.

They did not go into battle propelled by a horrible ideology of racial supremacy. They did not have Soviet commissars behind them with revolvers, waiting to blow their brains out if they hesitated. Perhaps the paradox is that the very freedoms they enjoyed and fought for made them less vicious as a fighting force. And I wonder whether the Tommy-bashers sometimes take a perverse pleasure in minimising their achievements—rather like the ingrained (and psychologically self-defensive) national pessimism about the England football team.

The British military performance wasn't as bad as all that. It was rare for the Germans to be beaten by anyone unless outnumbered, and often by a factor of two or three. El Alamein was a significant achievement, in that it made the North Africa landings much easier, and helped divert crucial German air support from Stalingrad; and there were many other great achievements, not least the essential one of fighting on and ending up conspicuously on the winning side.

As someone once said, the English lose every battle but the last. Perhaps they sometimes—though by no means always—lacked a fanatical spirit of semi-suicidal banzai bloodlust; that does not seem to me to be a wholly unattractive defect.

Churchill spoke to the depths of people's souls when Britain was alone, when the country was fighting for survival—and he reached them and he comforted in a way that no other speaker could have done. His language—stirring and old-fashioned—suited the moment. But as the country neared the end of six long and debilitating years of war, the people needed a new language, a new vision for a post-war Britain—and that an exhausted Churchill could not find.

AS HE APPROACHED the general election of 1945, he told his doctor, Lord Moran, 'I have a very strong feeling that my work is done. I have no message. I had a message. Now I only say "fight the damned socialists. I do not believe in this brave new world".' On the morning of 21 July, four days before the election results were due to be heard, he was in Berlin for a victory parade.

Hitler was dead. The Führer's bunker was in ruins along with all the other odious apparatus of Nazi rule. Europe could look forward to a new era of peaceful democracy; and everyone knew in their hearts that this was his achievement, and that without his iron resolve, at critical moments, this would not have been possible. This was what he had promised and fought for.

Churchill and Attlee drove in separate jeeps along a line of cheering British troops. Churchill's Private Secretary, John Peck, soon noticed something peculiar.

'It struck me and perhaps others as well, though nothing was said, as decidedly odd that Winston Churchill, the great war leader but for whom we should never have been in Berlin at all, got a markedly less vociferous cheer than Mr Attlee, who—however great his contribution to the coalition—had not hitherto made any marked personal impact upon the fighting forces.'

On the afternoon of 25 July Churchill left the Potsdam conference in Berlin, with both Stalin and Truman confident (publicly and privately) that he would be back as a triumphantly re-elected Prime Minister. The following morning, as the count was nearing completion, he awoke before dawn with 'a sharp stab of almost physical pain'.

A hitherto 'subconscious conviction that we were beaten broke forth and dominated my mind'. He was right. Labour had won by a colossal margin of 146 seats over all other parties. Churchill and the Conservatives had been routed. The outside world was amazed, and to this day people find it hard to understand how Churchill could have suffered such a rebuke.

Surely it is not surprising at all. Elections are won not on the basis of a politician's achievements, but on what is promised for the future. It was Churchill who in one of his protean incarnations had helped found the essentials of the welfare state; and in his wartime speeches he outlined the key reforms of the post-war Labour government. But it was Attlee who managed to claim the agenda.

In the very moment of his triumph, Churchill paid a price for his unique status—as a national figure who transcended party. He was after all the man so confident in himself that he had ratted and re-ratted. He was not coextensive with the Conservative Party; and therefore his achievements did not rub off on them. 'Cheer for Churchill; vote for Labour' was the Labour slogan. It worked.

It was perhaps not exactly how he saw it at the time, but there is a sense in which his very defeat was a triumph. He had fought for British democracy, and here it was: the ejection of a great war hero and leader, not by violence but by millions of small and unobtrusive strokes of the pencil.

As Clementine put it, 'It may well be a blessing in disguise.'

'At the moment,' replied Churchill, 'it seems quite effectively disguised.'

When someone else suggested that the electorate were guilty of 'ingratitude' Churchill said, 'I wouldn't call it that. They have had a very hard time.' That is what I mean by his greatness of soul.

He had been humiliated in his hour of glory, but Churchill ended the war with the crossover complete. Britain was exhausted and her global status diminished. Churchill was exhausted but with a global status that no other British politician has ever achieved: a moral giant. Not bad for a man who had been denounced in 1911, by the *Spectator*, as 'weak and rhetorical, without any principles or even any consistent outlook upon public affairs'.

A lesser man would have packed it in, and gone off to Chartwell to paint. Not Churchill. He never gave up; he never gave in. He now made a series of interventions that were to shape the world to this day.

# CHAPTER 19

# THE COLD WAR AND
# HOW HE WON IT

We have seen the room where he was born. Let me take you now to the room where Churchill spent his last few days as wartime Prime Minister. It is a sad sort of place—like the frowsty lounge of a 1920s golf club or hotel. Outside the sun is shining; there are glorious phloxes and roses in the beds; and yet it is a bit Stygian here at the heart of this bogus essay in supersized steel-framed stockbroker Tudor.

The decor is drab. The accent is on oak—heavy oaken chairs, oaken fireplace, and a great oak banister writhing up to a sinister minstrels' gallery. I stand looking at the table where they sat, the three little flags in the middle all drooping and dusty. I feel the unease and the hypocrisy of the occasion.

It was here that he came on 17 July 1945, to the Cecilienhof, one of the few buildings in Potsdam not damaged by Allied bombs. Originally intended for some minor offshoot of the Hohenzollern dynasty, it looked then as now like a vague German attempt to build an English country house. It was the last and least successful of his wartime conferences. He had tried and failed to hold the meeting in Britain—indeed, he never succeeded in persuading Roosevelt to visit Britain throughout the war. Now the summiteers were in the Russian zone of occupied Germany—in Potsdam, the home of German kings and kaisers.

This was the German Versailles, a place of palaces and pavilions, of lawns and lakes, a suburb of Berlin that today has UN world heritage status. In 1945 the greater part of the site was in ruins.

On the night of 14 April of that year the RAF had sent 500 Lancaster bombers, and dropped 1,780 tons of high explosive. Churchill was the author of this strategy; Churchill had insisted on area bombing—and with the specific and avowed intent of terrorising the civilian population. He pursued the aerial bombing—of doubtful military benefit—mainly because it was the only way he had of attacking Germany.

Short of launching a second front, it was the only means of expressing his pent-up aggression, of showing the Russians and the Americans that Britain, too, could inflict violence upon the enemy. It is true that he was himself seized by doubts. 'Are we beasts? Are we taking this too far?' he said suddenly one evening at Chartwell when he watched footage of burning German towns.

He was alarmed by the controversy over the Dresden fireball, in which 25,000 were killed and in many cases carbonised by British aerial bombing (and which he denounced in a suppressed memo as a 'mere act of terror and wanton destruction'), and he was furious when he found that the RAF had been so culturally insensitive as to attack the palaces of Potsdam. Now he came to see the results of a policy from which he could not easily dissociate himself.

More than 1,500 had died and 24,000 had been made homeless in Potsdam alone. As he picked his way through the rubble of Berlin he was filled with a typical compassion. 'My hate died with their sur-render,' he said in his memoirs. 'I was much moved by their thin haggard looks and threadbare clothes.'

Churchill's war was never with the German people. It was the 'Narzis' that he wanted to smash; and now that he was at the apogee of his success, he found himself in the presence of another enemy, and one he had feared long before Nazism was even born: just as savage; just as ideologically driven; and in some ways more difficult to fight.

The Potsdam table is large and round, about ten foot in diameter, and reputedly made for the occasion by Russian carpenters. The massive oak is covered, as it was then, by a thick red felt cloth: per-haps in honour of the Russians whose red flag had been hoisted over Berlin, and who had organised the conference. It looks like the per-fect place for poker; and there was one of the Big Three who seemed to have all the cards.

After four years of savage warfare, in which the Nazis and the So-viets had held each other by the throat like a pair of hydrophobic dogs, it is incredible to think that Stalin could still wield 6.4 million men in the European theatre alone. Russia had lost 20 million—and yet she ended the war as by far the most powerful military force in Europe.

In Stalin, the Soviet Union had a twinkling-eyed tyrant of total cynicism and ruthlessness. We have already seen how he baited Chur-chill in 1942, sneering at the alleged cowardliness of the British army. That was his style: sneer, flatter, fawn, bully, kill.

Stalin had risen to power by liquidating his enemies, and he main-tained power by systematic murder of entire groups of people—the Tsarist officer corps, the kulaks, counter-revolutionaries, Poles, who-ever stood in his way. He had the blood of hundreds of thousands of people on his hands before the Second World War had even begun.

It was in Tehran in November 1943 that Churchill got a flavour of his homicidal mania; and also of the eerie willingness of the Americans to indulge him.

The discussions of the Big Three had turned to Europe after the war. Stalin was already insisting that Poland should be bisected, and much of that country retained by Russia. Then, at the dinner in the evening, he sketched out his plans for post-war Germany.

Stalin: 'Fifty thousand Germans must be killed. Their General Staff must go.'

WSC: 'I will not be party to any butchery in cold blood. What happens in hot blood is another matter.'

Stalin: 'Fifty thousand MUST be shot.'

WSC (getting red in the face): 'I would rather be taken out now and shot than so disgrace my country.'

Franklin Delano Roosevelt: 'I have a compromise to propose. Not 50,000 but only 49,000 should be shot.'

At this hilarious sally, the President's son Elliott Roosevelt rose to say that he cordially agreed with Stalin's proposal, and that he was sure it would receive the full backing of Congress. Churchill then left the room in fury, and it was only with some difficulty that he could be persuaded to return.

What the Americans did not understand—or did not choose to understand—was that Stalin was only half joking; perhaps not even joking at all. To shoot 50,000 people in cold blood was nothing to Stalin; as he was said to have put it, not a tragedy but a statistic.

Things had been no better at Yalta in February 1945, where Stalin irresistibly and blandly continued to push his agenda: the Soviet domination of eastern Europe. Roosevelt was by now desperately ill, passing in and out of consciousness; and Churchill simply did not have the military muscle to oppose the Russian demands. Stalin was charm itself, comically showing off his limited command of English

('You said it!' and 'The toilet is over there' were among the few but surprisingly idiomatic phrases he deployed); but the message was increasingly clear. Russia was to retain all the gains of the odious Molotov–Ribbentrop pact, and to command all of eastern Europe and the Balkans—with the exception of Greece ('This brand I snatched from the burning,' as Churchill boasted, 'on Christmas day').

The Baltic states were to go to Russia. Poland was to go to Russia—Poland, the country whose very sovereignty and integrity had been the cause of the war; Poland was once again betrayed, sacrificed and carved up to please a totalitarian regime. Again and again, Churchill found himself isolated, as Roosevelt sided with the Russian dictator.

When that great American President finally died on 12 April 1945, Churchill took what seems now to be the astonishing decision not to go to his funeral: astonishing when you consider how integral their relationship had been to Allied success; not so astonishing when you think of the gradual estrangement that had begun between them. America was still driving a very hard bargain over British war loans, and had been responsible for such minor vexations as cancelling meat exports to Britain. But the fundamental divergence was on the matter of Stalin, Russia and the post-war world.

On 4 May 1945 Churchill wrote to Eden that the Russian coup over Poland 'constitutes an event in the history of Europe to which there has been no parallel'. On 13 May he cabled the new President Truman to say that an 'iron curtain' had descended across the Russian front—which shows that the phrase, later to become so controversial, had been used by Churchill almost a year before his Fulton, Missouri, speech. By the end of that month Churchill was so alarmed by the prospect of a communist and Russian-dominated eastern Europe that he proposed an operation that has only recently been disinterred, mainly by the historian David Reynolds. On 24 May he asked British military planners to look into what he called Operation

Unthinkable—by which British and American forces would actually turn on the Russians, and push them back from eastern Europe. How would they do it? They would enlist the fighters who had proved most effective of all: the Wehrmacht.

Churchill suggested to Montgomery that captured German weapons should be stored in such a way as to be capable of being conveniently returned to the de-Nazified German troops; and used for an assault against the Soviets. All that remained secret until 1998, and it is probably just as well that it did.

Even if it had been desirable, there was no way Churchill could have persuaded the Americans to take part in such a plan. To understand the comparative American indulgence of the Russians, you have to remember how the world looked to Washington in 1944 and early 1945. The war in the Pacific was by no means over. The Japanese were offering frenzied and suicidal resistance. The Japanese population was being schooled in guerrilla warfare—even to fight with spears. The Americans knew that eventually they would win—but they feared (in spite of possessing the bomb) that the loss of life would be horrific. They hoped that the Russians would come in decisively on their side.

And even if Churchill could have persuaded the Americans, there remains the prior question: what of his own army, and his own British electorate? What would they have said, if they had been told that it was now time to turn on the Russians? It is safe to say that if the British public had heard of Operation Unthinkable, they would have reacted with bewilderment and outrage. They knew little or nothing of Stalin's purges. In the minds of many British people, the Russians were heroes who had shown a courage and spirit of self-sacrifice that put other armies (including their own) to shame.

In popular imagination Stalin was not yet a blood-soaked tyrant; he was Uncle Joe, with his folksy pipe and moustache. If the British public had been told in 1945 that it was now time to turn their guns on Moscow, I am afraid they would have drawn the conclusion that Churchill had mounted his ancient hobby-horse of anti-communism—and that he was both wrong and deluded. The idea was never a runner, as British military planners made clear in their response to Churchill. Operation Unthinkable would require vast quantities of German troops and American resources; and I don't suppose that conclusion came as any real surprise to the British Prime Minister.

As ever, he was allowing his mind to roam, to go through all the logical options—no matter how mad-sounding they might be. It says something for his undiminished martial instinct—after six grinding and debilitating years—that he should even contemplate the possibility of such an action. However impractical, Operation Unthinkable also reveals the depths of his anxiety about the communist threat; and here at least he was surely right.

As he looked at the map of Europe, he saw Germany in ruins, France on her knees, Britain exhausted. He saw that Russian tanks were capable of advancing to the Atlantic and to the North Sea—if they chose. They had shown their willingness to engulf the capitals of eastern Europe, and to impose a form of government that he believed to be wicked. What could be done to stop them? That was the big strategic question he posed—and a question that many Americans, for the time being, seemed to have no interest even in asking.

By the time Churchill came to leave the Potsdam conference, on 25 July, he had achieved little or nothing. He had filled the air of the dingy room with some brilliant phrases—which the interpreters had struggled to translate; but it was as if Britain was visibly continuing to shrink in the shade of the two emerging superpowers.

On the American side, Truman revealed that Washington now had the capacity to wield an atomic weapon—and refused to share the technology with Britain: which you might think a slightly off-hand way to treat an ally that had honoured scrupulously the terms of the Anglo-American technology-sharing agreements. Most of the early theoretical work on nuclear fission was British, and it was all handed on a plate—along with radar and everything else—to America. In the end, Truman was to take the decision to bomb Hiroshima alone; the consultation of Churchill was a mere formality.

For the Russians, Stalin continued to play his hand with economy and skill. When he spoke, it was to the point. He was never at a loss for a fact (unlike Churchill, who sometimes had to lean back to allow his seconds to whisper in his ear); and when he thought it necessary the Russian tyrant continued to dispense his lethal charm. He told Churchill how sorry he was that he had not been more publicly effusive in thanking Britain for helping Russia. He made a great thing of gathering up the menus and going round to get Churchill's signature. 'I like that man,' Churchill was heard to say—being a bit of an old sucker for flattery.

And all the while the Bear was engulfing eastern Europe, smiling complacently as he chomped away, securing at Potsdam not just war reparations but war 'booty', carting away whatever he could to feed the Russian economy. The puppet Soviet-controlled Polish government appeared before the leaders at Potsdam. Churchill asked whether they might have some non-communists in their ranks. *Nyet*, was the answer.

Then on 26 July Churchill was back in London, to receive the Order of the Boot, first class, from the British public. It was now that he really showed what he was made of; as if there had been some previous doubt about the matter.

He was seventy years old; he had emerged victorious at the end of the most violent conflict humanity had ever seen. He had his memoirs to write. He had not even been to Chartwell during the war: the

271

place had been under dustcloths. He had his fishponds to restock, his pigs to tend. He could have left public life amid the applause of a grateful nation and of a world in his immortal debt. That was not his way.

It is true that at first he found it hard to cope with the loss of his status. A black cloud descended, as his daughter Mary has recorded. His family did their best to lift his spirits, playing him favourite old tunes such as 'Run, Rabbit, Run'. It wasn't much use. He quarrelled with Clementine, who spoke of 'our misery'.

Slowly, however, he began to get himself together. He went for long painting holidays to Italy (where on one occasion he tactlessly painted some bombed buildings, and got booed by the locals). He had his duties as Leader of the Opposition. He continued to denounce the 'Bolshevisation' of eastern Europe, and said that the Russians were 'realist-lizards of the crocodile family'. Towards the end of the year he received an interesting invitation from Truman, to come and give a speech at a 'wonderful school' called Westminster College at Fulton in his home state of Missouri.

On 4 March 1946 he and Truman left the White House to make the twenty-four-hour train journey to Missouri. It is important to note that the themes of the speech had now been long in gestation, and that Churchill had by no means kept his thoughts secret. He had shared the gist with James Byrne, the US Secretary of State, who 'seemed to like it very well'. He had discussed it with Clement Attlee, who wrote to him on 25 February to say, 'I am sure your Fulton speech will do good.' He had shown a draft before boarding the train to Admiral Leahy, Truman's senior Service adviser, who was (at least according to Churchill) 'enthusiastic'. He continued to polish the speech as they drew into Missouri, and as they chugged by that vast river he gratified his host's curiosity, and showed the whole thing to Truman. 'He told me he thought it was admirable,' reported Churchill. And so it is.

Churchill's speech at Fulton, Missouri, is unlike anything from modern political discourse. It has not been written on a word-processor. It has not been composed by a committee of speech writers. The thing is almost five thousand words long, and every phrase is redolent of the author.

He swoops from a Thomas Hardy-esque poetic style (the future is the 'after-time', for instance) to various hard-edged if batty proposals for defence cooperation. He at one stage proposes that every nation should commit a squadron to an international air force, to be directed by a world organisation—an idea that I have seen properly taken up only in the 1970s kids' TV programme *Thunderbirds*. He meditates on ideas that unite Britain and America:

> We must never cease to proclaim in fearless tones the great principles of freedom and the rights of man which are the joint inheritance of the English-speaking world and which through Magna Carta, the Bill of Rights, the Habeas Corpus, trial by jury, and the English common law find their most famous expression in the American Declaration of Independence . . .
>
> All this means that the people of any country have the right, and should have the power by constitutional action, by free unfettered elections, with secret ballot, to choose or change the character or form of government under which they dwell; that freedom of speech and thought should reign; that courts of justice, independent of the executive, unbiased by any party, should administer laws which have received the broad assent of large majorities or are consecrated by time and custom. Here are the title deeds of freedom which should

lie in every cottage home. Here is the message of the British and American peoples to mankind. Let us preach what we practice—let us practise what we preach.

The majority of the electorate may no longer live in 'cottage homes'—not unless they have a million or two—but these are still the ideals in which American and British democrats believe. They were the causes for which Churchill fought all his life. Finally he comes to the key point—the bombshell that he knows his audience is half expecting. 'There is a threat to the safety of the world, a threat to the Temple of Peace; and that threat is the Soviet Union.' He begins by insisting that he bears no ill-will either to the Russian people or towards his 'wartime comrade Marshal Stalin' . . .

We understand the Russian need to be secure on her western frontiers by the removal of all possibility of German aggression. We welcome Russia to her rightful place among the leading nations of the world. We welcome her flag upon the seas. Above all, we welcome constant, frequent and growing contacts between the Russian people and our own people on both sides of the Atlantic. It is my duty however, for I am sure you would wish me to state the facts as I see them to you, to place before you certain facts about the present position in Europe.

From Stettin in the Baltic to Trieste in the Adriatic, an iron curtain has descended across the Continent. Behind that line lie all the capitals of the ancient states of Central and Eastern Europe. Warsaw, Berlin, Prague, Vienna, Budapest, Belgrade, Bucharest and Sofia, all these famous cities and the populations around them lie in what I must call the Soviet sphere, and all are subject in one form or another, not only to Soviet influence but to a very high and, in many cases, increasing measure

of control from Moscow. Athens alone—Greece with its immortal glories—is free to decide its future at an election under
British, American and French observation. The Russian-
dominated Polish Government has been encouraged to make
enormous and wrongful inroads upon Germany, and mass
expulsions of millions of Germans on a scale grievous and
undreamed-of are now taking place. The Communist parties,
which were very small in all these Eastern States of Europe,
have been raised to pre-eminence and power far beyond their
numbers and are seeking everywhere to obtain totalitarian
control. Police governments are prevailing in nearly every
case, and so far, except in Czechoslovakia, there is no true
democracy.

He goes on in his *tour d'horizon*, taking in virtually everything
from the atomic bomb to the situation in Manchuria. He calls for a
'special relationship' between the UK and the USA, with 'similarity
of weapons and manuals of instruction'. He calls for a united Europe
and a brotherhood of man; a spiritually great Germany and a spiritually great France.

It is a magnificent speech and an inspiring vision—but it was of
course the commie-bashing which made the news.

Churchill was denounced as an 'alarmist'—just as he had been
accused of over-egging the threat from Nazi Germany. In London,
*The Times* sniffed that his sharp contrast between Western democracy
and communism was 'less than happy'. The two political creeds had
'much to learn from each other', said the fatuous editorial.

In New York the *Wall Street Journal* was appalled at the suggestion
that the USA might enter into some new period of close cooperation
with Britain. 'The United States wants no alliance, or anything that
resembles an alliance, with any other nation,' said the *Journal*; ab-

surdly, in view of what was about to happen in just a couple of years. The rumpus grew so loud that Truman was obliged to give a press conference, at which he weedily denied that Churchill had showed him the speech in advance.

In Moscow there were inevitable denunciations, with Churchill depicted as a crazed hand-grenade-toting warmonger. With his sinister racial theories about the superiority of the 'English-speaking peoples' he was the heir to the Nazis, said *Pravda*—a point explicitly echoed in an interview by Stalin himself.

At Westminster, Tory drips such as Butler (the old appeaser) and Peter Thorneycroft, later Tory Party chairman, used the kerfuffle as an excuse to start briefing against Churchill. 'Winston must go' was the word from the lunch tables. Labour MPs were so scandalised by his red-baiting that they called on Attlee to repudiate the speech, and when Attlee (with typical integrity) refused to do so, they tabled a motion of censure against Churchill, calling the speech 'inimical to the cause of world peace'. Among the ninety-three signatories of this motion was the future Labour Prime Minister James Callaghan.

I have not been able to discover any public act of contrition by Callaghan—but he must surely have eventually realised that he had made a fool of himself, and that Churchill, again, was right.

Within only a couple of years it was obvious that communism in eastern Europe did indeed mean a tyranny. Stalin shut off his dominions from economic integration with western Europe. He blockaded Berlin, and attempted to starve the population into surrender. A new entity was created—the Eastern bloc—in which brutal one-party states were forced to toe the Moscow line, and in which hundreds of thousands were killed or bullied into silence. With his Iron Curtain speech (as it became known) Churchill sketched out the whole moral and strategic framework of the world in which I was born; and it was emphatically not the world he wanted, but the world the Russians, in their paranoia, insisted upon.

Having disowned Churchill after Fulton, Truman saw that he was right—and adopted his famous doctrine of 'containment'. His successor, Dwight D. Eisenhower, was if anything even more hardline against the communists; and by the time Churchill came back to office as Prime Minister, in 1951, he was sufficiently alarmed by the state of global tension—and the new menace of the hydrogen bomb—that it was he, Churchill, who became the peace-monger.

He became obsessed by the idea of a 'summit', a frank and personal exchange of views between America, Russia and Britain (incarnated by himself). If only the world leaders could come together, he said, he was sure that world war could be avoided.

But by now he was seventy-six. He had led his country through five years of war; he had been Leader of the Opposition for six. He had marshalled his parliamentary troops heroically in the run-up to the election—staying up all night for debates, and in the course of the night he would make a series of brilliant little speeches, studded with jokes and sarcastic asides, and then at 7.30 a.m. he would top it all off with a truck driver's breakfast of eggs, bacon, sausages and coffee, followed, as Harold Macmillan noted, by a large whisky and soda and a huge cigar.

These things take their toll. The psychic urge to power was still as strong as ever but the mortal stuff of him was beginning to fail. He suffered from arterial spasms; he had skin irritations and eye complaints. He could no longer hear the voices of children or the call of birds. A splendidly named nerve specialist called Sir Russell Brain said that the reason he suffered from a 'tightness' in the shoulders was that the cells in his brain that received sensory messages from the shoulder were dead.

The story of Churchill's last years in office is not of some giant red sun, heat gone, sinking slowly out of sight. He is no volcano puttering himself to extinction. He is Tennyson's Ulysses—always struggling, striving, seeking: always convinced that some deed of note may yet be done. It is a story of unbelievable courage and willpower—and cunning.

In March 1953 Stalin was dead; Churchill seized the opportunity to call for a new start. I know what, he told Eisenhower: a summit! With the Russians! And let's build on the Anglo-American partnership as the foundation for world peace. Eisenhower wasn't interested.

On 5 June 1953 Winston Churchill sustained a serious stroke. His doctor thought he would die; and yet through sheer force of will he carried on. The following day he insisted on presiding at the cabinet, even though his mouth was twisted and he was finding it difficult to use his left arm. His colleagues didn't even notice that he was ill—just a bit pale and quiet.

The next day he was even worse: his left side was paralysed. He was taken to Chartwell to recover, and the press was given a message that the Prime Minister required a 'complete rest'. No one thought to ask why. A week after the stroke he received his Private Secretary, Jock Colville, and the Cabinet Secretary, Norman Brook. Churchill was in a wheelchair, and after dinner he said he was going to try to stand up. Brook recounted:

> Colville and I urged him not to attempt this, and when he insisted, we came up on either side of him so that we could catch him if he fell. But he waved us away with his stick and told us to stand back. He then lowered his feet to the ground, gripped the arms of his chair, and by a tremendous effort—with sweat pouring down his face—levered himself to his feet and stood

upright. Having demonstrated that he could do this, he sat down again and took up his cigar . . . He was determined to recover.

And he was utterly determined to get his meeting with the Soviets—the nuclear summit at which he could reinsert himself at the head of global events. The Russians were non-committal. Eisenhower was vague. His cabinet colleagues were more or less in a state of mutiny—secretly or openly hoping he would jack it in, and yet fearful of abandoning their talisman, the one British politician to be known around the world.

By 1954 he was under subtle and continuous pressure to go, and though he was capable of astonishing feats of exertion for a stroke victim, he was starting to feel, as he put it, 'like an aeroplane at the end of its flight, in the dusk, with the petrol running out, in search of a safe landing'. Still that plane flew on for almost a year, dodging and weaving through the flak of his enemies (and quite a lot from his friends) until finally, on 5 April 1955, at the age of eighty, he went to the Palace and resigned as Prime Minister.

'Man is spirit', he informed the cabinet at the last meeting, and gave them one piece of advice: 'Never be separated from the Americans.'

The so-called warmonger had spent his last years in office engaged in what was—for him—a futile mission to bring the great powers together and to promote a 'world easement': by which he meant abating what he saw as the unparalleled menace of thermonuclear weapons. And yet that summit did take place—three months after he finally left office, when Eisenhower, Eden, Faure and Bulganin met in Geneva.

Churchill knew instinctively what was wrong with communism—

that it repressed liberty; that it replaced individual discretion with state control; that it entailed the curtailment of democracy, and therefore that it was tyrannous. He also understood that only capitalism, for all its imperfections, was capable of satisfying the wants of human beings.

I am of the generation that saw communism in action, in that we were sometimes able to travel behind the Iron Curtain before 1989—and to see how right he was, in every particular, in that astoundingly prescient speech in Fulton, Missouri. We saw the fear, we heard the whispering, we read the ludicrous propaganda slogans of a failing system that could not supply basic needs, and which controlled the population by taking away the elementary freedom to travel.

Churchill foresaw all that with unerring clarity, just as he had understood the threat from Nazi Germany. He also prophesied that one day the whole thing would collapse—and with unexpected speed. He was right, and we lived to see that moment of joy, too.

OUTSIDE THE CECILIENHOF in Potsdam the sun seems very bright, after the gloom of the conference room. We get on our bikes and cycle through the meadows and gardens by the Wannsee.

I look at the name of the road. Mauerweg, it says. Of course! This is the place where the East German regime constructed the hideous wall that once divided the city, and which was felled in that glorious eruption in 1989. Once it was a symbol of terror and oppression: now there is nothing but a kingly cycle path.

On one side of the path, lounging brazenly in the sun, we suddenly come across a crowd of German nudists: nut-brown old men doing *Junker* calisthenics, young women in pairs communing mystically with nature. It occurs to me how different, in some ways, the Germans must be: this is not the sort of scene, after all, you would expect in Hyde Park on a Sunday afternoon—and we are in the Berlin equivalent. And yet these undraped and obviously defenceless people are the very personification of the pacifism and gentleness of modern Germany.

They vote for whom they choose. They say what they like. They pierce whatever portion of their body they please. They believe in free-market capitalism. They do not fear the knock on the door in the night. Their world has changed since the Wall came down. These sun-worshippers are much more obviously the children of Churchill's ideology than of Stalin's.

Who walked around the White House with no clothes on? I rest my case.

It was his ideas which were to prevail, his concepts of freedom and democracy which won. In that speech at Fulton he helped shape the essential architecture of the post-war world—the transatlantic alliance that in 1948 was to become NATO, and which was integral to the final defeat of communism in Russia and throughout eastern Europe.

He was also one of the very first to articulate an idea that is central to that security architecture—the vision of a reconciled France and Germany, and of a united Europe. That is an idea that remains in some ways exceedingly controversial today; and so is the question of what Churchill really meant by a united Europe, what he intended to happen, and what role he thought Britain would play.

# CHAPTER 20

# CHURCHILL
# THE EUROPEAN

I t is a measure of Churchill's prophetic numen that people will still
try to invoke him as the arbiter of various modern political dilem-
mas. Out of his voluminous sayings a text will be found to legitimate
some opinion or validate some course of action—and that text will be
brandished in a semi-religious way, as though the project had been
posthumously hallowed by Churchill the sage and wartime leader.

There is no question upon which his departed spirit has been
more regularly consulted than the intractable business of Britain's
relations with 'Europe'. It is a controversy that has bedevilled every
one of his successors as Prime Minister. In some cases the problem
has become so toxic as to lead to their political assassination, or attempted assassination.

Revolving as it does around the lofty questions of national sovereignty, democracy and British independence in the face of a great
continental alliance, 'Europe' would seem to be an exquisitely Churchillian dispute: just the sort of thing, you might think, that could be
settled by appeal to the example of the hero of 1940.

The trouble is that he is claimed by both sides. Europhiles and

Euro-sceptics: both factions believe in him. Both factions hail him as their prophet—and sometimes the argument as to his true meaning and intentions takes on the frenzy of a religious schism.

In November 2013, for instance, Manuel Barroso, then President of the EU Commission, made a speech in which he accurately quoted what Churchill had said in 1948 (and earlier, and *passim*) about the need to create a united Europe. This provoked a hail of abuse from the myriad denizens of the Euro-sceptic internet.

Some of them attacked Churchill, in one case calling him a 'fat, lying scumbag'. Some of them defended Churchill, and bashed Senhor Barroso. Perhaps we could sum up the general mood by quoting one of the anonymous Euro-sceptic correspondents, who on one newspaper website, at least, goes by the *nom de guerre* of 'stillpoliticallyincorrect'.

We don't need advice from this second-rate, unelected, unaccountable foreign politician [said stillpoliticallyincorrect of Barroso]. The sooner he is dangling from a Brussels lamp post the better. Why doesn't he clear off back to his own country and stop bossing us about? I hate the man and hope he dies soon, along with the rest of the EU commissars and most MEPs—including all the foreign ones! Then we can chuck out all the scrounging foreigners who have no real right to be here.

Leaving aside the merits of the points he (I bet it's a he) makes, there is a palpable rage here—a choking bile—at the very notion of this Portuguese fellow invoking the memory of Winston Churchill, to justify the programme of European integration.

In the imagination of most such people, Churchill is surely the embodiment of rock-ribbed British bulldoggery and independence. How can he be claimed by the Euro-federalists?

To see the origins of the feud, we need to probe the mind of the man himself, and to understand what he meant by European integration, what he wanted from it—and what role he saw for Britain. Let us go to the famous debate in the early days of June 1950, when the House of Commons is struggling to come to terms with the Schuman Plan—a sudden and audacious offer from the eponymous former French Prime Minister.

The UK has been challenged by France to join talks, with Germany, Italy and Benelux, on creating a new supranational body, to oversee the common European markets in coal and steel. This body will have a High Authority—the embryonic European Commission. It will have an assembly of national parliamentarians and a council of national ministers—the prelude to the eventual European Parliament and Council. It will have a court of justice, the beginnings of the all-powerful European Court in Luxembourg.

Here is Britain, in other words, being asked to assist at the very birth of the European Union. The clay is wet. The mould has yet to set. Now is the moment when Britain could have intervened decisively; accepted the invitation from France—and jointly seized the steering wheel.

Instead, the Labour government is suspicious, if not hostile. Britain is still the biggest coal and steel producer in all Europe—why should these industries submit to some inscrutable system of European control? 'The Durham miners won't wear it,' says one Labour cabinet minister; and so the Attlee government has told the French to hop it.

A letter has been dispatched to M. Schuman, thanking him for his interesting ideas, but politely declining to take part in the talks. In the minds of many on both sides of the English Channel, this is an absolutely critical turning-point in the history of Britain and Europe. This was when we missed the European bus, train, plane, bicycle, etc.

It was to be almost a quarter of a century before Britain finally joined—by which time the structures of the EU had been fixed in a way that was uncongenial to Britain, and to purist concepts of national democratic sovereignty.

What Churchill says now in this debate on the Schuman Plan—as Leader of the Opposition—is clearly vital to an understanding of his instincts. The first thing you notice about his parliamentary performances during this period is that he absolutely fizzes with energy. He is still zapping round the world making enormous, well-thought-out speeches on geopolitics. He is churning out his war memoirs, and indeed he will shortly receive the Nobel prize for literature.

He is almost seventy-five years old, and yet he is making countless interventions in Parliament, virtually every day, on every subject from railway freight charges, to Burma, to Korea, to the fishing industry, to the efficiency of the microphones they have just installed in the House.

It is fascinating to read the Hansard parliamentary record of the Schuman Plan debate, and see that age has done nothing to muffle his general irrepressibility. The Chancellor of the Exchequer is Sir Stafford Cripps (the austere figure ludicrously touted as his rival during the war), and it falls to Cripps to defend the government's negative response to Schuman. Churchill heckles him exuberantly. 'Utter rubbish!' he shouts. 'Nonsense!'

At one point poor Cripps has to ask him to have the politeness to be quiet, or else go and continue his conversation outside—like a badly rattled chemistry teacher confronted by the naughtiest boy in the class. When Churchill stands up to speak at 5.24 p.m., he has heard a debate that is virtually identical to the European debate today.

Labour Euro-sceptic MPs have denounced the suggestion that this 'High Authority' could have some bureaucratic control of the emerging common market, and that they could act without the strict approval of national governments. Who are these people? asks one Labour MP. What right would they have to tell us what to do?

'They would be an oligarchy imposed on Europe, an oligarchy which, with arbitrary power and with enormous influence, would be able to affect the lives of every person in this country.' There speaks the voice of the British Euro-sceptic, in words that might equally be used of M. Juncker and the EU Commission today.

To all of which the Tory Europhiles have responded, on this afternoon in 1950, with arguments that have become equally traditional.

'Do we really want to be isolated?' asks Bob Boothby, Churchill's former PPS. 'When all is said and done, unbridled national sovereignty remains the prime cause of the hideous disasters that have befallen us in this nightmare century.' Boothby ends by urging his Right Honourable Friend—Churchill—to lead the way and save western Europe for a second time, by helping the creation of a united Europe.

It is time for the Leader of the Opposition to sum up. Which side will he come down on? Churchill begins safely enough. He attacks the Attlee government for their incompetence: the French would never have been so rude as to spring this on us unawares if he had been Prime Minister, says Churchill. But on the key question, he soon makes himself clear. Yes, he thinks Britain should be there at the Schuman talks, and he lays into Attlee for his failure of leadership.

'He seeks to win for himself and his party popular applause by strutting around as a Palmerstonian jingo,' says Churchill, adopting the usual line of attack upon all British prime ministers who have sought in some way to distance Britain from the European project. Then he essentially takes Boothby's line: that Britain should not be left out.

... It will be far better for us to take part in the discussions than to stand outside and let events drift without us . . . The French have a saying: '*Les absents ont toujours tort*'. I do not know whether they learn French at Winchester [this is presumably a joke at the expense of Richard Crossman, the intellectual Labour MP, who has just made an anti-European speech] . . . The absence of Britain deranges the balance of Europe . . .

. . . and so on.

If Britain fails to engage, he warns, then there is a risk that the European bloc will become a neutral force, equidistant between Moscow and Washington; and that, he believes, would be a disaster. Would Britain have accepted Schuman's invitation, if he had been Prime Minister? Yes, is the resounding answer.

He addresses full-on the basic question of sovereignty, and he ends the speech with typical Churchillian internationalism. He makes the classic argument of the British Europhile: that the UK already shares sovereignty over defence with NATO and with America. Why should it be so unthinkable to share sovereignty with Europe?

The whole movement of the world is towards an interdependence of nations. We feel all around us the belief that it is our best hope. If independent, individual sovereignty is sacrosanct and inviolable, how is it that we are all wedded to a world organisation? It is an ideal to which we must subscribe. How is it that we have undertaken this immense obligation for the defence of Western Europe, involving ourselves as we have never done before in the fortunes of countries not protected by the waves and tides of the Channel? How is it that we accepted, and under the present Government eagerly sought, to live upon the bounty of the United States, thus becoming financially dependent upon them? It can only be justified and even tolerated because on either side of the Atlantic it is felt that inter-dependence is part of our faith and the means of our salvation . . .

. . . Nay, I will go further and say that for the sake of world organisation we would even run risks and make sacrifices. We fought alone against tyranny for a whole year, not purely from national motives. It is true that our lives depended upon our doing so, but we fought the better because we felt with conviction that it was not only our own cause but a world cause for which the Union Jack was kept flying in 1940 and 1941. The soldier who laid down his life, the mother who wept for her son, and the wife who lost her husband, got inspiration or comfort, and felt a sense of being linked with the universal and the eternal by the fact that we fought for what was precious not only for ourselves but for mankind. The Conservative and Liberal Parties declare that national sovereignty is not inviolable, and that it may be resolutely diminished for the sake of all the men in all the lands finding their way home together.

It is this sort of text which has been taken up and waved around as proof that Churchill was a rampant federalist—a believer in a United States of Europe. There is plenty more. He first seems to have articulated a vision of European union in 1930, after he had been travelling in the USA—and been much struck by the lack of borders and tariffs, and the way a single market helped economic growth. He wrote an article called 'A United States of Europe'; indeed, he is credited with coining the phrase.

In October 1942, in the depths of the war, he wrote a letter to Anthony Eden, in which he sketched out a vision for the post-war world. The best hope was a 'United States of Europe', excluding Russia, in which the barriers between the nations of Europe would 'be minimised and unrestricted travel will be possible'. After the war he made a series of rhapsodical speeches about this union of Gaul and Teuton, the foundation of the Temple of Peace, and so on.

At Zurich in 1946, Churchill said,

> We must build a kind of United States of Europe . . . The structure of the United States of Europe, if well and truly built, will be such as to make the material strength of a single state less important . . . If at first all the States of Europe are not willing or able to join the Union, we must nevertheless proceed to assemble and combine those who will and those who can.

But who were these states? Did he think that Britain should be part of it? Sometimes it seems that he did. In May 1947 he gave a speech at London's Albert Hall—addressing the crowd as the Chairman and Founder of the United Europe Movement, to 'present the idea of a United Europe in which our country will play a decisive part'. He concluded with what looks like an unmistakable commitment that 'Britain will have to play her full part as a member of the European family'.

By May 1950 he was making a speech in Scotland, and claiming credit for the very genesis of the Schuman Plan; and again he seems clear that Britain must be part of the programme.

> For more than forty years I have worked with France. At Zurich I appealed to her to regain the leadership of Europe by extending her hand to bring Germany back into the European family. We have now the proposal which M. Schuman, the French Foreign Minister, has made for the integration of French and

German coal and steel industries. This would be an important and effective step in preventing another war between France and Germany and lay at last to rest that quarrel of 1,000 years between Gaul and Teuton. Now France has taken the initiative in a manner beyond my hopes. But that by itself would not be enough. In order to make France able to deal on proper terms with Germany, we must be with France. The prime condition for the recovery of Europe is Britain and France standing together with all their strength and with all their wounds; and then these two nations offering their hands to Germany on honourable terms and with a great and merciful desire to look forward rather than back. For centuries France and England, and latterly Germany and France, have rent the world by their struggles. They have only to be united together to constitute the dominant force in the Old World and to become the centre of United Europe around which all other countries could rally. But added to this you have all the mighty approval of the great world power which has arisen across the Atlantic, and has shown itself in its hour of supremacy anxious only to make further sacrifices for the cause of freedom.

A united Europe, in other words, is not only good for France and Germany and Britain: it's what America wants, too.

I could cite other texts, from other speeches—at Brussels, Strasbourg, The Hague (many of them ending in tears from Churchill, ovations from his continental audiences, and at least one of them delivered in his own superb version of French); but I hope the point is nearly made. If you close one eye, and you listen with only half an ear, you can understand why Churchill is one of the presiding divinities of the European Union.

He is up there on his couch in the Euro-Olympus—alongside

European Union architects Monnet, Schuman, Spaak, De Gasperi—with Common Agricultural Policy grapes being dangled into his mouth. No wonder he has roundabouts and avenues named after him in Brussels; and no wonder you will find his face on the walls of the Strasbourg Euro-parliament.

So much for the case that Churchill was a visionary founder of the movement for a united Europe. It contains a very large dollop of truth. It is also true that he believed Britain should play a leading role in this process of unification. It is not, however, by any means the whole story, as the Euro-sceptics know full well.

That is what makes them so furious—because they, too, can point to Churchillian texts that plainly offer a different vision for Britain and the rest of the united Europe. Right back there in 1930, when he first had his brainwave about imitating America and creating a single European market, he entered this crucial reservation about his own country.

> But we have our own dream and our own task. We are with Europe, but not of it. We are linked, but not comprised. We are interested and associated but not absorbed. And should European statesmen address us in the words that were used of old: 'wouldest thou be spoken for to the King, or the Captain of the Host?', we should reply with the Shunammite woman, 'I dwell among my own people'.

Sometimes this is a little bit misquoted, for the sake of emphasis, and the words 'Nay, sir,' are put first into the mouth of the Shunammite woman—a rich lady who used to provide a spare room for the prophet Elisha; though not even the prophet Elisha could have prophesied that his generous female friend was to become most famous as the world's first British Euro-sceptic.

But the point stands. Churchill saw Britain as somehow dwelling apart from the European congeries; and in the course of one of his many bust-ups with General de Gaulle, he said that if Britain had to choose between Europe and the open sea, she would always choose the open sea.

In Churchill's universe, Britain was of course a European power—perhaps the greatest European power. But that was not the limit of her global role. Yes, he wanted a united Europe, and yes, he saw that Britain had an important role to help bring about that happy union—upon a continent that had seen such misery. But his role was to be a sponsor, a witness, rather than a contracting party.

Britain was certainly meant to be there in the body of the church, but as an usher or even as the priest rather than one of the partners in the actual marriage. If you want proof that he never saw Britain as a part of that federal union, it is there in his actions. It was only a few months after that 1950 debate on the Schuman Plan that he again became Prime Minister. If he had really wanted Britain to join the Coal and Steel Community, he could surely have entered an application then. He had the prestige; he had the support from men such as Macmillan and Boothby and the young Edward Heath, who made his maiden speech in that debate, with a powerful call for participation in the plan.

Some say Churchill effectively did a U-turn on gaining power, and dropped his fervent Europeanism as soon as it was obvious that it wasn't so popular with Anthony Eden and other Tories. On this analysis, there is a touch of the John Major about Churchill—trimming to appease the Euro-sceptics. I don't think this does justice to him, or to his vision. Go back to that crucial speech to the Commons of 27 June 1950, where he sets out his European views in full.

He comes to the nub of our anxieties today: the precise role of Britain.

. . . The question that we have to decide for ourselves—and there is certainly plenty of time for mature consideration of it—is, what association should Britain have with the Federal Union of Europe if such a thing should come to pass in the course of time?

It has not got to be decided today, but I shall give, with all humility, a plain answer. I cannot conceive that Britain would be an ordinary member of a Federal Union limited to Europe in any period which can at present be foreseen. We should in my opinion favour and help forward all developments on the Continent which arise naturally from a removal of barriers, from the process of reconciliation, and blessed oblivion of the terrible past, and also from our common dangers in the future and present. Although a hard-and-fast concrete federal constitution for Europe is not within the scope of practical affairs, we should help, sponsor and aid in every possible way the movement towards European unity. We should seek steadfastly for means to become intimately associated with it.

There you go: he wants the UK to be 'intimately associated' but cannot conceive that Britain will be 'an ordinary member'. There was no U-turn; there was no flip-flop. That was exactly the policy that he took with him into government.

It is not that he is against Europe, or inherently hostile to any continental power. On the contrary, he loved France with a passion, and was perhaps the most uninhibitedly Francophile prime minister Britain has ever had. It is just that he had an idea of Britain that transcended Europe, and which involved keeping Britain turned to face the rest of the world.

In this he was remarkably consistent all his political life. He ended his 1930 article with a vision for Britain as the intersecting set in a

three-circle Venn diagram. 'Great Britain may claim, with equal jus-
tification, to play three roles simultaneously, that of an European
nation, that of the focus of the British Empire, and that of a partner
in the English speaking world. These are not three alternative parts,
but a triple part . . .'

The empire has long gone, but the promiscuous internationalism
of the approach seems ever more sensible today. In a world where the
EU's share of global GDP is steadily diminishing, where the USA remains the world's largest economy, and where there is startling
growth in former Commonwealth countries, Churchill's circles are
still a reasonable way to look at Britain's place and role.

It is hard to know how Churchill would have handled the Schuman
Plan, if he had won the 1945 election. But one thing we can be sure
of: he would never have made Labour's mistake. He would certainly
have been there. Perhaps with his fearsome energy in debate, he
might have persuaded the other Europeans to go for an intergovern-
mental approach—dropping the idea, which remains so difficult and
occasionally so infuriating to this day, that national and democrati-
cally elected governments can be routinely overruled by a 'supranational' body.

If Churchill had been in power in 1948; if he had insisted on
being at the table; if the Churchill Factor had been at work in those
very early European talks—who knows, we might have a different
model of the EU today; more Anglo-Saxon, more democratic.

By 1950 it was probably already too late. Yes, Labour missed the
boat—and that was a mistake. But the truth is that Monnet and
Schuman didn't really want Britain at the table: otherwise they would
have given London a reasonable time to respond, rather than convening the talks at such breakneck speed, and they would not have
made agreement to supranationalism a condition of taking part.

When Churchill looked at what was unfolding in Europe in the

1950s, he didn't have any particular feeling of rancour, or regret, or exclusion. On the contrary, he looked at the developing plans for a common market with a paternal pride. It was his idea to bring these countries together, to bind them so indissolubly that they could never go to war again—and who can deny, today, that this idea has been a spectacular success?

Together with NATO (another institution for which he can claim joint credit) the European Community, now Union, has helped to deliver a period of peace and prosperity for its people as long as any since the days of the Antonine emperors. That is not to deny the many inadequacies and excesses of the system. Nor is it to minimise the strain—clearly foreseen by Churchill in 1950—of incorporating an ancient and proud democracy such as Britain into a type of 'supranational' government.

What would he have done today? What would he have made of the euro? What would he have thought of the working time directive? What would he have said about the Common Agricultural Policy? In a sense all these questions are absurd.

We cannot tax the great man in this querulous way. He cannot hear us. The oracle is dumb.

What we can do is examine his considerable and notably consistent body of thinking on this kind of question, and adduce some general principles.

He would have wanted a union between France and Germany as long as there was the slightest risk of conflict, and as a lifelong liberal free marketeer he would have supported free trade across a giant tariff-free zone.

He would have wanted the European organisation to be strongly and closely allied to America, with Britain actively helping to cement the relationship.

He would have seen the importance of that united Europe as a bulwark against an assertive Russia and other potential external threats.

He would have wanted to be personally involved at the head-of-government level. Knowing him as we do, it is impossible to imagine him allowing an important summit of world leaders to take place without him.

He would want as far as he possibly could to protect the sovereignty of the House of Commons, the democracy that he defended and that he served all his life.

On the evening of 5 March 1917, he left a darkened Commons Chamber in the company of Alexander MacCallum Scott, a Liberal MP. He turned and said: 'Look at it. This little place is what makes the difference between us and Germany. It is in virtue of this that we shall muddle through to success & for lack of this Germany's brilliant efficiency leads her to final disaster.'

Of course those desiderata now look self-contradictory. But if Churchill had been spared by the electorate in 1945—if he had helped paint the fresco when the plaster was still wet on the wall—then it seems possible that those contradictions would never have arisen.

Churchill's legacy on the continent of Europe is phenomenal and benign. Whatever exact role he meant Britain to play, he was one of those who created a seventy-year era in which there has been no war in western Europe—and the very idea seems ever more absurd.

And the impact of Churchill is felt to this day in places far beyond Europe—and many would say for the better.

# CHAPTER 21

# MAKER OF
# THE MODERN
# MIDDLE EAST

I n her heyday, the pleasure yacht *Christina* was the most ostenta-
tiously opulent if not downright vulgar private boat that had ever
floated on the sea. She had Impressionists on the wall and live lob-
sters in the pool and barstools upholstered with leather diligently
harvested from the foreskins of whales. But of all the exotic items
assembled by Aristotle Onassis, the most important were his guests—
prize lepidoptera that he caught in his gossamer net.

You might find Marilyn Monroe on board; or Frank Sinatra or
Elizabeth Taylor or Richard Burton—all toasting each other at the
taffrail and draping themselves over the deckchairs before going
off for whispering marital fisticuffs in the staterooms. Of all the
global superstars that Ari assembled, there was one who outshone
the rest; and on the morning of 11 April 1961, he had the proof of
his renown.

The white-hulled, yellow-funnelled *Christina*—in fact a converted
Canadian naval vessel that had been present at the Normandy

landings—had nosed up the Hudson River, towards her mooring point on 79th Street. There was an aquatic festival of welcome. There were blasts from liners and toots from tugs, and a New York fireboat joyfully ejaculated a jet of water to mark the arrival of the most popular Briton in America (the Beatles being still a couple of years away).

Now it was getting on for dinner time on the same day. With the help of two strong maids the eighty-six-year-old Winston Churchill was making his way down the deck. He had sustained another small stroke; his dentition was wonky. But his face was as cherubic as ever. His rheumy eyes were bright, his spotty bow tie was around his neck. He tapped over the polished boards with the same gold-topped cane that Edward VII had given him for his wedding in 1908, and there flickered within him the same old enthusiasm at the prospect of a meal and a spot of alcoholic refreshment.

It was true that he did not always find it easy to make conversation with Onassis, the Smyrna-born shipping tycoon, with his tales of the 'sons of bitches' who were interfering with his casinos. But then Churchill didn't mind much about that. In 1911 he had endured a six-week cruise with H. H. Asquith to the Mediterranean, during which he was heard to grunt that he had been asked to inspect too many ancient ruins. At least Onassis didn't make him feel bad about his relative lack of a classical education.

No, he liked the sensations of the cruise: the cosseting, the travel, the endless diversions—the landscapes and seascapes; and now he looked out at a scene he had first clapped eyes on in 1895—a lifetime away—when he had come as a twenty-year-old to stay with his mother's friend, Bourke Cockran, and learn his secrets of oratory.

When he had first seen New York it was physically a humbler place. There were some largish and handsome brick buildings, and there was all kinds of bustle, and smoke billowing from a thousand chimneys—and yet there were children in rags, and immigrant slums where the bodies of horses might lie in the streets for days. It was a city of energy and ambition, yes, but built on much the same sort of scale as late nineteenth-century Manchester or Liverpool or Glasgow. When Churchill first saw it, the skyline wasn't a patch on London.

Now, though, as he stood in the darkness in 1961, looking out at Manhattan, the transformation was enough to make him blink. The buildings had sprouted to undreamt-of heights, spindles and spires of glass and steel, and their reflections twinkled towards him on the water with the light of a million windows. It was London that now looked dowdy, and dingy, and a shade undernourished.

This New York skyline was the embodiment of the change he had seen in his lifetime, and over which he had very largely officiated. These skyscrapers were not just a new template for urban life: they represented the twentieth-century story of America's rise to greatness, and her eclipse of Britain. In his famous Mansion House speech of 1942, Churchill said he had not become the King's first minister in order to preside over the liquidation of the British Empire. And yet that, pretty much, was how things had panned out.

He felt it keenly. There is a sense in which Churchill's obsessive references to the triumph of the 'English-speaking peoples' were not just about ensuring a vital military and political Anglo-American alliance, though that was one of his purposes. They were also a psychological trick, a self-defence mechanism. The phrase was a way of masking and rationalising the humiliation of Britain's position. Britain had declined in relative importance; but that decline was salved by the rise of those close cousins, those fellow-English-speakers who shared, as he constantly pointed out, the same values: the language, democracy, free speech, independent judiciary and so on.

It was as though Churchill was trying to persuade himself (and the world) that the American triumph was somehow also a British triumph, and that the glory of these former colonies reflected on the mother country. It is valiant stuff, and of course not everyone sees it that way.

Many people might say that the story of Churchill's life was in part the *translatio imperii*—the passing of one global empire to another. As the Persians gave way to the Greeks, and the Greeks to the Romans, so the British had handed the imperial torch on to the Americans. It was A. J. P. Taylor who once said that the Second World War was 'the war of the British succession'—and if you accept that analysis it is obvious who won; and seventy years later it is astonishing to see that America, militarily, politically, economically, is still the most power-ful nation on earth.

During the meal that night on the *Christina*, a mysterious phone call came through for Sir Winston. His Private Secretary, Anthony Montague Browne, was asked to dial 'Operator 17' at the White House. It was the new President, John F. Kennedy, wondering whether Churchill would like to get in the presidential plane and come down to Washington—'to spend a couple of days' with JFK. Browne had to think quickly, and he decided to thank the President very much for his kind offer, but to say no. Churchill just wasn't mobile enough, and he was increasingly deaf.

It was perhaps a shame that they didn't meet, because Churchill still had passages of vigour and lucidity. They had met already, but before Kennedy was elected—once aboard the *Christina* when eyewit-nesses said he seemed to mistake the clean-cut Kennedy for a waiter, and once when they had a very friendly conversation about the young senator's presidential ambitions (Kennedy said he was worried about being a Catholic; Churchill said he could always sort that out and remain a good Christian). This was Churchill's last chance to sit in the Oval Office and meet a serving US President—and he had met most of them from William McKinley in 1900 onwards.

Here was Kennedy, the leader of the 'Free World'; here was

Churchill, physically bowed but with the vital spark still occasionally gleaming. Perhaps there was some hint that the old empire might have been able to pass to the new—because the problems confronting John F. Kennedy were certainly familiar to Churchill.

It was Churchill who pioneered the architecture of the Cold War, and the policy of standing up to Soviet communism. Now that policy was to be aggressively taken up by the young President: in Berlin, Cuba, and elsewhere. Churchill had been in the vanguard of the movement for a united Europe—a cause still supported by the USA and by Kennedy. Then there was a whole arena of geopolitics where the Americans were obliged to take up the imperial purple, after Britain had faltered after the war, and then collapsed at Suez. It is an arena where Churchill's role is now only hazily remembered; and yet it was critical.

Winston Churchill was one of the fathers of the modern Middle East. There is therefore at least a case for thinking that he helped create the world's number-one political disaster zone, and then passed that disaster zone on, like a cupful of quivering gelignite, to be the responsibility of America. It was John F. Kennedy who first provided the American security guarantee for Israel. There are many who would blame the British—and Churchill prime among them—for creating the territorial incoherencies that made that guarantee necessary. Was he guilty? If not, whom do we blame?

As I write these words today, Israel is bombing the positions of Arabs in Gaza; Hamas is firing rockets at Israel; the casualties in Syria mount higher and higher; fundamentalist fanatics have captured large parts of northern Iraq. Churchill's fingerprints are over the entire map.

Have a look at that map of Jordan—what do you see? The most striking feature is that weird triangular kink, a 400-mile salient from Saudi Arabia into modern Jordan. Some say that this fact of geography can be traced to one of Churchill's liquid lunches, and to this day it is called 'Winston's hiccup'. That story may or may not be true. What no one contests is Churchill's role in drawing that boundary. Kinky or not, it has lasted from that day to this.

He was integral to the creation of the modern state of Israel; and it fell to him, at the formative moment in the emergence of that nation, to try to make sense of the abjectly inconsistent commitments of the British government. He was the man who decided that there should be such a thing as the state of Iraq; it was he who bundled together the three Ottoman vilayets of Basra, Baghdad and Mosul—Shiite, Sunni and Kurd. If you wanted to put a single man in the frame for the agony of modern Iraq, if you wanted to blame anyone for the current implosion, then of course you might point the finger at George W. Bush and Tony Blair and Saddam Hussein—but if you wanted to grasp the essence of the problem of that wretched state, you would have to look at the role of Winston Churchill.

His epic career intersected with the Middle East at several key points (and remember that he is credited with pioneering the very term Middle East); but the most important was his role as Colonial Secretary. He was a little surprised to be offered the post, at the end of 1920; but it is easy to see why Lloyd George thought he was the right man for the job. He had shown immense energy and dynamism as Minister for Munitions—equipping Britain with the tanks, planes and other technology that helped win the war. As Secretary of State for War he had been masterly in his demobilisation strategy: quelling mutinies by ensuring that those who had served the longest were the first to be reunited with their families. He had shown his gifts of charm and persuasion in the pre-war Ulster talks—and those gifts would be needed in spades. The First World War had left some snortingly difficult problems, and especially in the Middle East.

———

THE POST OF Colonial Secretary might sound less grand than that of Foreign Secretary—a role still occupied by that most superior person, George Nathaniel Curzon. But that is to forget the scale of the British Empire in 1921. The First World War was not meant to be an acquisitive conflict; Britain went in with the explicit aim of *not* expanding her empire. But as Walter Reid has pointed out, between 1914 and 1919 the surface area of the world ruled by Britain expanded by 9 per cent.

When Churchill took the reins at the Colonial Office, he was at the apex of an empire that comprised fifty-eight countries covering 14 million square miles and he was responsible—one way or another—for the lives and hopes of 458 million people. It was by far the biggest empire the world has ever seen—six times the size of the Roman Empire at its apogee under Trajan. The British flag flew over a quarter of the land surface of the planet, and there was scarcely a sea or ocean that was not patrolled by the might of the British navy—a navy much modernised and improved by Churchill.

When you think about it that way, it is perhaps less surprising that Churchill threw himself into the job. He surrounded himself with the best and most famous experts, notably the Arabists T. E. Lawrence and Gertrude Bell. He boned up on such hitherto abstruse matters (to him) as the difference between Shia and Sunni. His first step was to summon a conference, at Cairo; and here he conducted himself with dazzling skill.

The press was sceptical about this venture. It was said that Churchill wanted a 'durbar'—a magnificent and ceremonial gathering of the imperial court. He was accused of wanting to govern 'on an oriental scale'. The truth was that someone had to take charge, because the situation in the Middle East was a total and utter shambles.

With the best possible intentions and motives, Britain had made a series of promises during the First World War, and those promises were now proving difficult to square with each other and indeed with reality. Perhaps it is a mitigation to say that they were made by a country in desperate straits, and with a population at risk of starvation from the German submarine campaign.

There were three British promises. The first was to the Arabs, in the form of the 1915 McMahon–Hussein correspondence. This was a series of fairly oleaginous letters from Sir Henry McMahon, British high commissioner in Egypt, to the Hashemite King Hussein—a bearded old worthy whose family claimed to be of the lineage of the prophet Mohammed. The gist of the letters was that the British government was all in favour of a big new Arab state—stretching from Palestine to Iraq and to the borders with Persia, with Hussein and his family on the throne; and the hope was that this promise would encourage the Arabs to revolt against the Turks, who were then allied with the Germans. The letters worked, in the sense that there was indeed such a revolt, a strategically piffling affair immortalised and wildly exaggerated in the film *Lawrence of Arabia*.

The next promise was to the French, who had been suffering appalling casualties on the Western Front. It was thought politic to paint them a picture of future French glory, once the war was over: and under the terms of the secret 1916 Sykes–Picot agreement, France was to have a zone of influence stretching from Syria to northern Iraq and including Baghdad—a strip of land, incidentally, that bears some resemblance to the 'caliphate' proclaimed in 2014 by the fanatics of the Islamic State of Iraq and Syria (ISIS). It was not at all clear how this secret undertaking to the French could be reconciled with the more public undertaking to the Arabs—and nor, frankly, was it capable of being so reconciled.

The third and most tragicomically incoherent promise of all was the so-called Balfour declaration. This was really a letter from A. J. Balfour to Lord Rothschild, dated 2 November 1917, and contained this exquisite masterpiece of Foreign Office fudgerama . . .

> His Majesty's government view with favour the establishment in Palestine of a national home for the Jewish people, and will use their best endeavours to facilitate the achievement of this object, it being clearly understood that nothing shall be done which may prejudice the civil and religious rights of existing non-Jewish communities in Palestine, or the rights and political status enjoyed by Jews in any other country.

Another way of putting it might have been that the British government viewed with favour the eating of a piece of cake by the Jewish people, provided nothing should be done to prejudice the rights of non-Jewish communities to eat the same piece of cake at the same time.

What prompted this bizarre declaration? Partly it was idealism. Ever since the vile pogroms in nineteenth-century Russia there had been a growing movement to find a homeland for the Jews. At one stage the British had even toyed with finding some space in Uganda; but Palestine, the land of the Hebrew Old Testament, was the obvious place. Palestine was still relatively underpopulated; and to some extent Balfour was merely adding the official British voice to the chorus that wanted to give 'a land without a people to a people without a land'.

Balfour may also have been moved by a more practical consideration: there was much anxiety in the First World War that Jewish sympathy might be inclined towards the Germans, because that was the best way of paying back the Russians for their anti-Semitism before the war. As Churchill himself later admitted, the Balfour declaration was partly intended to shore up Jewish support, especially in America—and its manifest muddle arose from the countervailing desire not to alienate the many millions of Muslims (not least in India) upon whose troops the British imperial forces relied.

Look at these three promises together, and there is no doubt about it: Britain had sold the same camel three times.

This was the mess that Churchill had to clear up, and in March 1921 he summoned all the key players to the splendour of the Semi-ramis Hotel in Cairo—then also, of course, an informal part of the British Empire. Soon the lobby echoed to the calls of Arabists in states of excitement.

'Gertie!' cried T. E. Lawrence, as he spotted the elegant but man-nish figure of Gertrude Bell.

'Dear boy!' said Gertrude Bell.

Churchill marched in, to cries of protest from a few Arabs outside, some of them carrying placards saying 'a bas Churchill'. He was holding an easel and followed by a member of staff carrying a bottle of wine in a bucket.

He established himself in the garden and began a spurt of cre-ative activity that was to produce enough paintings for him to hold an exhibition; but the biggest and most dramatic canvas of all was the political landscape of the Middle East.

At some point in the proceedings he organised a trip to see the Pyramids, and the entire party posed on camels in front of the Sphinx. Although he was an accomplished rider, Churchill managed to slip off the camel's hump. Thinking that their principal tourist was at risk, the dragoman offered him a horse instead.

'I've started on a camel, and I will finish on a camel,' he said, and there we see him today, firmly in the saddle—as he was throughout proceedings.

By the end of the Cairo conference he had gone some way to

making sense of the McMahon–Hussein letters. Of the four sons of King Hussein, Faisal was given the throne of Iraq (the French having chucked him out of Syria) and Abdullah was given the throne of Transjordan, now Jordan—where his family remains ensconced. T. E. Lawrence thought the summit was an outstanding success, and eleven years later he wrote to Churchill to point out that it had already delivered more than a decade of peace: not bad going.

Churchill's work was not done. Now he had to see whether he could massage away the inconsistencies of the Balfour declaration. The next stop was Jerusalem, where he conducted sessions of Solomon-like wisdom and impartiality.

He held two consecutive audiences, first with the Arabs and then with the Jews. The first group in to see him was the 'Executive Committee of the Arab Palestine Congress'. They did not make a good impression on Churchill; and it should be remembered that he already harboured the feeling that the Palestinians had failed to join the other Arabs in the revolt against the Turks.

The gist of the Palestinians' case was that the Jews should hop it. The Balfour declaration should be annulled. 'The Jews have been among the most active advocates of destruction in many lands . . . The Jew is clannish and unneighbourly, and cannot mix with those who live about him . . . the Jew is a Jew all the world over', and so on. They gave no sign of being willing to compromise, or to come to any sort of accommodation with the settlers. A condominium, shared rule, joint sovereignty, a federal solution—none of it was acceptable. Jews out, they said. As Abba Eban was later to say, the Palestinians never miss an opportunity to miss an opportunity, and they started as they meant to go on.

Churchill listened carefully, and then responded with practical advice. He stressed the two sides of the Balfour declaration—the protection that it afforded to the civil and political rights of the existing peoples. He noted that the declaration referred to 'a' national home for the Jews, rather than 'the' national home, with the indefinite article giving the suggestion that this was to be a shared abode and not exclusively Jewish property.

'If one promise stands, so does the other, and we shall be judged as we faithfully fulfil both,' he told them. But there could be no getting round the substance of what Balfour had promised the Jewish people, he said.

It was a declaration made while the war was still in progress, while victory and defeat hung in the balance. It must therefore be regarded as one of the facts definitely established by the triumphant conclusion of the Great War . . . Moreover it is manifestly right that the Jews, who are scattered all over the world, should have a national centre and a National Home where some of them may be reunited. And where else could that be but in this land of Palestine, with which for more than three thousand years they have been profoundly and intimately associated?

He then heard from the Jewish deputation. Their speech, as you might perhaps expect, was couched in words much more calculated to appeal to Winston Churchill.

' . . . Our Jewish and Zionist programme lays special stress on the establishing of sincere friendship between ourselves and the Arabs. The Jewish people returning after 2000 years of exile and persecution, to its homeland, cannot suffer the suspicion that it wishes to deny another nation its rights . . .'

Churchill replied gravely, with the tones of a Roman proconsul arbitrating in a dispute. One tribe might be more advanced, more civilised—but they had a duty to those unrulier tribes that faced the prospect of dispossession. The Jewish settlers must show 'prudence' and 'patience', he warned. They must allay the alarm of others, no matter how unjustified that alarm might be.

Later, in a speech at the Hebrew University, he repeated his message. The Jews had a great responsibility, he said. They had indeed the chance to create a land flowing with milk and honey. But he warned them that 'every step you take must therefore be for the moral and material benefit of all Palestinians'.

He was then given a symbolic tree to plant. Symbolically, it broke. There was nothing else to plant except a palm, and the sapling did not flourish.

There are those who say that Churchill was naive in his handling of the Arab–Jewish question, some that he was positively disingenuous. In March 1921 he took the crucial decision that the west bank of the Jordan was emphatically outside the terms of the McMahon–Hussein promises. It was not to be part of the Kingdom of Abdullah, the son of Hussein.

This was the beginning of the creation of that Jewish homeland promised by Balfour—and in taking that step there have been plenty of people who have accused Churchill of being a tool of the great global Jewish conspiracy.

There are loonies out there who will tell you that Churchill's mother Jennie Jerome was of Jewish stock (she wasn't; her father was descended from Huguenots. She may have been partly Native American, but she wasn't Jewish). A little more plausibly, they will tell you that his views were warped by the very substantial donations he received from Jewish bankers and financiers: Ernest Cassel, Sir Henry Strakosch, Bernard Baruch. It is perfectly true that Churchill's personal finances would not today pass the *Private Eye* test. They would not look good if splashed on the front page of the *Guardian*. He did indeed take money from these men, sometimes in considerable sums.

But those were very different times, when parliamentarians and ministers were paid much less—and expected to have a private income—and it was by no means unusual for politicians to receive financial support from their admirers.

As it happens, I don't think these donations made a bean of difference to Churchill's views about Jewry, nor to his decisions about Palestine. He was basically philo-Semitic, like his father Randolph, and had been all his life. He admired the Jewish characteristics that he shared in such abundance—energy, self-reliance, hard work, family life.

As he wrote in a newspaper article in 1920, 'Some people like the Jews and some do not, but no thoughtful man can doubt the fact that they are beyond all question the most formidable and the most remarkable race which has ever appeared in the world.' He has from time to time been accused of adopting some off-colour sentiments—such as in an unpublished article in which he seems to suggest that Jewish people may be partly responsible for some of the resentment they inspire, and the feeling that they are 'Hebrew bloodsuckers'. But the authorship of the article is contested (a ghostly hand alleged) and it is surely important that it was never published.

As Sir Martin Gilbert has demonstrated beyond the slightest doubt, Churchill admired Jews, employed Jews, enjoyed the company of Jews, and believed in a Jewish homeland. He was not a Zionist, he once said, but he was 'wedded to Zionism'.

All that is true. On the other hand, it does not mean that Churchill was in any sense anti-Arab, let alone anti-Muslim. Indeed, there were times both in 1904 and in the 1920s when his general 'tendency to orientalism' encouraged him to join Wilfrid Scawen Blunt in actually wearing Arab-style robes. He hero-worshipped the head-dress-sporting Lawrence of Arabia, and as Warren Dockter points out in his new survey, *Winston Churchill and the Islamic World*, he was always mindful that the British Empire was the greatest Muslim power on earth: the home in 1920 of 87 million Muslims.

He inveighed against the loss of India not just because of the blow to British prestige, but also because he worried about future Hindu oppression of the Muslims; and since Muslim troops were invaluable for the empire, Muslim goodwill was vital. He tended to side with the Turks over the Greeks, even though the Turks had been his opponents in the First World War.

Remember what he did in the depths of 1940, when Britain was most desperate for friends: he found £100,000 to build the Regent's Park mosque in London—a gesture that was intended to be noted in the Muslim world.

So when Churchill paved the way for Jewish entry to Palestine—and his 1922 White Paper encouraged more immigration—it was because he genuinely believed that it would be the best thing for that otherwise arid and neglected part of the world, and that it would be the best thing for both communities. He saw Jew and Arab living side by side.

He imagined the technically expert Schlomo giving eager young Mohammed a hand with his tractor, and teaching him the art of irrigation. He saw orchards blossoming over the desert, and prosperity for all. Indeed, he had some support for this vision from the old King Hussein himself, who wrote in his publication *al-Qibla* that Palestine was a 'sacred and beloved homeland of its original sons—the Jews'. The Hashemite King went on to make precisely the same starry-eyed prediction as Churchill.

'Experience has proved their capacity to succeed in their energies and their labours . . . The return of these exiles to their homeland will prove materially and spiritually an experimental school for their Arab brethren in the field, factories and trade.' Alas, things did not work out that way. As the years rolled on, tensions got worse;

Jewish immigration increased, especially as the Nazi persecutions began.

As it turned out, Churchill was too optimistic about the caring, sharing spirit of the early Zionists. They did not tend to employ Arabs on their farms. There were Arab riots and protests, and the poor soldiers of the British mandate were caught in the middle, driven to shoot Arabs—when many in Britain were starting to feel that a serious injustice was being done.

In 1937 the position had got so bad that it was decided to set up the Peel Commission, to understand what had gone wrong in Palestine. Churchill gave some secret testimony to that Commission—and here we can see exactly what he imagined he was doing when he opened the door to substantial Jewish immigration, and created that homeland on the west bank of the Jordan.

' . . . We committed ourselves to the idea that some day, somehow, far off in the future, subject to justice and economic convenience, there might well be a great Jewish state there, numbered by millions, far exceeding the present inhabitants of the country . . .' (Today we can see how his vision has come true. There are more than eight million Israelis, and 75 per cent of them are Jews.)

Of course it would be right to protect the Arabs, he told the Peel Commission, and it was wrong of the Jews not to hire them; but he saw the Zionist project as something that was fundamentally progressive, enlightened and civilising. It made no sense to allow the Arabs to get in the way of that progress—when ultimately it would be to the advantage of all.

'I do not admit that the dog in the manger has the final right to the manger,' he said. It was like saying that America should be reserved for the Native Americans or Australia for the Aborigines. It was absurd, in his view—an offence against his Whiggish concepts of social improvement.

In any event, he denied that he had imported a 'foreign race' to Palestine. 'Not at all,' he said: it was the Arabs who were the conquerors. Churchill pointed out that in the time of Christ the population of Palestine was much greater—and the people had been mainly Jews. That all changed in the seventh century AD. 'When the Mohammedan upset occurred in world history, and the hordes of Islam swept over these places they broke it all up, smashed it all up. You have seen the terraces on the hills which used to be cultivated, which under Arab rule have remained a desert.'

The Commission pressed Churchill: when did he imagine that this would be reversed? When would the Jews become a majority again? 'The British government is the judge, and should keep the power to be the judge.'

There he was being overoptimistic, if not romantic; and at some level he must have known it. Britain could not conceivably have kept power in Palestine for long enough to ensure that there was lasting fair play between Jew and Arab.

When Churchill became Colonial Secretary in 1921, he was responsible for the greatest empire the world has ever seen, but also one where the financial elastic was already stretched fit to bust. What was his mission, in fulfilling the British mandate in Mesopotamia? Yes, it was partly to secure oil interests—though it is interesting that Middle Eastern oil had not yet acquired its dominance in British strategic thinking. In 1938, 57 per cent of British oil came from America and only 22 per cent from the Middle East.

His main purpose was to cut the costs of patrolling a place that he described—in words that will not endear him to the Iraqi tourist board—as 'a score of mud villages sandwiched in between a swampy river and a blistering desert, inhabited by a few hundred half naked families, usually starving'. Why waste infantry on this dump, he said, when they could be in India? So he cut military expenditure, and decided to rely on the RAF—which could well achieve British objectives by strafing and bombing. This was to lead to some ugly episodes later on, for which he was not directly responsible and which he deplored, when British planes bombed civilians.

He also favoured (that's right, you guessed it) the use of gas—the very sin for which the world most abominated Saddam Hussein. He was, thankfully, frustrated in this ambition, though he protested: 'I can't understand why it should be thought legitimate to kill people with bullets and barbarism to make them sneeze.'

Whatever Britain did in Mesopotamia, he decided it should be done as cheaply as possible: indeed, he at one stage proposed abandoning Baghdad altogether, and to cut costs to only £8 million a year by restricting the mandate to Basra in the south.

The point is that Britain did not want to hang on to the place out of some misplaced desire for prestige, or colonial swagger. Before he was even Colonial Secretary Churchill suggested in 1919 that the mandates for both Mesopotamia and Palestine should be handed over to Turkey: and after he had some experience of dealing with Iraq he said: 'I hate Irak and wish we had never gone there. It is like living on top of an ungrateful volcano'—words that the US-led Coalition forces might have heeded before they invaded in 2003.

The British mission in Iraq and Palestine was to bring as much order to the area as was compatible with the straitened financial circumstances in which they found themselves: to fulfil the mandate, and then to ensure that the successor regime was as friendly to Britain as was possible, given their diminished powers of military projection overseas. The Iraqi mandate continued officially until 1932, though British influence persisted for much longer. By the end of the Second World War it was obvious that the British efforts to hold Palestine were doomed.

Jewish immigration was now morally and physically unstoppable;

and since the Arab reaction was as violent as ever, the British troops found themselves desperately trying to uphold the principles of Balfour, and to be fair to both sides. The British still tried to restrict the pace of Jewish immigration, and there were awful scenes as the victims of Nazi concentration camps were themselves detained, in British-organised camps, rather than being allowed into Palestine.

Jewish terrorists began to turn their guns and bombs on the British themselves—the very people who had created the homeland. They murdered Lord Moyne, the British minister in Palestine, on whose yacht Clementine Churchill had dallied in the South Seas with the suave art dealer Terence Philip. They killed British soldiers who were only doing their job, to the black fury of Ernest Bevin, the Labour Foreign Secretary.

Even Winston Churchill was shaken in his Zionism. He described the attacks as 'an odious act of ingratitude'. His relations with Chaim Weizmann, the Manchester-born father of the Zionist movement, were never the same. In the end the British simply scarpered from Palestine, literally leaving the key under the mat. The flag came down, and a new nation was born.

It was a procedure that took place—with a bit more dignity—in India in the same year; and it happened around the world in the great recessional that marked the last phase of Churchill's life. Across the planet he saw the Union Jack come down, from Malaya to Malawi, from Singapore to Suez—where the Americans finally pulled the rug in 1956 from under the military pretensions of the tottering old empire.

As he said bitterly towards the end of his life, 'I have achieved a great deal to achieve nothing in the end'. That is rot, of course (as he surely knew). Consider his achievements in the Middle East alone.

Jordan has been amazingly stable, from that day to this, even if his arm wobbled as he drew it. Iraq was to remain broadly in the British sphere of influence for forty years after the Cairo conference, and Iraqi oil was to prove invaluable in helping Britain to survive and win the Second World War. As for the birth of Israel, at which he performed the role of midwife, well: your view will depend on the existential question of whether or not you believe in the value of the Jewish state.

If you are among those who hold that the Balfour declaration was the biggest single error of British foreign policy, then you will obviously think that Churchill was wrong to give it practical effect. There again, if you think that on the whole it was right after 2,000 years of persecution to give the Jews a homeland in a place they had once occupied and that was now relatively sparsely populated; if you think it was a visionary idea to hope that their talents would let the desert bloom; if you think that it is not a bad idea to have at least one democracy—no matter how imperfect—in that part of the world, then you will perhaps think Churchill a bit of a hero.

He could not have known in the 1920s that his vision of a land 'flowing with milk and honey' would be so betrayed by the short-sightedness and selfishness of both sides. He can't be blamed for the shameful way Israelis have treated Palestinians, nor for Palestinian terrorism, nor for the generally woeful quality of Palestinian leadership. Nor can he really be blamed for the apparent disintegration of Iraq, if that is indeed what is now happening.

It was as good an idea as any to amalgamate the three vilayets, following the collapse of the Ottoman Empire. It was what the Arab leaders said they wanted—and it was what they had been promised: a strong unitary Arab state. It was hardly Churchill's fault that no Iraqi leader has arisen with the greatness and generosity to unite the country.

Churchill certainly understood and denounced the perils of Islamic extremism, but he can't be blamed for the failure of Arab leadership. Perhaps the only way to end intercommunal and schismatic conflict in the patchwork of the Middle East would be to install a new Roman Empire, complete with ruthless proconsular violence and a system of compulsory loyalty to the central power. That would be unacceptable for many reasons—and it didn't work that well for the Romans, either (they had a hell of a drubbing near Baghdad).

Far from achieving nothing, Churchill's ideals actually helped not to perpetuate the British Empire, but to ensure that it was unbundled in a relatively dignified and effective way. It was one of the paradoxes of his life that Churchillian goals, of freedom and democracy, were espoused by the very children of the empire as they campaigned for their own independence.

As Richard Toye has pointed out, the Atlantic Charter of 1941 may not have cut much ice in Washington. But it was heard by Nelson Mandela and other African leaders.

When he stood on that yacht in 1961, there was certainly a case for saying that Churchill and his country had been diminished. He was old and frail; Britain had been bankrupted by the war, and greatly reduced in financial and military muscle—an outcome that had surely been anticipated and connived at by the Americans.

His own country was now so short of millionaires that he had to rely on the hospitality of the gangsterish social climber Aristotle Onassis. He stood beneath the long shadow of New York's Empire State Building, a tower that dwarfs Big Ben in London as the American defence budget dwarfs that of the whole of western Europe, Britain included.

He knew that the fate of the world now lay in America's hands—and he was right. In our own time it has fallen to the Americans to try to hold the ring in Palestine, to reason with the Israelis, to try to cope with the ungrateful volcano of Iraq. As a British imperialist, he was inevitably a failure. As an idealist, he was a success.

That handy conceptual elision of 'the English-speaking peoples' has helped to carry Churchillian ideas around the world. The English-speaking peoples are now far more numerous than the peoples of the old British Empire—perhaps 2 billion, and they are growing in number every day. There are more Chinese English-speakers than there are in England; even the EU Commission, in the last ten years, has unofficially adopted English.

There are more democracies around the world, and there are fewer wars. Whatever you may think about the American-led imperium of free markets and free trade, they are lifting billions of people out of poverty. Those are all ideals for which Churchill fought, and which he identified as common to Britain and America.

Those nights on the *Christina* were the last time he saw the land of his mother. The next day he went to Idlewild airport and boarded a flight home that had been equipped with two bottles of cognac, seven bottles of wine, one bottle of brandy and two pounds of Stilton. That should have seen him through.

The yacht *Christina*, incidentally, has lately been put up for sale. She can be found in a dockyard in East London.

So, too, can people from countries around the world, with 300 languages spoken in the city. Churchill not only transformed much of the world; by the time he left office he had begun the process— not altogether intentionally, perhaps—of creating the modern multicultural Britain.

# CHAPTER 22

# THE MEANING OF HIS NAME TODAY

I f you were ever tempted to doubt the strength of the love between Winston and Clementine Churchill, you should look at the countless notes and billets-doux they sent each other all their married life. On the day of her seventy-eighth birthday in 1963, he wrote as follows:

*My darling one,*

> *This is only to give you
> my fondest love and kisses
> a hundred times repeated*

> *I am a pretty dull and
> paltry scribbler; but my
> stick as it writes carries my
> heart along with it.*

> *Your ever & always*

> *W*

He was now eighty-eight, and in other letters he lamented the passing of that old facility of expression—and recorded his amazement at what he now saw as the speed of others. He still went to the House of Commons, though other MPs were shocked by how frail he had become. It was only after quite some pressure from Clementine that he agreed finally not to seek re-election, and on 24 July 1964 he went to the House for the last time.

When you think of the punishment he had given his mortal frame—the toxins he had ingested all his life—you can see in that very longevity his essential character: his instinct to hold on, fight on, never give in. But he also knew that his work was done, and that his career was beginning to merge with history. As he said to his daughter Diana, 'My life is over, but it is not yet ended.' He liked to be gloomy about his accomplishments—possibly because he was fishing for compliments. Really he had no right to such gloom.

In those days his legacy was everywhere, his very name a meme that spread through all levels of society. In that year students were already graduating from Churchill College, Cambridge. Communities in Britain were voluntarily anointing some of the 430 roads, closes, squares and cul-de-sacs that bear his name to this day. When he left the Commons in 1964 a young John Winston Lennon was celebrating the sale of 1.5 million copies of a record called 'I Want to Hold Your Hand'.

Lennon had been born in October 1940—the year of the country's maximum peril and Churchill's supreme leadership. For more than ten years Churchill had shared the House of Commons with a man who in 1964 became Defence Secretary—Denis Winston Healey. Healey had been born in 1917 to Churchill fans in Mottingham, south-east London—and he entered the House of Commons in 1952 with the unique distinction of having been named at birth after the man who was then still serving as Prime

Minister; which tells us something about the sheer span of Churchill's life.

Can anyone beat Healey's record of being named after Churchill in 1917, when he was only forty-two? Step forward Winston Graham, author of the Poldark novels, who was born in Manchester in 1908—the year Churchill fought the North-West Manchester by-election; the year he entered the cabinet at the age of thirty-three, as President of the Board of Trade, and began his campaign to create Labour Exchanges and end the exploitation of child labour.

Then across post-war Britain and the world there were hundreds if not thousands of young Winstons—many of them Afro-Caribbeans—who were surely named with the war leader in mind.

There are Churchillian eponyms to be found in great works of literature—Winston Smith, hero of George Orwell's dystopia, *1984*. Of famous cinematic Winstons we might mention *Pulp Fiction*'s superbly confident Mr Winston Wolf, played by Harvey Keitel, who is called upon to clear up the mess when John Travolta accidentally shoots someone's brains out in the back of a car.

There are Churchill night clubs and bars and pubs—about twenty pubs in Britain bear his name and pug-like visage, far more than bear the name of any other contemporary figure.

Sometimes it is easy to understand the semiotic function of the name: you can see why a pub-owner might want to go for Churchill. He is the world's greatest advertisement for the benefits of alcohol. But why is there a Churchill escort agency? And what do they offer, apart from blood, toil, tears and sweat?

The other day I was cycling through Harefield in the rural far west of London, and I came across Churchill's Barbers. I looked inside, and saw a tattooed chap with an earring having the back of his neck shaved, and an oil painting of Churchill in a hat. Why, I asked myself, would you fill a little barbershop with pictures of Winston

Churchill? He had many outstandingly good points—but he was not exactly famous for his hairstyle; quite the reverse.

Then it occurred to me, of course, that there are millions of men who have a haircut not unlike Sir Winston's. Oi Baldy! is the message of Churchill the Barbers: you can be a hero, too. Come inside and have a proper trim of what is left.

Whatever the Churchill brand is intended to signify—and it means all kinds of things—the associations are mainly positive; but they are not exclusively positive.

How many babies would be called Winston in Britain today? The value of his name and brand is strong, but it has perceptibly shifted, and that is because in the fifty years since he died there has been a more or less continuous assault on his reputation. One by one they have fired their missiles in his general direction.

Some of the artillery fire has been wielded by right-wingers like David Irving, who have accused him not just of unnecessarily waging war on Hitler, but of colluding in such crimes as the bombing of Coventry (untrue) and assassinating the Polish leader Władysław Sikorski (rubbish).

In recent years, however, the most damaging attacks have come from well-meaning people who object that Churchill's speeches, letters and articles are riddled with ideas and language that today consign him to a leper colony of rank political incorrectness. He is accused of being a racist, a sexist, an imperialist, a Zionist, an Aryan and Anglo-Saxon supremacist and a believer in eugenics; and as he recedes from us in time the unpasteurised Churchill can seem a bit ripe for our delicate modern taste.

If his words are cleverly filleted, they can indeed be made to appear unacceptable ('All my daughter's friends think he is a racist', one London mother told me); and there is enough truth in the charges against him to cause some embarrassment to the educational establishment. When the Department of Education sent out a com-memorative VE Day video to all schools in 1995, they managed to give Churchill only fourteen seconds in a thirty-five-minute history of the Second World War.

There are all sorts of defences against those who seek to apply modern standards to Churchill. He did have what is now considered to be a racist interpretation of the difference between one society and another; but he hated the mistreatment of anyone of any race. See his anger at Kitchener's butchery of the Dervishes; remember his rage at the Lugards, and their disdainful and murderous treatment of the natives of West Africa. He didn't believe that the white man should hold the whip hand, as if by genetic right. He believed in merit.

As Colonial Secretary in 1921 he announced that within the British Empire 'there should be no barrier of race, colour or creed which should prevent any man from reaching any station if he is fitted for it'. It must also be said that his views on racial distinctions—though widely attacked—were by no means exceptional for a man born in 1874; and there were plenty of others who consciously or unconsciously held the same sort of opinions.

Sometimes he delighted in skewering the hypocrisy of his opponents. In the middle of the war Roosevelt attempted to wind him up at a White House lunch, by seating him next to Mrs Ogden Reid, a publisher and fierce campaigner for the independence of India.

This woman duly asked him: 'What are you going to do about those wretched Indians?'

Churchill replied: 'Before we proceed further let us get one thing clear. Are we talking about the brown Indians in India, who have multiplied alarmingly under the benevolent British rule? Or are we speaking of the red Indians in America who, I understand, are almost extinct?'

Churchill one, Mrs Ogden Reid nil, I feel.

Those who continue to bash him for being out of date on race might also remember that the USA continued with a system of active racial segregation, of a kind he would never have tolerated in Britain, until the late 1960s.

Yes, it is also true that he said some things that now sound very sinister about eugenics and the need to sterilise the feeble-minded. As a young minister in 1910 he wrote to Asquith warning that 'the unnatural and increasingly rapid growth of the Feeble-Minded and Insane classes, coupled as it is with a steady restriction among all the thrifty, energetic and superior stocks constitutes a national and race danger which it is impossible to exaggerate'.

But again, he was by no means alone: Bills for the segregation of 'morons' were overwhelmingly passed in Parliament. It was an age when people were themselves feeble-minded on the subject of feeble-mindedness, and had a very poor understanding of psychology and genetics.

Perhaps it gives a flavour of the context if I point out that in 1927 the great American jurist Oliver Wendell Holmes recorded a judgement agreeing with the sterilisation of a woman called Carrie Buck, who had been labelled feeble-minded, along with her mother and daughter. 'Three generations of imbeciles is enough,' he said. Between 1907 and 1981 the USA forcibly sterilised 65,000 people.

Churchill may indeed have said such things, a decade or two previously: but—thankfully—he never actually put these whacky ideas into practice.

And yes, it was true that by today's standards he was pretty much a male chauvinist pig—at least ideologically; no doubt of that.

Nancy Astor was the first woman to enter the House of Commons, and when in 1919 she asked him why he was so cold towards her, he gave this psychologically rich reply: 'I feel you have come into my

bathroom and I have only a sponge with which to defend myself.'
There speaks an alumnus of an all-male English public school.

There was a truly terrible moment in March 1944, when the
House was debating Butler's Education Bill, and a female Conservative MP called Thelma Cazalet-Keir had successfully moved an
amendment calling for equal pay for women teachers. Churchill decided to use this as a pretext for humiliating his backbench critics.
He turned the matter into a confidence vote—which few would want
to oppose—and forced his MPs to overturn equal pay for women
teachers by 425 votes to 23.

He was rightly pilloried at the time; and yet no one could accuse
him of being a misogynist—he loved clever women (Pamela, Violet);
and he got there in the end. He redeemed himself when one of his
last parliamentary measures, announced at the beginning of 1955,
was equal pay for women in teaching, the civil service and local government. As he said to Jock Colville in 1958, when proposing that
women should be admitted on equal terms to Churchill College,
Cambridge, 'When I think of what women did in the war, I feel sure
they deserve to be treated equally.' (The college eventually admitted
women in 1972.)

You can criticise Churchill for being an imperialist and a
Zionist—as he certainly was, both—but a fair-minded person would
have to admit that he supported both these projects because he conceived that they entailed the advance of civilisation. His language on
India sometimes seems unhinged ('Gandhi ought to be bound hand
and foot at the gates of Delhi and then trampled by an enormous
elephant . . .'); but you have to bear in mind that he saw the Raj as a
restraint on barbarous practices—suttee, bride-price, the shunning
of the Untouchables, and so on.

Those who despise the empire have to ask themselves whether
they hate it more than they hate, say, slavery, or female genital muti-

lation. In Churchill's imperialism there was much more than just the extended egotism of the super-patriot. He was unlike so many other politicians, of every age, in that I think he was at heart a genuine idealist. He believed in the greatness of Britain and her civilising mission, and that led him to say some things that seem quite bonkers today.

All these embarrassing quotations have been picked over for years by the anti-Churchillians. Their bones lie bleached and shocking in the corner of the picture. But they are only a part of a vast and glorious landscape; and they have done nothing to put off politicians from every part of the spectrum, who have tried to ape him, to invoke him or somehow to channel his genius—from Harold Wilson to Margaret Thatcher to Kwame Nkrumah to Fidel Castro to Nelson Mandela.

That is because the story of Churchill is bigger and more inspiring than a mere political creed. It is about the indomitability of the human spirit. He may seem horribly unfashionable in his views to us today, but in his essential character he is a source of eternal—and perhaps growing—inspiration.

Look at the hordes of visitors tramping through the gardens of Chartwell: 212,769 of them in 2013—a record. With the greatest respect to that famous house, it is not an architectural masterpiece. If you were being mean, you might say it was rather dumpy in style, and heavy on the red brick. The grounds are rolling and pleasant enough, but not a patch on those of most stately homes.

People go to Chartwell because it is redolent of the spirit of Churchill; and that is why they go to the underground Churchill war rooms by the Cabinet Office—a record half a million last year, 38 per cent more than the previous year. They go to feel the almost physical presence of the former Prime Minister: to see the camp bed he used for his power naps, the map of Britain's coastal defences in front of him, the cigar like a strange brown coprolite in the ashtray beside him.

They feel his greatness and his bravery in that moment of desperation; and that is why not a single one of the revisionists has really got a shot on target. Year after year the little puffs of their gunfire explode around him, and he sails through it all on his white pony, waving his hat in the air, as serene and unscathed as when he came through the musketfire of Malakand.

I WAS THINKING about this quality of Churchill's—this megalopsychia, greatness of heart—when I remembered that there was an aspect of his creative life that we haven't properly discussed. So one hot afternoon I decided to drive down to Chartwell again, to join the crowds of pilgrims.

As I sat in the South London traffic I remembered a story about how he would leave London at 4.30 p.m. on a Thursday, and he would collect the typist and Rufus the poodle, and every week he would stop to buy the *Evening Standard* at the same place by Crystal Palace. Every time the vendor would step forward and salute, and he would refuse to accept any payment; so every time Churchill would give him the remains of whatever cigar he happened to be smoking (you will recall that another beneficiary of his stubs was the gardener at Chartwell; the poor fellow died of cancer). Is there any politician in the world today who could pay someone in half-chewed cigars?

When we arrived at Chartwell we went straight through the grounds, past his vast round swimming pool, to the studio by the ponds.

Churchill got into painting in 1915, in his state of post-Gallipoli gloom, at a rented house called Hoe Farm near Godalming. He later described how he took it up, in a passage that shows his journalistic flair for making something wonderful out of not very much . . .

Some experiments one Sunday on the country with the children's paint-box led me to procure the next morning a complete outfit for painting in oils.

Having bought the colours, an easel, and a canvas, the next step was *to begin*. But what a step to take! The palette gleamed with beads of colour; fair and white rose the canvas; the empty brush hung poised, heavy with destiny, irresolute in the air. My hand seemed arrested by a silent veto. But after all the sky on this occasion was unquestionably blue, and a pale blue at that. There could be no doubt that blue paint mixed with white should be put on the top part of the canvas. One really does not need to have had an artist's training to see that. It is a starting-point open to all.

So very gingerly I mixed a little blue paint in the palette with a very small brush, and then with infinite precaution made a mark about as big as a bean upon the affronted snow-white shield. It was a challenge, a deliberate challenge; but so subdued, so halting, indeed so cataleptic, that it deserved no response. At that moment the loud approaching sound of a motor car was heard in the drive. From this chariot there stepped swiftly and lightly none other than the gifted wife of Sir John Lavery. 'Painting! But what are you hesitating about? Let me have a brush, the big one.'

Splash into the turpentine, wallop into the blue and the white, frantic flourish on the palette, clean no longer, and then several large, fierce strokes and slashes of blue on the absolutely cowering canvas. Anyone could see that it could not hit back. No evil fate avenged the jaunty violence. The canvas grinned in helplessness before me. The spell was broken. The sickly inhibitions rolled away. I seized the largest brush and fell upon my victim with Berserk fury. I have never felt any awe of a canvas since.

The studio takes up the entire interior of an old cottage, with high windows and his easel facing the fireplace. There next to it is the painting of Randolph, looking prawn-eyed and haughty, with the rent still in the canvas: the one that he was meant to be repairing when he had 'The Dream'.

A tall open-shelved chest rests against the wall, once a vast cigar collection from the people of Havana, now containing hundreds of tubes of paint, squeezed and streaked and laid out in rows. One has a sense of the energy with which he threw himself into his art: the military-style planning of the stools and easels and palettes and umbrellas and smocks and turps and linseed oil—all the paraphernalia of the artist with which he equipped himself before assaulting the canvas.

But when your eye ranges over the room, you realise that this was no pose. He wasn't fooling around, here. There are canvases running in rows round the room, from floor to ceiling—some of the 539 that he did in his lifetime.

Not even his most fanatical admirers would call him a technical virtuoso; he is no freehand master of the human form. To get a likeness he sometimes uses a peculiar device called an epidiascope, which beams a photograph on to the canvas—and he has employed this to do some slightly frozen studies of rugby players at a line-out, and A. J. Balfour and his wife looking a bit like capuchin monkeys. But there are plenty of others that express his personality, and sometimes they are lovely.

I am here with a couple of friends, and we soon work out what gets him going. He likes colour, the brighter and lusher the better—and any excuse nature will give him to bring them together. He loves a pink palace wall, or a gorgeous ochre ruin, and then an azure sky and preferably a line of snow-capped mountains somewhere in the distance.

He can't get enough of the shadows on the Pyramids, or the light on the waves as they crash on some Mediterranean shore. Anything involving dark green cypresses, lime-green lawns, bright blue skies, and pinky old buildings—Churchill is your man.

You can feel the release and the enthusiasm with which he has splodged that pigment on. One of my colleagues tries to sum up her response. 'They are so light, and so optimistic,' she says. That seems about right. He sets out to please and reward the viewer, and he succeeds. One Churchill landscape has just been sold for $1 million—as much as a Monet, for heaven's sake.

People feel drawn to his works not because they are polished masterpieces, but precisely because they are not. He was willing to try it out, to court ridicule, to make mistakes—but the crucial point is that he is at least willing to throw himself into it and to run that risk.

Sometimes it doesn't work; sometimes it comes off triumphantly. That was the spirit that he took with him into that dark and tobacco-filled room in the early summer of 1940. Other hands dithered in front of the blank and terrifying canvas. Churchill took the plunge, loaded up his brush and applied his bright-hued and romantic version of events in broad and vigorous strokes. And that, amigos, is the final rejoinder to all his earnest doubters and critics.

BRITAIN BY 1964 was in so many ways an incomparably better country than it had been when Churchill entered Parliament at the beginning of the century. There was less deference, less class-consciousness—of course there was, when you consider that the pilots of the Battle of Britain had been state school boys. The few came from the ranks of the many.

The grinding poverty that Churchill had seen in his youth, the slums he had surveyed in Manchester as he strolled in his top hat—most of that had been wiped out. Women were in the process of emancipation, higher education was beginning its massive post-war expansion, a National Health Service had been created and a welfare state intended to help everyone in adversity.

People will differ as to Churchill's role in this transformation, though it strikes me that the Labour government of 1945–50 owes a huge amount to him; not just to the work done by Churchill and Lloyd George in the first decades of the twentieth century, but also to Churchill's own instincts in the wartime coalition government. He made a speech on 21 March 1943, called 'After the War', that more or less anticipated the big changes in health, pensions and social security. As Attlee was later to say, 'he had sympathy, an incredibly wide sympathy, for ordinary people all over the world'.

He did not much rejoice in the prospect of mass immigration to Britain (he spoke of 'Hottentots', and so on). But as Andrew Roberts has rightly pointed out, that very immigration was partly the product of Churchill's continuing and romantic vision—well into the 1950s—of Britain as the great imperial motherland.

That was why he and the Tory cabinet found it so hard to wrap their heads round the question, and to slam the door shut; and the paradox therefore is that in his imperialist conception of Britain he was actually one of the founders (if unwittingly and grudgingly) of the multiracial society of today.

Overall, a revolution had taken place in Britain—but a benign revolution in which the essentials of the constitution had been preserved. He had first met Queen Elizabeth II in 1928, when she was two years old. He remarked to Clementine that she was a 'character' with an 'air of authority and reflectiveness astonishing in an infant'.

You might think there was something a bit smarmy about detecting an air of authority in a two-year-old, but he lived to be Prime Minister when she was crowned, and it is almost certainly true to say that she was crowned only because he had lived to be Prime Minister. That is the point to send his critics into final confusion and rout: none of those changes and improvements—none of them—could have been taken for granted if Britain had folded in the face of the Nazi threat.

There would have been no great reforming Labour government, because there would have been no democracy to install it. There would have been no unions, because they would have been repressed, along with free speech and civil rights; and London would not have been emerging as the swinging capital of the world but as a dingy and put-upon satellite where the parents of pop stars—if there were any—were encouraged to christen their children Adolf rather than Winston.

If there is such a thing as the British character (and there probably is, more or less), then it has morphed around the features of Winston Churchill—broadly humorous but occasionally bellicose; irreverent but traditionalist; steadfast but sentimental; rejoicing in language and wordplay of all kinds; keen to a fault on drink and food.

He means something not just to the politicians who claim to espouse his ideals, but to a huge spread of humanity. He is there as a role model for anyone who wasn't much good at school, anyone who never made it to university, anyone who wasn't much cop at maths.

He speaks for all those who have worried about living up to the expectations of their parents, anyone who has felt that they are a failure, anyone who has struggled with depression, anyone who has ever eaten or smoked or drunk more than was strictly good for them, anyone who feels that they must battle on against the odds.

Add those categories together, and you have a lot of human beings.


ON 24 JANUARY 1965 Winston Churchill died, at the age of ninety. An estimated 300,000 people filed past his coffin as it lay in state in Westminster Hall—the first such lying-in-state to be accorded to a commoner since the Duke of Wellington. You can see them in the footage—the Britain of my parents' generation: old men with sunken chaps and trilby hats, women with heavy coats and headscarves; but also young men in drainpipe trousers, and women with short skirts and mascara and peroxide hair and red lipstick; people crying, staring, holding up their primitive cameras.

After the funeral in St Paul's, his body was taken on a launch called the *Havengore* from Tower Pier to Waterloo, and as she passed the docks of the Pool of London, the cranes bowed in salute. A special train took him to Bladon in Oxfordshire, where he was buried in the grounds of the church—the church whose spire can be seen from the window of the room where he was born.

There is quite properly no particular sign in the village that this is his resting-place, certainly no advertisement on the roads. I go through the lychgate and stand over the grave. Already lichen and other natural changes have started slightly to blur the inscription on the great slab.

He lies with his wife and his mother and his father and his brother and his children. It is time to meditate, for one last time, on the greatness of that spirit: not what he did, or how he did it, but where that vast energy came from.

# CHAPTER 23

# THE
# CHURCHILL FACTOR

The truth is that though I love writing and thinking about Winston Churchill, the old boy can sometimes be faintly intimidating. I hasten to say that he is always brilliant fun—but as you try to do justice to his life you are acutely conscious of being chained to a genius, and a genius of unbelievable energy and fecundity.

For those of us who have tried feebly to do just some of the things he did, it can be a little bit crushing. If you have ever wanted to be a politician or a journalist or a historian—or even a painter—you end up wondering where on earth he got it all from.

By now my long lunch with Churchill's grandson Nicholas Soames is coming to an end. The Savoy Grill produces the bill—fairly Churchillian in scale; and I try to tackle this last big question. His grandfather was the man who changed history by putting oil instead of coal into the superdreadnoughts. What sort of fuel did Churchill run on? What made him go?

Soames broods, and then surprises me by saying that his grandfather was an ordinary sort of chap. He did what other Englishmen like doing: mucking about at home, hobbies and so forth. 'You know, in many ways he was quite a normal sort of family man,' he says.

Yes, I say, but no normal family man produces more published words than Shakespeare and Dickens combined, wins the Nobel prize for literature, kills umpteen people in armed conflict on four continents, serves in every great office of state including Prime Minister (twice), is indispensable to victory in two world wars and then posthumously sells his paintings for a million dollars. I am trying to grapple with the ultimate source of all this psychic energy.

What, indeed, do we mean by mental energy? Is it something psychological or something physiological? Was he genetically or hormonally endowed with some superior process of internal combustion, or did it arise out of childhood psychological conditioning? Or perhaps it was a mixture of the two. Who knows—depends on your answer to the mind–body problem, I suppose.

'Some burn damp faggots,' says William Butler Yeats at his vatic best. 'Others may consume/ The entire combustible world in one small room.' If ever you wanted a 12-cylinder, 6-litre entire combustible world consumer, that man is Churchill. I remember when I was about fifteen reading an essay by the psychologist Anthony Storr, in which he postulated that Churchill's biggest and most important victory was over himself.

What he meant was that Churchill was always conscious of being small and runty and cowardly at school—remember the episode when they throw cricket balls at him, and he runs away. So by an act of will he decided to defeat his cowardice and his stammer, and to be the 80-pound weakling who uses dumb-bells to acquire the body of Charles Atlas. Having vanquished his own cowardice, goes the argument, it was easy to vanquish everything else.

I always thought this analysis was all very well, but vulnerable to charges of circularity. I mean: why did he decide to master his fear?

Was he really a coward? Does a cowardly schoolboy kick the awful headmaster's straw hat to pieces? By now I expect most readers will have picked up quite enough of the data they need to form a pretty good idea of Churchill's psychology, and perhaps we don't need to push all the points much farther.

What have we got in the mix? There was the father, no doubt about it: the pain of Randolph's rejections and criticism, the terror of not living up to him; the need after his timely death (from Winston's point of view) both to avenge and excel him. Then there is the mother—boy, what a woman. Jennie is obviously crucial in the way she pushed and helped Churchill, his glory being at least partly her glory, after all. We can only wonder to what extent it spurred his derring-do and heroics at Malakand, to think his mother had probably slept with Bindon Blood to get him there.

There was the general historical context in which he emerged. He was born not just when Britain was at her peak, but when his generation understood that it would require superhuman efforts and energies to sustain that empire. The sheer strain of that exertion helped make the Victorians somehow bigger than we are now, constructed on a grander scale.

'They were harder, tougher people,' says Soames. 'Mind you, my grandfather always had someone to look after him, wherever he went.'

And then there was the natural egotism that is shared to a greater or lesser extent by every human being, and the desire for prestige and esteem. I have always thought Churchill had a secret syllogism in his head:

Britain = greatest empire on earth

Churchill = greatest man in British Empire

Therefore Churchill = greatest man on earth

Andrew Roberts says this is right, but too modest. The correct syllogism should be:

Britain = greatest empire the world has ever seen

Churchill = greatest man in British Empire

Therefore Churchill = greatest man in the history of the world.

This is in one sense true, but it is also in a way unfair on Churchill. He did possess a titanic ego, but one that was tempered by humour, and irony, and by deep humanity and sympathy for other people, and by a commitment to public service and a belief in the democratic right of people to kick him out—as they did—at elections. Remember his instant forgiveness both at Dundee in 1922 and after the humiliation of 1945.

That is what I mean by his greatness of heart. Just before we go, Soames tells me a last story, to make the point about his sentimentality and generosity.

One evening during the war a lady who was a cleaner at the Ministry of Defence came down to go home, and as she was going for her bus she spotted something in the gutter. It was a file covered with pink ribbon and notices saying 'Top Secret'.

So she quickly picked it out of the puddle and tucked it under her raincoat, and took it home. She showed it to her son, and he immediately realised it was terribly secret and important. Without opening it he went straight back to the MOD.

By the time he got there it was quite late at night, and everyone had gone—and this young fellow was treated pretty insolently by the people on the door.

They kept telling him just to leave the file there, and someone would deal with it in the morning. He said no, and he would refuse to go until he had seen someone of flag officer rank.

Finally someone senior came down, and took the file—and of course it was the battle orders for Anzio.

Well, the War Cabinet was called the following day, and they had to work out how serious the security breach was, and whether they could proceed with the Anzio landings.

They looked at the file carefully, and decided that it had only been in the water for a few seconds, and that the cleaning lady's story was true—and so on balance they decided to go ahead with the invasion of Italy.

Churchill then turned to the Chief of the Imperial General Staff and he said, 'Pug, how did this happen?' Ismay told him about the woman, and her son, and as he did so, Churchill started to cry.

'She shall be a Dame Commander of the British Empire!' he said. 'Make it so!'

His Private Secretary Jock Colville followed up, and he got on to Tommy Lascelles, the King's Private Secretary, to see if he could push it through. It was one of the few things the King got wrong, because when the Birthday Honours came out she got an MBE.

But I tell you something, when he finally lost office in 1945, there it was in his own resignation honours. Number five on that list was the MOD cleaning lady—DBE.

That story, alas, has withstood all my efforts to verify it at the Churchill Archive or elsewhere. But it illustrates a fundamental truth. Winston Churchill liked to get his way. And thank God he did.

LIKE THE GENERATIONS of leaves, so are the generations of men, says Homer. That seems about right to me: we are like leaves not only in our mortality, but in our similarity.

I have always thought that an alien looking cursorily at this planet might conclude that we human beings are not strictly speaking individuals, but all really part of the same organism: like leaves connected by invisible twigs and branches.

We look very much the same, we rustle together, we are blown about by the same winds, and so on. It is easy to see why so many historians and historiographers have taken the Tolstoyan line, that the story of humanity is not the story of great men and shining deeds.

For several decades now it has been fashionable to say that these so-called great men and women are just epiphenomena, meretricious bubbles on the vast tides of social history. The real story, on this view, is about deep economic forces, technological advances, changes in the price of sorghum, the overwhelming weight of an infinite number of mundane human actions.

Well, I think the story of Winston Churchill is a pretty withering retort to all that malarkey. He, and he alone, made the difference.

It is easy to think of a few other people who have made a colossal impact on world history—but almost always for the worse: Hitler, Lenin, etc. How many others can you think of who have been decisive for the better, who have personally tilted the scales of fate in the direction of freedom and hope?

Not many, I bet; and that is because when history needed it, in 1940, there was only one man who possessed the Churchill Factor; and having spent quite some time now considering the question, I am finally with those who think there has been no one remotely like him before or since.

# TIMELINE OF EVENTS

**1874** Born, 30 November

**1876** Churchill family moves to Dublin

**1880** Churchill family returns to England

**1882** Enrolled at St George's School at Ascot

**1884** Enrolled at Brunswick School in Hove

**1886** Father becomes Chancellor of the Exchequer

**1887** Enrolled at Harrow

**1893** Enrolled at Royal Military College at Sandhurst

**1894** Commissioned cavalry officer in the 4th Queen's Own Hussars

**1895** Father dies

Writes for the *Daily Graphic* covering the Spanish American
War in Cuba

First visit to the United States

**1896** Stationed in India and undergoes self-education

**1897** Covers siege of the Malakand for the *Daily Telegraph* and sees
action in the Malakand Field Force on the North-West
Frontier of India

**1898** Publishes first book

Participates in and covers the Battle of Omdurman in Sudan
for the *Morning Post*

**1899** Unsuccessfully stands for Parliament in Oldham by-election

Becomes prisoner of war in South Africa and a national hero
when he escapes

**1900** Successfully stands for Oldham

Visits United States and Canada on lecture tour

**1901** Maiden speech in Parliament

**1904** Switches from Tories to Liberals

**1905** Becomes Colonial Under-Secretary

**1907** Tours Africa

**1908** Promoted to President of the Board of Trade

Marries Clementine Hozier

**1909** Diana Churchill born

**1910** Becomes Home Secretary

**1911** Siege of Sidney Street

Randolph Churchill born

Becomes First Lord of the Admiralty

**1913** Founds Royal Naval Flying Corps

**1914** Outbreak of the First World War

Commands Defence of Antwerp

Sarah Churchill born

**1915** The Dardanelles

Dismissed from the Admiralty

Demoted to Chancellor of the Duchy of Lancaster

**1916** Commissioned as lieutenant-colonel and commands

6th Battalion of the Royal Scots Fusiliers

**1917** Rejoins the Government as Minister for Munitions

**1918** First World War armistice

Marigold Churchill born

**1919** Becomes Secretary for War and Air

**1921** Becomes Colonial Secretary

Founds Middle East Department in Colonial Office

Chairs Cairo Conference, founding Jordan and Iraq

Death of Marigold Churchill

**1922** Chanak crisis and fall of the Lloyd George coalition

Loses Dundee election

Mary Churchill born

**1924** 'Re-rats' to the Tory Party

Appointed Chancellor of the Exchequer

**1925** Returns Britain to the Gold Standard

**1926** General Strike

**1929** Churchill returns to the USA on a tour

**1931** Not invited to join the cabinet because of his views on Indian
    independence

    Hit by motor car in New York

**1932** Enters political wilderness

    Nearly meets Adolf Hitler in Germany

**1933** Hitler appointed Chancellor of Germany

**1935** Stanley Baldwin appointed Prime Minister

**1936** Abdication crisis

**1937** Neville Chamberlain becomes Prime Minister

**1938** Munich Agreement

**1939** 'Churchill is Back!' He is named First Lord of the Admiralty

    Molotov–Ribbentrop pact signed, 23 August

    Hitler invades Poland starting the Second World War,
    1 September

**1940** Churchill is named Prime Minister, 10 May

    Churchill convinces the cabinet to fight on, 28 May

    Dunkirk evacuation, May/June

    Fall of Paris, June

    Establishment of Vichy France, 22 June

    Churchill orders attack on French fleet at Mers-el-Kébir,
    3 July

    Battle of Britain begins, 10 July

**1941** British troops evacuate Greece, 30 April

    Hitler breaks the Molotov–Ribbentrop pact and unleashes
    Operation Barbarossa, 22 June

    Atlantic Charter signed, 14 August

    Japan bombs Pearl Harbor, bringing the USA into the war,
    7 December

**1942** Fall of Singapore, February

Beginning of the Battle of Stalingrad, 22 August

Battle of El Alamein, November

**1943** First Quebec Conference, August

Invasion of the Italian mainland, 3 September

Teheran Conference, November

**1944** D-Day invasion of Normandy, 6 June

Second Quebec Conference, September

**1945** Yalta Conference, February

Death of Franklin D. Roosevelt, 12 April

Hitler commits suicide, 30 April

VE Day, 8 May

Potsdam Conference, July

Conservatives lose general election and Churchill loses his
    premiership, July

End of the Second World War, 2 September

**1946** Describes the 'Iron Curtain' in 'Sinews of Peace' speech at
    Fulton, Missouri, 5 March

Gives the 'United States of Europe' speech in Zurich, 19
    September

**1951** Tories win the 1951 general election and Churchill returns as
    Prime Minister, 25 October

**1953** Churchill suffers significant stroke, June

**1955** Retires as Prime Minister, 6 April

**1961** Visits the USA for the last time on Aristotle Onassis's yacht
    *Christina*

**1963** Named first honorary citizen of the United States by John F.
    Kennedy

**1964** Stands down as MP for Woodford, 15 October

**1965** Dies seventy years to the day after his father's death,
    24 January

# ACKNOWLEDGEMENTS

This book was the brainchild of my superb editor, Rupert Lancaster at Hodder. A few years ago he approached the Churchill Estate and suggested that there should be a new appreciation to mark the fiftieth anniversary of Sir Winston's death. The Churchill Estate was keen, and somehow I was fingered as the man for the job—so I am grateful both to Rupert and to Gordon Wise and everyone else at the Churchill Estate; and of course to my wonderful agent, Natasha Fairweather.

It has been a privilege to labour in the Churchill vineyard, as Martin Gilbert once put it. I should record my prime debt to the omniscient Dr Allen Packwood of the Churchill Archives, who was willing to take calls at the most inconvenient times—trying to take his children swimming, and so on—and who pointed me in the direction of all sorts of extraordinary documents.

I was given unstinting guidance by the magnificent staff and curators at Chartwell, the Cabinet War Rooms and Blenheim Palace.

Andrew Roberts gave me two long and alcohol-fuelled tutorials at 5 Hertford Street.

David Cameron did some invaluable devilling into the exact locations of the pivotal meetings in May 1940—not at all clear in Lukacs, for instance.

Of the Churchill family, Nicholas Soames and Celia Sandys were very helpful in discussing their grandfather, and I wrote one chapter in the Greek home of Churchill's great-grandson Hugo Dixon.

Above all, this book could not have been written without the dynamic researches and encouragement of the great Warren Dockter (or Doctor Dockter, as he is inevitably known in our family) of Tennessee and Cambridge. Together we explored everything from Churchill's bunker to his bedroom to his bivouac in the First World War, and as we bandied our theories, the whole exercise was given colour and excitement by Warren's inexhaustible knowledge.

Churchill famously said: 'Writing a book is an adventure. To begin with it is a toy and an amusement. Then it becomes a mistress, then it becomes a master, then it becomes a tyrant. The last phase is that just as you are about to be reconciled to your servitude, you kill the monster and fling him to the public'.

He's right about servitude. So I particularly want to thank my wife, Marina, for putting up with the tyrant Churchill—occupying our house and making constant demands like some giant inflatable lodger—and for all her excellent suggestions.

## PUBLISHERS' ACKNOWLEDGEMENTS

The publishers would like to acknowledge the support and advice of the Churchill Archives Centre in Cambridge and the members of the Churchill Alliance in the publishing of this book. Thanks also to Cecelia Mackay for her picture research and Natalie Adams and Sarah Lewery for their help with images from the collections at the Churchill Archives Centre.

To find out more about Winston Churchill, the plans for Churchill 2015 and the organisations that form his living legacy, go to www.churchill.com.

# NOTES ON SOURCES

## 1. THE OFFER FROM HITLER

Page 13. **'The Prime Minister said . . . into this position'** Cabinet meeting minutes, 28 May 1940, confidential annex; CAB 65/13. See also John Lukacs, *Five Days in London, May 1940* (New Haven, Conn.: 1999).

Page 15. **'The gist . . . destroyed our aircraft factories'** Cabinet meeting minutes, 28 May 1940, confidential annex; CAB 65/13.

Page 16. **'tender to the Nazis'** Lady Nelly Cecil; Lynne Olson, *Troublesome Young Men: The Rebels Who Brought Churchill to Power and Helped Save England* (London: 2008), p. 66.

Page 16. **Hitler was a 'born leader'** Lloyd George, *The Daily Express*, 17 September 1936.

Page 16. **'a man of his supreme quality . . . today'** Lloyd George to T. Phillip Cornwell-Evans, 1937; William Manchester, *The Last Lion: Winston Spencer Churchill, Alone: 1932–1940* (London: 1988), p. 82.

Page 17. **'If Hitler did not exist . . . champion'** Ward Price, *Daily Mail*, 21 September 1936; also see Olson, *Troublesome Young Men*, p. 123.

Page 18. **'frightful rot'** Lord Halifax Diary, 27 May 1940; see Andrew Roberts, *'The Holy Fox': The Life of Lord Halifax* (London: 2011), p. 221.

Pages 18–19. **'I have thought . . . immense reserves and advantages'** Hugh Dalton, *Memoirs: The Fateful Years, 1931–1945* (London: 1957), pp. 335–36.

Page 20. **'Holy Fox'** See Roberts, *'The Holy Fox.'*

## 2. THE NON-CHURCHILL UNIVERSE

Page 23. **'like to see as the culmination . . . English people'** Lord Halifax, July 1938 (date unconfirmed); John Lukacs, *Five Days in London, May 1940* (New Haven, Conn.: 1999), p. 64.

Page 24. **'Democracy is finished in England'** Joe Kennedy, *Boston Globe*, 10 November 1940.

Page 25. **nightmarish structure . . . had been expelled** Albert Speer, *Inside the Third Reich* (London: 1970).

Page 26. **deportation meant liquidation** See Hannah Arendt, *Eichmann in Jerusalem:*

347

*A Report on the Banality of Evil* (London: 1963); David Cesarani, *Becoming Eichmann: Rethinking the Life, Crimes and Trial of a "Desk Murderer"* (Boston: 2006).

Pages 26–27. **'the abyss of a new Dark Age . . . perverted science'** Winston Churchill, House of Commons, 18 June 1940; *Hansard*, HC Deb, vol. 362, cc51–64; http://hansard.millbanksystems.com/commons/1940/jun/18/war-situation.

Page 27. **the worst system . . . except for all the others** Winston Churchill, House of Commons, 11 November 1947; Robert Rhodes James, ed., *Winston S. Churchill: His Complete Speeches, 1897–1963*, vol. 7 (1974), p. 7566.

Page 29. **Hitler's Operation Sealion . . . British population** Otto Brautigam, *So hat es sich zugetragen: Ein Leben als Soldat und Diplomat* (Wurzburg: 1968), p. 590.

## 3. ROGUE ELEPHANT

Page 32. **'I shan't last long'** Winston Churchill, 13 May 1940; Norman Rose, *Churchill: The Unruly Giant* (London: 1995), p. 327.

Page 32. **'sullen silence'** Lynne Olson, *Troublesome Young Men: The Rebels Who Brought Churchill to Power and Helped Save England* (London: 2008), p. 330.

Page 33. **'WC they regard . . . feel about it'** Nancy Dugdale; Andrew Roberts, *Eminent Churchillians* (London: 2010), ebook edition.

Page 33. **'glamour boys'** David Margesson coined the phrase. See Graham Stewart, *Burying Caesar: The Churchill-Chamberlain Rivalry* (London: 2003).

Page 33. **'rogue elephant'** Lord Hankey to Samuel Hoare, 12 May 1940; HNKY 4/32, Hankey Papers, Churchill College, Cambridge.

Page 34. **'oozes with port . . . cigar'** Lord Halifax; Julian Jackson, *The Fall of France: The Nazi Invasion of 1940* (London: 2004), p. 210.

Page 34. **'fat baby'** Lady Alexandra Metcalf; Roberts, *Eminent Churchillians*, Kindle edition.

Page 34. **'Is there no poverty at home?'** Winston Churchill, House of Commons, 13 May 1901; Virginia Cowles, *Winston Churchill: The Era and the Man* (London: 1953), p. 86.

Page 35. **'My prognostication . . . at the Election'** See Martin Gilbert, *Churchill: A Life* (New York: 1991), p. 169.

Page 35. **'Blenheim rat'** Rose, *Unruly Giant*, p. 66.

Page 35. **'I am an English Liberal . . . methods'** Winston Churchill to Hugh Cecil, 24 October 1903 (letter not sent); R. C. Kemper, ed., *Winston Churchill: Resolution, Defiance, Magnanimity, Good Will* (Columbia, Mo.: 1996), p. 145.

Page 36. **Oscar Wilde variety** Papers on WSC's successful libel action against A. C. Bruce-Pryce, CHAR1/17, Churchill Papers.

Page 36. **'I understand what the photographer . . . gentleman doing'** A. J. Balfour; Roy Jenkins, *Churchill: A Biography* (London: 2001), p. 145.

Page 37. **'man enveloped in a cloak . . . looked satisfied'** Rose, *Unruly Giant*, p. 136.

Page 37. **'unfit for the office he now holds'** Jenkins, *Churchill*, p. 251.

Page 37. **'half-naked fakir'** Winston Churchill, 'A Seditious Middle Temple Lawyer' Speech at Winchester House, 23 Febuary 1931, Robert Rhodes James, ed., *Winston S. Churchill: His Complete Speeches, 1897–1963* (New York: 1974), pp. 4982–6.

Page 39. **'wonderfully pretty and very healthy'** Lord Randolph to Mrs Leonard

Jerome, 30 November 1874, Randolph Churchill, *Winston S. Churchill: Youth, 1874–1900* (London: 1966), p. 1.

Page 41. **'pantherine'** Mary Lovell, *The Churchills: A Family at the Heart of History* (London: 2011), p. 65.

Page 41. **'She shone for me . . . at a distance'** Winston Churchill, *My Early Life* (London: 1996 edition), p. 28.

Page 41. **'Papa' . . . 'Father' is better** Lord Randolph Churchill to Winston Churchill, 13 June 1894; CHAR 1/2/83.

Page 41. **'become a mere social wastrel . . . existence'** Lord Randolph Churchill to Winston Churchill, 9 August 1893; CHAR 1/2/66–68.

Page 41. **'young stupid' . . . 'not to be trusted'** Lord Randolph Churchill to Winston Churchill, 21 April 1894; CHAR 1/2/78.

Page 42. **Recent scholarship** See John H. Mather, 'Lord Randolph Churchill: Maladies Et Mort', The Churchill Centre, http://www.winstonchurchill.org/learn/myths/myths/his-father-died-of-syphilis. Accessed 26 August 2014.

Page 42. **'He is completely untrustworthy . . . before him'** Lord Derby to Lloyd George, August 1916; Gilbert, *Churchill: A Life*, p. 365.

Page 42. **'cheap fellows'** Teddy Roosevelt to Theodore Roosevelt Jr, 23 May 1908; *Theodore Roosevelt Papers*, Manuscripts division, Library of Congress. Martin Gilbert, *Churchill and America* (London: 2005), p. 50.

## 4. The Randolph Factor

Page 44. **'Of course you are too old. . . name for yourself'** Winston Churchill, 'The Dream'; Martin Gilbert, *Winston S. Churchill, vol. 8: 'Never Despair' 1945–1965* (London: 1988), pp. 364–72.

Page 45. **'Stop that now . . . snub-nose radical!'** Lady Randolph to Lord Randolph Churchill, 15 February 1886; CHAR 28/100/12–14.

Page 45. **'He has much smartened up . . . wonders for him'** Lord Randolph Churchill, 23 October 1893; Norman Rose, *Churchill: The Unruly Giant* (London: 1995), p. 29.

Page 47. **'Since I have been in parliament . . . to do so'** Lord Randolph Churchill to Sir Stafford Northcote, 3 March 1883; Winston Churchill, *Lord Randolph Churchill* (New York: 1907), p. 192.

Page 47. **'looking down on the Front Benches . . . sublime'** Sir Stafford Northcote, ibid., p. 177.

Page 48. **'opportunism, mostly'** John Charmley, *A History of Conservative Politics Since 1830* (London: 2008), p. 59.

Page 48. **'Little Randy' . . . they cried** Mary Lovell, *The Churchills: In Love and War* (London: 2012), p. 88.

Page 48. **'an old man in a hurry'** Lord Randolph Churchill, 1886; Winston Churchill, *Lord Randolph Churchill*, p. 860.

Page 49. **'the forest laments . . . perspire'** Winston Churchill, *Lord Randolph Churchill*, p. 229.

Page 49. **'I always believed . . . mantle of Elijah'** Winston Churchill, 'The Dream', Gilbert, *Churchill, vol.8, 'Never Despair'*, pp. 364–72.

Page 50. **'I still have my father's robes'**  Rose, *Unruly Giant*, p. 287.

Page 51. **'I had forgotten Goschen'**  Anne Sebba, *American Jennie: The Remarkable Life of Lady Randolph Churchill* (London: 2010), p. 158.

Page 52. **'What Price Churchill?'**  Rose, *Unruly Giant*, p. 287.

Page 52. **'We must have a new Prime Minister . . . must be you"**  Lynne Olson, *Troublesome Young Men: The Rebels Who Brought Churchill to Power and Helped Save England* (London: 2008), p. 298.

Page 52. **'I felt . . . this hour and this trial'**  Winston Churchill, 10 May 1940; Martin Gilbert, *Churchill: A Life* (New York: 1991), p. 645.

## 5. NO ACT TOO DARING OR TOO NOBLE

Page 55. **'She is out of control'**  Winston Churchill, 'In the Air', CHAR 8/319.

Page 56. **'This is very likely death'**  Ibid.

Page 56. **'We are in the Stephenson age . . . value to our country'**  Winston Churchill said this to his pilot, Ivon Courtney; Martin Gilbert, *Churchill: A Life* (New York: 1991), p. 248.

Page 57. **one flight in five thousand**  See Gilbert, *Churchill: A Life*, p. 248.

Page 57. **'I do not suppose . . . wrong of you'**  Sunny Marlborough to Winston Churchill, March 1913; Gilbert, *Churchill: A Life*, p. 248.

Page 57. **'foolish' . . . 'unfair to his family'**  F. E. Smith to Winston Churchill, 6 December 1913; Michael Sheldon, *Young Titan: The Making of Winston Churchill* (London: 2013), p. 294.

Page 57. **His cousin . . . 'evil'**  Lady Londonderry to Winston Churchill, July 1919; Gilbert, *Churchill: A Life*, p. 414.

Page 57. **'I have been very naughty . . . flying'**  Winston Churchill to Clementine Churchill, 29 November 1913; Mary Soames, *Clementine Churchill: The Biography of a Marriage* (London: 2003), p. 116.

Pages 57–58. **'I started Winston . . . practice'**  Captain Gilbert Lushington to Miss Hynes, 30 November 1913; Gilbert, *Churchill: A Life*, p. 252.

Page 58. **an eerie letter . . . doomed flight**  For correspondence, see Martin Gilbert, *In Search of Churchill* (London: 1995 edition), pp. 28–84.

Pages 58–59. **He was constantly nipping . . . presentiments of doom**  See Winston Churchill, *Thoughts and Adventures: Churchill Reflects on Spies, Cartoons, Flying, and the Future* (London: 1949), pp. 133–49.

Page 60. **'within a foot of my head'**  Douglas Russell, *Winston Churchill: Soldier—The Military Life of a Gentleman at War* (London: 2005), p. 121.

Page 60. **'The bullets . . . our heads'**  Winston Churchill, *My Early Life: A Roving Commission* (New York: 1930), p. 84.

Page 60. **'I cannot be certain . . . they fell'**  Norman Rose, *Churchill: The Unruly Giant* (London: 1995), p. 47.

Page 61. **'I rode my grey pony . . . too noble'**  Winston Churchill to Lady Randolph Churchill, 22 December 1897; Randolph Churchill, *Winston S. Churchill: Youth, 1874–1900* (London: 1966), p. 350.

Pages 61–62. **The Dervishes . . . twelve deep** For Churchill's account, see Winston Churchill, 'The Sensations of a Calvary Charge', *My Early Life*, pp. 182–96.

Page 62. **'rode up to individuals . . . one very doubtful'** Gilbert, *Churchill: A Life*, p. 97.

Page 62. **'the most dangerous . . . to see'** Winston Churchill to Ian Hamilton, 16 Sept 1898; BRDW V 1/1, Broadwater Collection, Churchill College, Cambridge.

Page 63. **He later cycled . . . Diamond Hill** See Winston Churchill, *The Boer War: London to Ladysmith via Pretoria and Ian Hamilton's March* (London: 2008 edition), p. 287.

Page 63. **served with the troops . . . hear them talking** See A. Dewar-Gibb, 'Captain X', *With Winston Churchill at the Front* (London: 1924).

Page 64. **'Being in many ways . . . personal courage'** Winston Churchill to Jack Churchill, 02 December 1897; CHAR 28/152A/122.

# 6. The Great Dictator

Page 70. **'Master of sham-Augustan prose'** Martin Stannard, *Evelyn Waugh* (London: 2013), p. 440.

Page 70. **'No specific literary talent . . . self-expression'** Geoffrey Wheatcroft, 'Winston Churchill, the Author of Victory,' review of Peter Clarke, *Mr. Churchill's Profession: Statesman, Orator, Writer'* in *Times Literary Supplement*, 18 July 2012.

Page 70. **'Shifty barrister's case . . . literature'** Evelyn Waugh, *Letters of Evelyn Waugh* (London: 2010), p. 627.

Page 70. **'He had an ignorance . . . staggering proportions'** J. H. Plumb, taken from Michael Cohen, *Churchill and the Jews, 1900–1948* (London: 2013), p. 4.

Page 70. **'Curiously old-fashioned . . . 5th avenue'** See J. H. Plumb, 'The Historian,' in A.J.P. Taylor et al., eds., *Churchill: Four Faces and the Man* (London: 1969), p. 130.

Pages 70–71. **'Rarely can an author's . . . 1953'** Peter Clarke, 'Prologue,' *Mr. Churchill's Profession: Statesman, Orator, Writer* (London: 2012), p. ix.

Pages 72–74. **'It was from the very beginning . . . double sixes again'** Winston Churchill, 'The Morning Post', from F. Woods, ed., *Winston S. Churchill: War Correspondent, 1895–1900*, pp. 300–2.

Page 74. **His description . . . 400 yards a day** Winston Churchill, 10 September 1898, Camp Omdurman; Woods, *War Correspondent*, pp. 143–47.

Page 74. **'the wounded dervishes . . . ridiculous'** Winston Churchill, *The River War: An Historical Account of the Reconquest of the Soudan*, vol. II (London: 1899), p. 225.

Page 75. **'financially it is ruinous . . . a blunder'** Winston Churchill to Lady Randolph, 21 October 1897. C.V. I, part 2, p. 807.

Page 75. **'It is with regret . . . barbarism unrelieved'** Winston Churchill, dispatch from Nowshera, 16 October 1897, in Woods, *War Correspondent*, p. 85.

Page 76. **'Hope . . . he won't write'** Lady Jeune to H. Kitchener, 1898; Martin Gilbert, *Churchill: A Life* (New York: 1991), p. 90.

Page 76. **'cannot really tell lies'** Norman Rose, *Churchill: The Unruly Giant* (London: 1995), p. 154.

Page 77. **his first ever essay at Harrow**   Gilbert, *Churchill: A Life*, p. 19.

Page 78. **'suspiciously round'**   Roy Jenkins, *Churchill: A Biography* (New York: 2001), p. 80.

Page 78. **his income from writing**   Clarke, *Mr. Churchill's Profession*, Appendix: 'Churchill and the British Tax System'.

Page 80. **'The old Whig claptrap . . . chapter'**   J. H. Plumb, *The Making of an Historian: The Collected Essays of J. H. Plumb* (New York: 1988), p. 240.

Page 80. **'The past is a pasteboard . . . signpost the future'**   J. H. Plumb, quoted in A.J.P. Taylor, *Churchill Revised: A Critical Assessment* (London: 1969), p. 169.


# 7. HE MOBILISED THE ENGLISH LANGUAGE

Page 84. **'I thank the House for having listened to me'**   For the entire ordeal, see Virginia Cowles, *Churchill: The Era and the Man* (London: 1953), p. 102; Martin Gilbert, *Churchill: A Life* (New York: 1991), p. 163.

Page 84. **'defective cerebration'**   Gilbert, *Churchill: A Life*, p. 164.

Page 86. **'Ladies . . . I stand for liberty!'**   Douglas Russell, *Winston Churchill, Soldier: The Military Life of a Gentleman at War* (London: 2005), p. 65. See also Cowles, *Churchill: The Era and the Man*, p. 40. However, Churchill himself says that 'no very accurate report of my words has been preserved.' Winston Churchill, *My Early Life: A Roving Commission* (New York: 1930), p. 71.

Page 86. **'Sometimes a slight . . . attention of the audience'**   See Winston Churchill, 'The Scaffolding of Rhetoric,' November 1897, https://www.winstonchurchill.org/images/pdfs/for_educators/THE_SCAFFOLDING_OF_RHETORIC.pdf. Accessed 29 August 2014.

Page 86. **'The cheers become louder . . . all direction'**   Ibid.

Page 87. **'scholarly and limp'**   Michael Sheldon, *The Young Titan: The Making of Winston Churchill* (London: 2014), p. 31.

Page 87. **'Mr Churchill does not inherit . . . help him'**   H. W. Massingham, *The Daily News*; Roy Jenkins, *Churchill: A Biography* (New York: 2001), p. 75.

Page 87. **'Mr. Churchill and oratory . . . ever will be'**   Quoted from Richard Toye, *The Roar of the Lion: The Untold Story of Winston Churchill's World War Two Speeches* (London: 2013), p. 18.

Pages 87–88. **'What was there to say . . . a coward'**   Winston Churchill, *Savrola: A Tale of Revolution in Laurania* (London: 1897), pp. 88–91.

Page 89. **'rhetorician . . . influence crowds'**   Colin Cross, ed., *Life with Lloyd George: The Diary of A. J. Sylvester, 1931–45* (London: 1975), p. 148.

Page 89. **'Winston is not yet . . . said'**   Edwin Montagu to H. H. Asquith, 20 January 1909; Toye, *Roar of the Lion*, p. 21.

Page 89. **'I do not care . . . words produce'**   Winston Churchill to Lady Randolph Churchill, 1898, quoted from Norman Rose, *Churchill: An Unruly Life* (New York: 1998), p. 45.

Pages 89–90. **'terminological inexactitude'**   Winston Churchill, 22 February 1906, *Hansard*, HC Deb, vol. 152, cc531–86.

Page 90. **'foul race . . . their due'**   Jock Colville, *Fringes of Power: Downing Street Diaries 1939–1955* (London: 2004), p. 563.

Page 91. 'Rallied . . . despised his orations' Evelyn Waugh to Ann Flemming, 27 January 1965; Toye, *Roar of the Lion*, p. 70.

Page 91. 'radio personality' Ibid.

Pages 91–92. 'he gives the impression . . . fails miserably' Ibid., pp. 69–70.

Page 92. 'fucking liar' or 'fucking bullshit' Ibid, pp. 95, 131.

Page 92. 'He's no speaker, is he?' Ibid., p. 126.

Page 92. 'The ceremony at Gettysburg . . . Lincoln' Ibid., p. 69.

Page 93. 'There are two people . . . I am' Ibid., p. 28.

Page 93. 'The winning formula . . . never fails' Harold Nicolson to Ben and Nigel Nicolson, 21 September 1943; Nigel Nicolson, ed., *Harold Nicolson: Diaries and Letters 1939–1945* (London: 1967), p. 321.

Page 94. 'Audiences prefer . . . Latin and the Greek' Winston Churchill, 'The Scaffolding of Rhetoric.' November 1897, https://www.winstonchurchill.org/images/pdfs/for_educators/THE_SCAFFOLDING_OF_RHETORIC.pdf. Accessed 29 August 2014.

Page 94. Churchill's 'finest hour' speech See *Hansard*, HC Deb, 18 June 1940, vol. 362, cc51–64.

Page 94. 'liberated . . . freed' Winston Churchill speech notes, CHAR 9/172.

Page 94. 'I felt sick . . . so many to so few' Lord Ismay, *The Memoirs of Lord Ismay* (London: 1960), pp. 179–80.

Page 96. 'the end of the beginning' speech For the whole speech, see http://www.winstonchurchill.org/learn/speeches/speeches-of-winston-churchill/1941-1945-war-leader/987-the-end-of-the-beginning. Accessed 29 August 2014.

## 8. A PROPER HUMAN HEART

Page 101. 'Where were you educated . . . book' Elizabeth Nel, *Winston Churchill by His Personal Secretary* (London: 2007), p. 40.

Pages 101–2. 'I want to see Buffalo Bill . . . too much for that' Winston Churchill to Lady Randolph Churchill, 11 June 1886; Martin Gilbert, *Churchill: A Life* (New York: 1991), p. 13.

Page 102. 'orientalism' Lady Gwendoline Bertie to Churchill, 27 August 1907; Randolph Churchill, ed., *Winston S. Churchill Companion*, vol. 2, part 1 (London: 1969), p. 672.

Page 102. To the front . . . 'ordinary people' Norman Rose, *Churchill: An Unruly Life* (London: 1994), pp. 203–4.

Page 103. 'Winston, like all really self-centred . . . boring people' Margot Asquith, 23 January 1915; Michael and Eleanor Brock, eds., *Margot Asquith's Great War Diary 1914–1916: The View from Downing Street* (London: 2014), p. 74.

Page 104. 'I wonder . . . speaking terms with me' Winston Churchill, June 1941, Martin Gilbert, ed., *The Churchill War Papers, vol. 3: The Ever-Widening War 1941* (London: 1993), p. xxxvii.

Page 104. 'When you first meet Winston . . . virtues' See http://www.winstonchurchill.org/support/the-churchill-centre/publications/finest-hour/issues-109-to-144/no-138/863-action-this-day-fh-138. Accessed 29 August 2014.

Page 105. 'without a large cigar . . . Col Churchill.' A. Dewar-Gibb, 'Captain X', *With Winston Churchill at the Front* (London: 1925), chapter 8.

Page 105. **'After a very brief . . . sheer personality'**   Douglas Russell, *Winston Churchill, Soldier: The Military Life of a Gentleman at War* (London: 2005), p. 377.

Page 106. **'practices of the Oscar Wilde variety'**   CHAR 1/17.

Page 106. **Ralph Wigram**   For the Wigram story, see Gilbert, *Churchill: A Life*, pp. 542–60.

Page 107. **worrying about . . . Noah's ark animals**   Mary Soames, *Clementine Churchill: The Biography of a Marriage* (London: 2003), p. 95.

Page 108. **'Colonel Churchill . . . greatest admiration'**   A. Dewar-Gibb, *With Winston Churchill at the Front*, chapter 8.

Page 108. **Churchill was always . . . a girlfriend**   Soames, *Clementine Churchill*, p. cxix.

Page 109. **'flying buttress'**   Mary Soames, Crosby Kemper Lecture, 1991; John Perry, *Winston Churchill* (New York: 2010), p. 157.

Page 110. **'My nurse . . . my many troubles.'**   Winston Churchill, *My Early Life: A Roving Commission* (New York: 1930), p. 5.

Page 110. **'cruel and mean'**   Winston Churchill to Lady Randolph Churchill, 29 October 1893; CHAR 28/19/24–27.

Page 110. **'Take plenty . . . good for my sake'**   Gilbert, *Churchill: A Life*, pp. 42–43.

Page 111. **'The jacket . . . calm again'**   Gilbert, *Churchill: A Life*, p. 53.

Page 111. **'We saw a snake . . . Everest would not let me'**   Winston Churchill to Lord Randolph Churchill, 10 April 1882; CHAR 28/13/8.

## 9. MY DARLING CLEMENTINE

Page 113. **'I want so much . . . talk about'**   Winston Churchill to Clementine [Hozier] Churchill, 7 August 1908; Mary Soames, ed., *Speaking for Themselves: The Personal Letters of Winston and Clementine Churchill* (London: 1999), p. 11.

Page 113. **'those strange mysterious . . . arrive at loneliness'**   Winston Churchill to Clementine [Hozier] Churchill, 8 August 1908; ibid, p. 12.

Page 114. **'If that beetle reaches . . . not going to'**   Norman Rose, *Churchill: An Unruly Life* (London: 1994), p. 61.

Page 115. **'I always hear . . . I doubt it'**   Rose, *Unruly Life*, p. 60. The lady friend of Lloyd George has been only identified as Miss G- G-, 'whose family was quite well-known in Liberal circles.' See Rose, *Unruly Life*, p. 356.

Page 115. **'You brute! . . . properly'**   Martin Gilbert, *Churchill: A Life* (New York: 1991), p. 210.

Page 116. **Nor do most historians**   See Paul Addison, 'Churchill and Women', http://www.churchillarchive.com/education-resources/higher-education?id=Addison. Accessed 30 August 2014.

Page 116. **'the beautiful Polly Hacket'**   Gilbert, *Churchill: A Life*, p. 42.

Page 116. **'the most beautiful girl I've ever seen'**   Winston Churchill to Lady Randolph Churchill, 4 November 1896; CHAR 28/22/18–23.

Page 116. **Muriel Wilson**   See Michael Sheldon, *The Young Titan: The Making of Winston Churchill* (London: 2014), pp. 181–92.

Page 118. **'our days of hansom cabs'**   Pamela Plowden to Winston Churchill, May 1940; Gilbert, *Churchill: A Life*, p. 645.

Page 118. **'lived happily ever after'**   Winston Churchill, *My Early Life: A Roving Commission* (New York: 1930), p. 370.

Page 118. **'His wife could never . . . both**   Jenkins, *Churchill: A Biography*, p. 138.

Page 119. **'without an office . . . without an appendix'**   Winston Churchill, *Thoughts and Adventures* (London: 1949), p. 213.

Page 119. **'A lot of people . . . peace-making'**   Gilbert, *Churchill: A Life*, p. 459.

Page 119 **'It always makes me unhappy . . . prevail'**   Roy Jenkins, *Churchill: A Biography* (New York: 2001), p. 362.

Pages 120–21. **'My Darling . . . here it is now'**   Clementine Churchill to Winston Churchill, 27 June 1940; Soames, *Speaking for Themselves*, p. 454.

Pages 121–22. **'If the country . . . lost the war'**   Andrew Roberts, *Hitler and Churchill: Secrets of Leadership* (London: 2010), p. 68.

Page 122. **'Here lies a woman . . . required'**   Mary Soames, *Clementine Churchill: The Biography of a Marriage* (London: 2003), p. 284.

Page 122. **'first, second and third'**   Mary Soames, 'Father Always Came First, Second and Third', *Daily Telegraph*, 16 August 2002.

Page 122. **'We are still young . . . warming'**   Gilbert, *Churchill: A Life*, p. 357.

Pages 122–23. **'a figure of panache . . . little child'**   See Christopher Wilson, 'The Most Wicked Woman in High Society', *Daily Mail*, 29 March 2014.

Page 123. **'It's an enchanted island . . . isn't it?'**   Soames, *Clementine Churchill*, p. 298.

Pages 123–24. **'He lived in a beautiful wicker . . . people he liked'**   Ibid., pp. 269–70.

Page 125. **'Oh my darling . . . folded in your arms'**   Clementine Churchill to Winston Churchill, 20 April 1935; Soames, *Speaking for Themselves*, p. 399.

Page 125. **'I think a lot . . . want you back'**   Winston Churchill to Clementine Churchill, 13 April 1935; ibid, p. 398.


## 10. The Making of John Bull

Page 130. **'Young lady . . . had a choice'**   Dominique Enright, *The Wicked Wit of Winston Churchill* (London: 2011), Kindle edition.

Page 130. **'I want every box . . . master race'**   Susan Elia MacNeal, *Mr. Churchill's Secretary* (London: 2012).

Page 131. **'Winston . . . I would drink it'**   Martin Gilbert, *In Search of Churchill: A Historian's Journey* (London: 1994), p. 232.

Page 131. **'This is the kind of English . . . will not put'**   http://www.winstonchurchill .org/learn/speeches/quotations/famous-quotations-and-stories. Accessed 31 August 2014.

Pages. 131–32. **'In the future . . . anti-fascists'**   See http://standuptohate.blogspot. co.uk/p/winston-churchill-and-anti-fascist.html. Accessed 31 August 2014.

Page 132. **'The hardest cross . . . Cross of Lorraine'**   See http://www.winston churchill.org/learn/speeches/quotations/quotes-falsely-attributed. Accessed 31 August 2014.

Page 132. **'bring a friend, if you have one'**   Derek Tatham to Winston Churchill, 19 September 1949; G. B. Shaw to Derek Tatham, 16 September 1949. See CHUR 2/165/72–82.

Page 132. **'mouthwash'**   Michael Richards, 'Alcohol Abuser'. See http://www.winston churchill.org/learn/myths/myths/he-was-an-alcohol-abuser. Accessed 31 August 2014.

Page 133. **'Never forget your trademark'**   Andrew Roberts, *Hitler and Churchill: Secrets of Leadership* (London: 2010), p. 137.

Page 134. **'Winston . . . sober in the morning'**   See 'Drunk and Ugly: The Rumour Mill', http://www.winstonchurchill.org/support/the-churchill-centre/publications/ chartwell-bulletin/2011/31-jan/1052-drunk-and-ugly-the-rumor-mill.   Accessed 31 August 2014.

Pages 134–35. **'Churchill has spent . . . impromptu remarks'**   Clayton Fritchley, 'A Politician Must Watch His Wit', *New York Times Magazine* (3 July 1960), p. 31.

Page 135. **'Tell the Lord Privy Seal . . . shit at a time'**   Andrew Marr, *A History of Modern Britain* (London: 2009), p. 19.

Page 135. **'beginning of the end . . . beginning'**   Winston Churchill, 10 November 1942, Richard Toye, *The Roar of the Lion: The Untold Story of Winston Churchill's World War Two Speeches* (London: 2013), p. 148.

Page 135. **'I am ready . . . another question'**   Winston Churchill on his seventy-fifth birthday. Celia Sandys, *From Winston with Love and Kisses: The Young Churchill* (College Station, Tex.: 2013), p. 12.

Page 135. **'we shape . . . shape us'**   Winston Churchill, 28 October 1943. See http://www.winstonchurchill.org/learn/speeches/quotations/famous-quotations -and-stories. Accessed 31 August 2014.

Page 135. **'I have taken . . . out of me'**   Michael Richards, 'Alcohol Abuser'. See http://www.winstonchurchill.org/learn/myths/myths/he-was-an-alcohol-abuser. Accessed 31 August 2014.

Page 135. **'May I have . . . white meat'**   Dominique Enright, *The Wicked Wit of Winston Churchill* (London: 2011), Kindle edition.

Page 136. **'And mark my words . . . liquidate you'**   Winston Churchill, 5 July 1943; Nigel Nicolson, ed., *Harold Nicholson Diaries and Letters: 1939–1945*, vol.2, p. 303.

Page 136. **'sheep in sheep's clothing'**   See D. W. Brogan, *Safire's Political Dictionary* (London: 2008), p. 352.

Page 136. **'I remember . . . Treasury Bench'**   Winston Churchill, 28 January 1931, House of Commons; *Hansard*, HC Deb, vol. 247, cc999–1111.

Page 136. **'There but for the grace . . . goes God'**   Winston Churchill, quoted in *Life*, 16 February 1948, p. 39.

Page 136. **'no more . . . pink pansies'**   Richard Langworth, ed., *Churchill: By Himself* (New York: 2013), p. 57.

Page 136. **'Tell them . . . instruction literally'**   Enright, *Wicked Wit of Winston Churchill*, p. 139.

Page 137. **'When I warned . . . some neck!'**   Winston Churchill, 30 December 1941, Canadian Parliament, Ottawa; Richard Langworth, *Churchill: By Himself*, p. 24.

Page 137. **'triphibian', 'unsordid'**   Ibid, p. 48.

Page 137. **'Gimme . . . klop'**   Ibid, p. 54.

Page 138. **'Christ!'**   John Pearson, *The Private Lives of Winston Churchill* (London: 1991), p. 155.

## 11. 'THE MOST ADVANCED POLITICIAN OF THE TIME'

Page 141. **'Fancy living . . . clever!'**  Michael Sheldon, *The Young Titan: The Making of Winston Churchill* (London: 2014), pp. 127–28.

Page 141. **'like blacks'**  Winston Churchill to Clementine Churchill, 17 April 1924; Mary Soames, *Speaking for Themselves: The Personal Letters of Winston and Clementine Churchill* (London: 1999), p. 281.

Page 141. **'no interest . . . yellow peoples'**  Winston Churchill to Neville Chamberlain, 27 March 1939; see 'Did Singapore Have to Fall?' http://www.winstonchurchill.org/support/the-churchill-centre/publications/finest-hour/issues-109-to-144/no-138/903-part-5-did-singapore-have-to-fall. Accessed 31 August 2014.

Page 142. **'bomb or machine-gun'**  John Pearson, *The Private Lives of Winston Churchill* (London: 1991), p. 183.

Page 142. **'baboons'**  Martin Gilbert, *Winston S. Churchill, vol. 4: The Stricken World, 1916–1922*, p. 227.

Page 142. **'horrible . . . moral disease'**  Paul Addison, *Churchill: The Unexpected Hero* (Oxford: 2005), p. 93.

Page 142. **'one might as well . . . Bolsheviks'**  See Martin Gilbert, *Churchill: A Life* (New York: 1991), p. 408.

Page 142. **'feeding cat's meat to a tiger'**  Madhusree Mukerjee, *Churchill's Secret War: The British Empire and the Ravaging of India During World War II* (London: 2010), p. 14.

Page 142. **'a bit of bloodshed . . . throat'**  Paul Addison, *Churchill on the Home Front, 1900–1955* (London: 1992), p. 216.

Page 143. **'It is a national evil . . . degeneration'**  Winston Churchill, 28 April 1909, House of Commons, *Hansard*, HC Deb, vol. 4, cc342–411.

Page 144. **'a striking illustration . . . legislation'**  Alan S. Baxendale, *Winston Leonard Spencer-Churchill: Penal Reformer* (London: 2010), p. 191, n. 66.

Page 144. **'Insurance . . . rescue of the masses'**  Randolph Churchill and Martin Gilbert, *Winston S. Churchill: Young Statesman 1901–1914*, p. 294.

Page 145. **'All this picture . . . industry'**  Winston Churchill to Clementine Churchill, 14 September 1909; Addison, *Home Front*, p. 86.

Page 145. **'survival of a feudal . . . forever'**  Gilbert, *Churchill: A Life*, p. 211.

Page 146. **'The prisoner . . . habits in prison'**  Ibid., pp. 212–13.

Page 146. **'I wanted to draw . . . inconvenience'**  Roy Jenkins, *Churchill: A Biography* (New York: 2001), p. 182.

Page 147. **'vendetta'**  See 'Winston Churchill' *Daily Telegraph*, 2 March 2010.

Page 147. **'They are very poor . . . starving'**  Gilbert, *Churchill: A Life*, p. 231.

Page 147. **'had a real grievance . . . civilisation'**  Ibid., p. 232.

Page 148. **'no worker . . . trade dispute'**  Ibid., p. 377.

Page 148. **'recalcitrant . . . unreasonable'**  Ibid., p. 478.

Page 148. **'aboriginal . . . Tory'**  Addison, *Home Front*, p. 101.

Page 148. **'Winston has no convictions'**  Richard Toye, *Lloyd George and Churchill: Rivals for Greatness* (London: 2012), p. 47.

Page 149. **'made his hair stand on end'**  Jenkins, *Churchill*, p. 81.

Page 151. **'It was the world . . . very few'**  James C. Humes, *Churchill: The Prophetic Statesman* (New York: 2012), p. 68.

Page 152. **'he desired in Britain . . . working class'** James Muller, *Churchill as a Peace-maker* (London: 2003), p. 14.

Page 152. **great central party . . . on the other** Addison, *Home Front*, p. 26.

Page 152. **'Conservative in principle . . . sympathy'** Norman Rose, *Churchill: An Unruly Life* (London: 1994), p. 208.

Page 153. **'the existing capitalist . . . necessities'** Gilbert, *Churchill: A Life*, pp. 465–68.

## 12. No Glory in Slaughter

Page 157. **'could not help . . . before that'** Martin Gilbert, *Churchill: A Life* (New York: 1991), p. 393.

Page 158. **'The economic clauses . . . futile'** Winston Churchill, *The Second World War, vol. 1: The Gathering Storm* (London: 1986), p. 6.

Page 159. **'a man with such power . . . confronted'** Martin Gilbert, *Winston S. Churchill, vol. 5: Prophet of Truth 1922–1939*, p. 805.

Page 160. **'Churchill had seen more . . . army'** Pat Buchanan, *Churchill, Hitler and the Unnecessary War: How Britain Lost Its Empire and the West Lost the World* (New York: 2008), p. 59.

Page 160. **'seldom . . . minimise its horrors'** Peregrine Worsthorne, 'Why Winston Churchill Is Not Really a War Hero', *The Week*, 22 October 2008.

Page 161. **'Winston has got . . . with sadness'** Roy Jenkins, *Churchill: A Biography* (New York: 2001), p. 240.

Page 161. **'Winston . . . delicious'** Michael and Eleanor Brock, eds., *Margot Asquith's Great War Diary 1914–1916: The View from Downing Street* (London: 2014), p. 54; Gilbert, *Churchill: A Life*, pp. 294–95.

Page 162. **'your father . . . Dardanelles'** Andrew Roberts, review of Carlo D'Este, *Warlord: A Life of Churchill at War, 1874–1945*, *Daily Telegraph*, 10 April 2009.

Page 162. **'criminal and cowardly'** Norman Rose, *Churchill: An Unruly Life* (London: 1994), p. 39.

Page 163. **'boy . . . Russia'** Michael Sheldon, *The Young Titan: The Making of Winston Churchill* (London: 2014), pp. 129–31.

Page 164. **'If I were a Boer . . . field'** Winston Churchill's maiden speech in the House of Commons, 18 February 1901; Jenkins, *Churchill*, p. 72.

Page 164 **'What is going on . . . bloody rags'** Richard Langworth, *Churchill: By Himself* (New York: 2013), p. 251.

Page 165. **'I saw the daylight . . . death'** Churchill, *The Second World War*, vol. 1, p. 201.

## 13. The Ships That Walked

Page 170. **'moveable machine gun . . . trench'** Winston Churchill to John French, 10 April 1915; Winston Churchill, *The World Crisis, 1911–1918* (London: 2005), pp. 313–14.

Page 170. **'The spectacle . . . self-binder'**   Ibid., p. 314.

Page 171. **'landships'**   H. G. Wells, 'The Land Ironclads', *The Strand Magazine*, December 1903.

Page 171. **he wrote to Asquith**   See Winston Churchill to H. H. Asquith, 5 January 1915, CHAR 13/44/32–35.

Pages 171–72. **'so that they are . . . people in them'**   Winton Churchill, 'Statement on the Introduction of the Tank', CHAR 2/109.

Page 172. **'The rollers . . . rolling process'**   Ibid.

Page 173. **'a tractor . . . enemy trenches'**   Tennyson d'Eyncourt to Winston Churchill, 22 February 1915; Martin Gilbert, *Winston S. Churchill, vol. 4: The Challenge of War* (London: 1973), p. 553.

Page 173. **'As proposed . . . WSC'**   Martin Gilbert, *Churchill: A Life* (New York: 1991), p. 298.

Page2 174–75. **'After losing . . . at the front'**   Tennyson D'Eyncourt to Winston Churchill, 14 February 1916, CHAR 2/71/14.

Page 175. **'a grave danger . . . as a whole'**   Gilbert, *Churchill: A Life*, p. 373.

Pages 175–76. **'That dangerous and uncertain . . . Whitehall'**   Ibid., p. 376.

Page 177. **'bellybando'**   Norman McGowan, *My Years with Churchill* (London: 1958), p. 94.

Page 178. **'Machines . . . slaughter'**   Gilbert, *Churchill: A Life*, p. 370.

## 14. The 100-Horsepower Mental Engine

Page 184. **'KBO'**   See 'Churchill: Leader and Statesman', http://www.winston churchill.org/learn/biography/biography/churchill-leader-and-statesman. Accessed 1 September 2014.

Page 185. **'They say . . . take the chance?'**   Lou Channon, *Ronald Reagan: The Presidential Portfolio—A History Illustrated from the Collection of the Ronald Reagan Library and Museum* (London: 2001).

Page 186. **try counting . . . parliamentary record**   Traditionally referred to as 'Hansard', for Thomas Curson Hansard (1776–1833), a London printer and publisher, the record of parliamentary proceedings in the United Kingdom may be accessed at http://hansard.millbanksystems.com.

Page 186. **'My husband . . . quite beyond us'**   Eleanor Roosevelt, 'Churchill at the White House' in *The Atlantic*, 1 March 1965 (published posthumously). http://www.theatlantic.com/magazine/archive/1965/03/churchill-at-the-white-house/305459. Accessed 1 September 2014.

Pages 187–88. **'limited . . . matters'**   Norman Rose, *Churchill: An Unruly Life* (London: 1994), p. 173.

Page 188. **'damned dots'**   Winston Churchill, *Lord Randolph Churchill*, vol. 2 (London: 1906), p. 184.

Page 188. **'speaking Persian'**   William Manchester, *The Last Lion—Winston Spencer Churchill: Visions of Glory, 1874–1932*, p. 786.

Page 188. **'There comes . . . horsepower mind'**   Stanley Baldwin, 'Churchill & His Contemporaries' http://www.winstonchurchill.org/learn/myths/churchill-trivia/528-contemporaries. Accessed 1 September 2014.

Page 188. **'Black dog'** Martin Gilbert, *In Search of Churchill* (London: 1995), p. 210.

Page 189. **'You know . . . brushing your teeth'** Ibid., p. 26.

Page189–90. **'The principle . . . St. George's Day'** Winston Churchill, *The Second World War*, vol. 4 (London: 1950), pp. 623–24.

Page 191. **'The ferment of ideas . . . difficulties'** Max Hastings, *Finest Years: Churchill as Warlord, 1940–45* (London: 2009), p. 93.

## 15. Playing Roulette with History

Page 194. **'I tried to give . . . professions'** Martin Gilbert, *Churchill and the Jews: A Lifelong Friendship* (London: 2007), pp. 98–99.

Page 194. **'Tell your boss . . . bad sticker'** Ernst Hanfstaengel, *Hitler—The Missing Years* (London: 1957), p. 185.

Page 195. **'very glad'** Winston Churchill, *The Second World War, vol. 1: The Gathering Storm* (London: 1986), p. 40.

Page 195. **'I had no national . . . character'** Ibid.

Page 195. **'Heil . . . Boothby'** Robert Rhodes James, *Robert Boothby: A Portrait of Churchill's Ally* (London: 1991), p. 138.

Page 196. **'Why is your chief . . . born'** Churchill, *The Second World War*, vol.1, p. 40.

Page 196. **'What part . . . same about you'** Hanfstaengel, *Hitler*, p. 187.

Page 196. **'what is the sense . . . born'** Roy Jenkins, *Churchill: A Biography* (New York: 2001), p. 469.

Page 197. **'All these bands . . . weapons'** Martin Gilbert, *Churchill: The Power of Words: His Remarkable Life Recounted Through His Writings and Speeches* (London: 2012), p. 101.

Pages 197–98. **'the ability to foretell . . . happen'** Richard Langworth, *Churchill: By Himself* (New York: 2013), p. 505.

Page 199. **'gross example . . . lives'** Martin Gilbert, *Churchill: A Life* (New York: 1991), p. 286.

Page 200. **'soft under-belly'** Winston Churchill, House of Commons, 11 November 1942, *Hansard*, HC Deb, vol. 385, cc8–56.

Page 200. **'I thought he would die . . . finished'** Gilbert, *Churchill: A Life*, p. 321.

Page 201. **'chewing barbed wire in Flanders'** Mary Soames, *Clementine Churchill: The Biography of a Marriage* (London: 2003), p. 134.

Page 202. **'foul baboonery'** Gilbert, *Churchill: A Life*, p. 410.

Page 202. **'civilisation . . . victims'** Clifford Kinvig, *Churchill's Crusade: The British Invasion of Russia, 1918–1920* (London: 2007), p. 85.

Page 202. **'Nothing . . . regime'** Gilbert, *Churchill: A Life*, p. 415.

Page 203. **'I will not submit . . . baboons'** Kinvig, *Churchill's Crusade*, p. 154.

Page 203. **'He hunts lions . . . cats'** David Low, 'Winston's Bag', *The Star*, 21 January 1920.

Page 204. **'Stop This New War'** *Daily Mail*, 18 September 1922; Andrew Mango, *Ataturk* (London: 2004), p. 352.

Page 205. **'I had the greatest difficulty . . . teasing her'** Gilbert, *Churchill: A Life*, p. 465.

Page 206. **Keynes wrote a denunciation**   See J. Maynard Keynes, *The Economic Conse-quences of Mr Churchill* (London: 1925).

Page 206. **'I would rather . . . content'**   Geoffrey Best, *Churchill: A Study in Greatness* (London: 2001), p. 119.

Page 206. **'You shall not press . . . cross of gold'**   Michael Kazin, *A Godly Hero: The Life of William Jennings Bryan* (New York: 2006), p. 61.

Page 206. **'I will make you . . . Chancellor'**   Liaquat Ahaned, *Lords of Finesse: 1929, The Great Depression, and the Bankers Who Broke the World* (New York: 2011), p. 235.

Page 207. **'nauseating'**   Winston Churchill, 23 February 1931, Richard Toye, *Chur-chill's Empire: The World That Made Him and the World That He Made* (London: 2011), p. 176.

Page 209. **'We are a sort . . . fought for Britain'**   Gilbert, *Churchill: A Life*, p. 501.

Page 209. **'Make a success . . . much more'**   Toye, *Churchill's Empire*, p. 188.

Page 210. **'Winston collapsed . . . years'**   Paul Addison, *Churchill on the Home Front 1900–1950* (London: 1992), p. 323.

Page 212. **'failure'**   Robert Rhodes James, *Churchill: A Study in Failure, 1900–1939* (London: 1981).

Page 213. **'ridiculous . . . memorandum'**   James C. Humes, *Churchill: The Prophetic Statesman* (New York: 2012), p. 32.

Page 213. **'declare war . . . Pagan times'**   Langworth, *Churchill: By Himself*, pp. 122–23.

## 16. An Icy Ruthlessness

Page 217. **'Shooting fish in a barrel'**   Robert Philpott interviewed in Philip Graig, 'Mass Murder or a Stroke of Genius That Saved Britain? As Closer Ties with France Are Planned, the 'Betrayal' They Still Can't Forgive', *Daily Mail*, 5 Febru-ary 2010.

Page 218. **'I leave it . . . to history'**   Winston Churchill, 4 July 1940, House of Com-mons, *Hansard*, HC Deb, vol. 362, cc1043–51.

Page 219. **'France is civilisation'**   Lord Moran, interview in *Life*, 22 April 1966, p. 106.

Page 219. **'in other directions'**   Gilbert, *Churchill: A Life*, p. 180.

Pages 219–20. **'to hell with that . . . weather'**   Martin Gilbert, *Winston S. Churchill, vol. 6: Finest Hour, 1939–1941* (London: 1983), p. 526.

Page 221. **'the war . . . Masonic plot'**   Michael Cohen, *Britain's Moment in Palestine: Retrospect and Perspectives, 1917–1948* (London: 2014), p. 14.

Page 221. **'blasted rhetoric'**   Jonathan Rose, *The Literary Churchill* (New Haven, Conn.: 2014), p. 296.

Page 221. **'fetch Seal . . . floes'**   Max Hastings, *Finest Years: Churchill as Warlord, 1940–45* (London: 2009), p. 106.

Page 224. **a fascinating study . . . 'butchery'**   Richard Lamb, *Churchill as War Leader* (London: 1991).

Page 224. **'All efforts . . . success'**   Sheila Lawlor, *Churchill and the Politics of War, 1940–1941* (London: 1994), pp. 57–58.

Page 225. **'at all costs, at all risks . . . to ruin'**   Winston Churchill, *The Second World War: Their Finest Hour*, pp. 197–98.

Page 226. **'Honourable discussions'**   See 'Battle Summary no.1', http://www.hmshood .org.uk/reference/official/adm234/adm234-317.htm. Accessed 2 September 2014.

Page 226. **'If we had known . . . all the difference'**   David Brown, *The Road to Oran: Anglo-French Naval Relations, September 1939–July 1940* (London: 2004), p. xxix.

Page 226. **'Settle matters quickly'**   'Diary of Events', 3 July 1940, CHAR 9/173A–B.

Page 226. **'It was a terrible decision . . . state'**   Winston Churchill, 4 July 1940, House of Commons, *Hansard*, HC Deb, vol. 362, cc1043–51.

Page 228. **'unending suffering and misery'**   Adolph Hitler, 19 July 1940, in David Jablonsky, *Churchill and Hitler: Essays on the Political-Military Direction of Total War* (London: 1994), p. 220.

Page 228. **'Hitler must invade . . . fail he will'**   Gilbert, *Winston S. Churchill, vol.6: Finest Hour*, p. 663.

Page 231. **that speech on Oran**   Winston Churchill, 4 July 1940, House of Commons, *Hansard*, HC Deb, vol. 362, cc1043–51.

## 17. THE WOOING OF AMERICA

Page 232. **'Sit down . . . drag the United States in'**   Martin Gilbert, *Winston S. Churchill, vol.6: Finest Hour, 1939–1941* (London: 1983), p. 358.

Page 235. **'It is 27 years ago . . . enough'**   David Roll, *The Hopkins Touch: Harry Hopkins and the Forging of the Alliance to Defeat Hitler* (London: 2013), p. 137.

Page 237. **'Not a single . . . ourselves'**   John Keegan, *The Second World War* (New York: 1989), p. 539.

Page 237. **'left . . . dissatisfaction'**   Richard Toye, *The Roar of the Lion: The Untold Story of Winston Churchill's World War Two Speeches* (London: 2013), p. 114.

Page 239. **'kiss Uncle Sam . . . not on all four'**   Norman Rose, *Churchill: An Unruly Life* (London: 1994), p. 183.

Page 239. **'Strong drink . . . all my life'**   John Ramsden, *Man of the Century: Winston Churchill and His Legend Since 1945* (London: 2009), p. 132.

Page 240. **'As one former . . . to another'**   See Admiral Boyce, 'Formal Naval Persons', http://www.winstonchurchill.org/support/the-churchill-centre/publications/finest-hour-online/1305-qformer-naval-personsq. Accessed 2 September 2014.

Pages 240–41. **'Even though . . . liberation of the old'**   Winston Churchill, 'We Shall Fight Them on the Beaches', 4 June 1940, http://www.winstonchurchill.org/learn/speeches/speeches-of-winston-churchill/128-we-shall-fight-on-the-beaches. Accessed 2 September 2014.

Page 241. **the Oran speech**   Winston Churchill, 4 July 1940, *Hansard*, HC Deb, vol. 362, cc1043–51.

Page 241. **'the most unsordid act in history'**   Winston Churchill, 24 August 1945, *Hansard*, HC Deb, vol. 413, cc955–8.

Page 241. **Britain was being skinned . . . to the bone**   Martin Gilbert, *Churchill and America* (London: 2005), p. 219.

Page 243. **'There is nothing . . . kill anything'**   Martin Gilbert, *The Churchill War Papers, vol.3: The Ever-Widening War* (London: 1993), p. 1399.

Page 244. 'The British Prime Minister . . . United States' Richard Langworth, *Churchill's Wit: The Definitive Collection* (New York: 2009), p. 16.

Page 244. 'Sure I am . . . forefront of the battle' Winston Churchill, 'Address to the Congress of the United States', 26 December 1941; Martin Gilbert, ed., *Churchill: The Power of Words: His Remarkable Life Recounted Through His Writings and Speeches* (London: 2012), p. 294.

Page 244. 'No one . . . war at all' Martin Gilbert, *Winston S. Churchill, vol. 7: Road to Victory, 1941–1945* (London: 2000), p. 553.

Page 245. 'Saturated . . . thankful' Martin Gilbert, *Churchill and America* (London: 2005), p. 245.

## 18. The Giant of the Shrunken Island

Page 247. 'This will never do' Alan 'Tommy' Lascelles, *King's Counsellor, Abdication and War: The Diaries of Sir Alan Lascelles* (London: 2006), p. 224.

Page 247. a letter for the King King George VI to Winston Churchill, 31 May 44; CHAR 20/136/10.

Page 248. 'To this the unfortunate . . . violently' Lascelles, *King's Counsellor*, p. 226.

Page 249. 'Tommy's face . . . longer' Ibid.

Page 249. 'I was thinking . . . risk is 100–1' Ibid.

Page 249. 'in this instance . . . selfishness' Ibid.

Page 249. a second and firmer reprimand King George VI to Winston Churchill, 2 June 44; CHAR 20/136/4.

Page 251. 'That is certainly a strong argument' Lascelles, *King's Counsellor*, p. 227.

Page 251. 'the most ghastly . . . whole war' Max Hastings, *Overlord: D-Day and the Battle for Normandy 1944* (London: 2012), p. 1.

Page 252. 'front page stuff' Lascelles, *King's Counsellor*, p. 228.

Page 253. 'unnecessary battle' For instance, see Correlli Barnett, *The Battle of El Alamein* (London: 1964).

Page 253. 'I can't get the victories . . . hard to get' Vincent O'Hara, *In Passage Perilous: Malta and the Convoy Battles of June 1942* (Bloomington, Ind.: 2012), p. 67.

Page 254. 'Many British officers . . . Japanese' Max Hastings, 'After a Series of Military Defeats Even Churchill Started to Fear That Our Army Was Simply Too Yellow to Fight', *The Daily Mail*, 21 August 2009.

Page 255. 'Father . . . soldiers won't fight' Andrew Roberts, *Masters and Commanders: The Military Geniuses Who Led the West to Victory in World War II* (London: 2009), p. 287.

Page 255. 'We had so many . . . done better' Max Hasting, 'On Churchill's Fighting Spirit', *Financial Times*, 4 September 2009, http://www.ft.com/cms/s/0/e6824d52-98e2-11de-aa1b-00144feabdco.html#axzz3CBVtTd9C. Accessed 3 September 2014.

Page 255. 'Defeat is one thing . . . another' Robert Dallek, *Franklin D. Roosevelt and American Foreign Policy, 1932–1945* (Oxford: 1995), p. 347.

Page 255. 'He wins . . . battle' Norman Rose, *Churchill: The Unruly Giant* (New York: 1995), p. 389.

Page 255. **'You British . . . fighting'**  Martin Gilbert, *Winston S. Churchill, vol. 7: Road to Victory, 1941–1945* (New York: 1986), p. 185.

Page 257. **'a tumbler . . . cigars!!'**  Arthur Bryant, *The Turn of the Tide: A History of the War Years Based on the Diaries of Field-Marshal Lord Alanbrooke, Chief of the Imperial General Staff* (New York: 1957), p. 464.

Page 258. **'had a plug'**  Winston Churchill to President Roosevelt, 14 June 1944; *Winston S. Churchill, The Second World War, vol. 6: Triumph and Tragedy* (London: 1953), p. 28.

Page 258. **'Let's do it . . . graphically'**  See account of Ralph Martin; Additional Churchill Papers, WCHL 15/2/6.

Page 258. **'I shall never forget . . . critical moment'**  Martin Gilbert, *Churchill: A Life* (New York: 1991), p. 829.

Page 259. **'Prime Minister . . . come away'**  Ibid., p. 832.

Page 259. **'The look on Winston's face . . . by his nurse'**  Ibid., p. 832.

Page 261. **'I have a very strong feeling . . . brave new world'**  Norman Rose, *Churchill: An Unruly Life* (London: 1994) p. 394.

Page 261. **'It struck me . . . fighting forces'**  Gilbert, *Churchill: A Life*, p. 852.

Pages 261–62. **'a sharp stab . . . dominated my mind'**  Martin Gilbert, *Winston S. Churchill, vol. 8: 'Never Despair' 1945–1965*, p. 106.

Page 262. **'Cheer for Churchill . . . Labour'**  Adrian Fort, *Nancy: The Story of Lady Astor* (London: 2012), p. 304.

Page 262. **'It may well be . . . effectively disguised'**  Paul Addison, *Churchill: The Unexpected Hero* (Oxford: 2005), p. 215.

Page 262. **'I wouldn't call . . . hard time'**  John Severance, *Winston Churchill: Soldier, Statesman, Artist* (New York: 1996), p. 115.

Page 263. **'weak and rhetorical . . . public affairs'**  *The Spectator* upon news of Churchill's appointment to First Lord of the Admiralty; quoted from Rose, *Unruly Life*, p. 88.

## 19. The Cold War and How He Won It

Page 265. **'Are we beasts . . . too far?'**  Norman Rose, *Churchill: An Unruly Life* (London: 1994), p. 337.

Page 265. **'mere act . . . wanton destruction'**  Winston Churchill Cabinet minutes, 28 March 1945; David Reynolds, *In Command of History: Churchill Fighting and Writing the Second World War* (London: 2005), p. 481.

Page 266. **'My hate died . . . clothes'**  Martin Gilbert, *Churchill: A Life* (New York: 1991), p. 850.

Page 267. **he sketched out his plans**  Lord Moran, *Winston Churchill: The Struggle for Survival, 1940–1965* (London: 1966), p. 163.

Page 268. **'You said it! . . . over there'**  Richard Collier, *The War That Stalin Won: Tehran–Berlin* (London: 1983), p. 240.

Page 268. **'This brand . . . on Christmas Day'**  Geoffrey Best, *Churchill: A Study in Greatness* (London: 2001), p. 271.

Page 268. **'constitutes . . . parallel'**  Winston S. Churchill, *The Second World War, vol. 6: Triumph and Tragedy*, p. 438.

Page 269. **All that remained secret**  See David Reynolds, *From World War to Cold War: Churchill, Roosevelt, and the International History of the 1940s* (Oxford: 2006).

Page 271. **'I like that man'**  David Carlton, *Churchill and the Soviet Union* (Manchester: 2000), p. 144.

Page 272. **'our misery'**  Rose, *Unruly Life*, p. 255.

Page 272. **'realist-lizards of the crocodile family'**  Martin Gilbert, *Winston S. Churchill, vol.8: 'Never Despair' 1945–1965*, p.161.

Page 272. **'wonderful school'**  Gregory Sand, *Defending the West: The Truman-Churchill Correspondence, 1945–1960* (London: 2004), p. 6.

Page 272. **'seemed to like it very well'**  Martin Gilbert, *Churchill and America* (London: 2005), p. 367.

Page 272. **'I am sure . . . good'**  Fraser J. Harbutt, *The Iron Curtain* (Oxford: 1988), p. 172.

Page 272. **'enthusiastic'**  Ibid., p. 180.

Page 273. **'He told me . . . admirable'**  Ibid.

Page 272. **Churchill's speech at Fulton**  Winston Churchill, 5 March 1946, Fulton, Missouri.  See  http://www.winstonchurchill.org/learn/speeches/speeches-of-winston-churchill/120-the-sinews-of-peace. Accessed 3 September 2014.

Page 275. **'special relationship . . . manuals of instruction'**  Ibid.

Page 275. **'less than happy . . . each other'**  Gilbert, *Churchill: A Life*, p. 867.

Page 275. **'The United States . . . any other nation'**  Ibid., p. 868.

Page 276. **'inimical . . . peace'**  Geoffrey Williams, *The Permanent Alliance: The Euro-American Relationship, 1945–1984* (London: 1977), p. 19.

Page 277. **'tightness'**  Lord Moran, *Winston Churchill: The Struggle for Survival, 1940–1965* (London: 1966), p. 337.

Page 278. **'complete rest'**  Gilbert, *Churchill and America*, p. 421.

Pages 278–79. **'Colville . . . recover'**  Gilbert, *Winston S. Churchill, vol. 8, 'Never Despair'*, p. 856.

Page 279. **'like an aeroplane . . . safe landing'**  James Muller, *Churchill as a Peacemaker* (London: 2003), p. 323.

Page 279. **'Man is spirit . . . Americans'**  Gilbert, *Churchill: A Life*, p. 939.

## 20. CHURCHILL THE EUROPEAN

Page 283. **'We don't need . . . right to be here'**  See 'stillpoliticallyincorrect', http://disqus.com/telegraph-795480a5f59311af7dfc5b92f96f73d7/. Accessed 3 September 2014.

Page 284. **'The Durham miners won't wear it'**  Alex May, *Britain and Europe Since 1945* (London: 2014), p. 18.

Page 285. **'Utter rubbish! . . . Nonsense!'**  Winston Churchill, House of Commons, 26 June 1950, *Hansard,* HC Deb, vol. 476, cc1907–2056.

Page 285. **'High Authority'**  For instance, see James Carmichael, House of Commons, 26 June 1950, *Hansard,* HC Deb, vol. 476, cc1907–2056.

Page 286. **'They would be . . . in this country'**  Maurice Edelman, 27 June 1950, *Hansard,* HC Deb, vol. 476, cc2104–59.

Page 286. 'Do we really . . . nightmare century' Robert Boothby, ibid.

Pages 286–87. 'He seeks to win . . . balance of Europe' Winston Churchill, ibid.

Pages 287–88. 'The whole movement . . . home together' Winston Churchill, ibid.

Page 289. 'United States of Europe . . . possible' Martin Gilbert, *Churchill: A Life* (New York: 1991), p. 731.

Page 289. 'We must build . . . those who can' Winston Churchill, 'Speech to the Academic Youth', 19 September 1946; http://www.churchill-society-london.org. uk/astonish.html. Accessed 3 September 2014.

Page 289. 'the idea of . . . European family' Winston Churchill, *Winston Churchill's Speeches: Never Give In!* (London: 2007), pp. 439–42.

Page 289. a speech in Scotland Robert Rhodes James, *Churchill Speaks: Winston S. Churchill in Peace and War: Collected Speeches, 1897–1963* (London: 1980), p. 930.

Page 291. 'But . . . dwell among my own people' Winston Churchill, 'Why Not the United States of Europe', *News of the World*, 29 May 1938; quoted from Martin Gilbert, *Churchill: The Power of Words: His Remarkable Life Recounted Through His Writings and Speeches* (London: 2012), pp. 199–200.

Page 293. 'The question . . . associated with it' Winston Churchill, House of Commons, 27 June 1950, *Hansard*, HC Deb, vol. 476, cc2104–59.

Page 294. 'Great Britain . . . triple part' Winston Churchill, 'Why Not the United States of Europe', *News of the World*, 29 May 1938.

Page 296. 'Look at it . . . final disaster' Kevin Theakston, *Winston Churchill and the British Constitution* (London: 2004), p. 132.

## 21. Maker of the Modern Middle East

Page 300. 'the war of the British succession' C. J. Wrigley, *A.J.P. Taylor: Radical Historian of Europe* (London: 2006), p. 315.

Page 302. 'Winston's hiccup' See 'Frank Jacobs, 'Winston's Hiccup' *New York Times*, 6 March 2013; http://opinionator.blogs.nytimes.com/2012/03/06/winstons-hiccup/?_php=true&_type=blogs&_r=0. Accessed 3 September 2014.

Page 303. surface area . . . ruled by Britain See Walter Reid, *Empire of Sand: How Britain Made the Middle East* (London: 2011).

Page 303. 'on an oriental scale' *Spectator*, 'The Question of the Mandates', 28 August 1920.

Page 305. a letter from A. J. Balfour A. J. Balfour to Walter Rothschild, 2 November 1917; Gudrun Krämer, *A History of Palestine: From the Ottoman Conquest to the Founding of the State of Israel* (Princeton: 2011), p. 149.

Page 305. 'a land without . . . without a land' Israel Zangwill, "The Return to Palestine", *New Liberal Review* (December 1901), p. 615.

Page 306. 'Gertie! . . . Dear boy!' Shareen Brysac and Karl Meyer, *Kingmakers: The Invention of the Modern Middle East* (London: 2009), p. 176.

Page 306. 'a bas Churchill' Jack Fishman, *My Darling Clementine: The Story of Lady Churchill* (London: 1966), p. 92.

Page 306. 'I've started . . . finish on a camel' Janet Wallach, *Desert Queen: The Ex-*

*traordinary Life of Gertrude Bell: Adventurer, Adviser to Kings, Ally of Lawrence of Arabia* (New York: 2005), p. 300.

Page 307. **'The Jews have been . . . the world over'**  Michael J. Cohen, *Churchill and the Jews, 1900–1948* (London: 2013), p. 90.

Page 307. **'the Palestinians never miss . . . opportunity'**  Oded Balaban, *Interpreting Conflict: Israeli–Palestinian Negotiations at Camp David II and Beyond* (New York: 2005), p. 60.

Page 308.  **'If one promise . . . fulfil both'**  Winston Churchill's reply to Mousa Kasem El-Hussaini; Howard Grief, *The Legal Foundation and Borders of Israel Under International Law: A Treatise on Jewish Sovereignty Over the Land of Israel* ( Jerusalem, 2008), p. 446.

Page 308. **'It was a declaration . . . intimately associated'**  Winston Churchill's reply to Mousa Kasem El-Hussaini, in Gilbert, *Winston S. Churchill, vol. 4; The Stricken World*, p. 565.

Page 308. **'Our Jewish and Zionist . . . rights'**  Gilbert, *Winston S. Churchill, Vol. 4; The Stricken World*, p. 567.

Page 309. **'prudence . . . patience'**  Norman Rose, 'Churchill and Zionism', in Robert Blake and William Roger Louis, eds., *Churchill: A Major New Reassessment of His Life in Peace and War* (London: 1996), p. 156.

Page 309. **'Every step . . . all Palestinians'**  Gilbert, *Churchill: A Life*, p. 435.

Page 309. **'Some people . . . appeared in the world'**  Michael Makovsky, *Churchill's Promised Land: Zionism and Statecraft* (New Haven, Conn.: 2007), p. 85.

Page 310. **'Hebrew bloodsuckers'**  Cohen, *Churchill and the Jews*, p. 138.

Page 310. **'tendency to orientalism'**  Lady Gwendoline Bertie to Churchill, 27 August 1907; Randolph Churchill and Martin Gilbert, *Winston S. Churchill, vol. 2, Companion Part 1*, p. 672. See also Warren Dockter, 'The Influence of a Poet: Wilfrid S. Blunt and the Churchills', *Journal of Historical Biography*, vol. 10 (Autumn 2011), pp. 70–102.

Page 310. **in his new survey**  Warren Dockter, *Winston Churchill and the Islamic World: Orientalism, Empire and Diplomacy in the Middle East* (London: 2014).

Page 311. **'sacred and beloved homeland . . . trade'**  Isaiah Freidman, *Palestine, a Twice-Promised Land: The British, the Arabs & Zionism : 1915-1920* (London: 2000), p. 171.

Page 312. **'We committed ourselves . . . inhabitants of the country'**  Paul Addison, *Churchill: The Unexpected Hero*, p. 101.

Pages 312–13. **'I do not admit . . . power to be the judge'**  Palestine Royal Commission, Minutes of Evidence, 12 March 1937; CHAR/2/317/8666, 8728, pp. 503, 507.

Page 313. **'a score of mud villages . . . usually starving'**  Cohen, *Churchill and the Jews*, p. 67.

Page 314. **'I can't understand . . . make them sneeze'**  Winston Churchill in War Office minutes, 22 May 1919, Gilbert, *Winston S. Churchill, vol. 4, Companion Part 1*, p. 649.

Page 314. **'I hate Irak . . . ungrateful volcano'**  Ronald Hyam, 'Churchill and the British Empire' in Blake and Louis, *Churchill*, p. 174.

Page 315. **'an odious act of ingratitude'** Martin Gilbert, *Winston S. Churchill, vol. 8: 'Never Despair' 1945–1965* (London: 1988), p. 1233.

Page 315. **'I have achieved . . . nothing in the end'** Rose, *Unruly Life*, p. 424.

Page 317. **As Richard Toye has pointed out** Richard Toye, *Churchill's Empire: The World That Made Him and the World That He Made* (London: 2011), p. 316.

## 22. THE MEANING OF HIS NAME TODAY

Page 319. **'My darling one . . . Your ever & always W'** Martin Gilbert, *Winston S. Churchill, vol. 8: 'Never Despair' 1945–1965* (London: 1988), p. 1342.

Page 320. **'My life is over . . . not yet ended'** Martin Gilbert, *Churchill: A Life* (New York: 1991), p. 956.

Page 323. **'there should be no barrier . . . fitted for it'** Richard Toye, *Churchill's Empire: The World That Made Him and the World That He Made* (London: 2011), p. xii.

Page 323. **'What are you going to do . . . almost extinct'** Richard Langworth, *Churchill: By Himself* (New York: 2013), p. 569.

Page 324. **'the unnatural . . . impossible to exaggerate'** See Gilbert, 'Churchill and Eugenics' http://www.winstonchurchill.org/support/the-churchill-centre/publications/finest-hour-online/594-churchill-and-eugenics. Accessed 4 September 2014.

Page 324. **'Three generations . . . is enough'** Martin Gilbert, ibid.

Pages 324–25. **'I feel you have come . . . defend myself'** Langworth, *Churchill's Wit: The Definitive Collection* (New York: 2009), p. 101.

Page 325. **'When I think . . . treated equally'** Richard Langworth, *Churchill: By Himself* (New York: 2013), p. 442.

Page 325. **'Gandhi . . . elephant'** Arthur Herman, *Gandhi & Churchill: The Epic Rivalry That Destroyed an Empire and Forged Our Age* (London: 2009), p. 273.

Page 328. **'Some experiments . . . canvas since'** Winston Churchill, *Thoughts and Adventures* (London: 1949), pp. 234–35.

Page 331. **'He had sympathy . . . all over the world'** Gilbert, *Winston S. Churchill, vol. 8, 'Never Despair'*, p.1361.

Pages 331–32. **'character . . . in an infant'** Gilbert, *Churchill: A Life*, p. 487.

## 23. THE CHURCHILL FACTOR

Page 335. **an essay by the psychologist Anthony Storr** See Anthony Storr, 'The Man' in A.J.P. Taylor, ed., *Churchill: Four Faces and the Man* (London: 1969), pp. 210–11.

# BIBLIOGRAPHY

The bibliography has been compiled by Dr Warren Dockter, Research Fellow at the University of Cambridge, to cover not only works quoted or cited in the text, but also material consulted during the preparation of this book.

## Primary Sources

### *Unpublished Sources*

#### The National Archives
Cabinet papers (CAB)
Hansard: House of Common Debates
Prime Minister's papers (PREM)

#### Personal papers
(Leo) Amery papers, Churchill College, Cambridge (AMEL)
(Julian) Amery papers, Churchill College, Cambridge (AMEJ)
Broadwater Collection, Churchill College, Cambridge (BRDW)
Chartwell Manuscripts, Churchill College, Cambridge (CHWL)
(Clementine) Churchill papers, Churchill College, Cambridge (CSCT)
(Lord Randoph) Churchill papers, Churchill College, Cambridge (RCHL)
(Randolph) Churchill papers, Churchill College, Cambridge (RCDCH)
(Winston) Churchill papers, Churchill College, Cambridge (CHAR & CHUR)
Churchill Additional Collection, Churchill College, Cambridge (WCHL)
(John) Colville papers, Churchill College, Cambridge (CLVL)

### *Published Sources*

#### Major works by Winston Churchill
Churchill, Winston, *A History of the English-Speaking Peoples*, Vols I–IV. London: Cassell and Company Ltd., 1956.
———— *Amid These Storms: Thoughts and Adventures*. London: Thornton Butterworth, Ltd., 1932.
———— *Great Contemporaries*. London: Thornton Butterworth, Ltd., 1932.
———— *Ian Hamilton's March*. London: Longmans, Green, & Co., 1900.
———— *India-Speeches*. London: Thornton Butterworth, Ltd., 1931.

—— *London to Ladysmith Via Pretoria*. London: Longmans, Green, & Co., 1900.

—— *Lord Randolph Churchill*, Vols I–II. London: Macmillan and Co., 1906.

—— *Marlborough: His Life and Times*, Vols I–IV. London: George C. Harrap & Co., 1933–38.

—— *My African Journey*. London: Hodder and Stoughton, 1908.

—— *My Early Life: A Roving Commission*. London: Thornton Butterworth, Ltd., 1930.

—— *Painting as a Pastime*. London: Odhams Press, 1948.

—— *Savrola: A Tale of Revolution in Laurania*. London, Longmans, Green, & Co., 1900.

—— *The River War: An Account of the Reconquest of the Sudan*, Vols I–II. London: Longmans, Green, & Co., 1899.

—— *World War II*, Vols I–VI. London: Cassell & Co., 1948–54.

—— *The Story of the Malakand Field Force: An Episode of Frontier War*. London: Longmans, Green, & Co., 1898.

—— *The World Crisis*, Vols I–V. London: Thornton Butterworth, Ltd., 1923–31.

### The official biography

Churchill, Randolph S., *Winston S Churchill Vol. I: Youth 1875–1900*. London: Heinemann, 1966.

Churchill, Randolph S. (ed.), *Companion Volume I, Parts 1 and 2*. London: Heinemann, 1967.

—— *Winston S Churchill Vol. II: Young Statesmen 1901–1914*. London: Heinemann, 1967.

—— (ed.), *Companion Volume II, Parts 1, 2, and 3*. London: Heinemann, 1969.

Gilbert, Martin, *Winston S Churchill Vol. III: 1914–1916*. London: Heinemann, 1971.

Gilbert, Martin (ed.), *Companion Volume III, Parts 1 and 2*. London: Heinemann, 1972.

—— *Winston S Churchill Vol. IV: 1916–1922*. London: Heinemann, 1975.

—— (ed.), *Companion Volume IV, Parts 1, 2, and 3*. London: Heinemann, 1977.

—— *Winston S Churchill Vol. V: 1922–1939*. London: Heinemann, 1976.

—— (ed.), *Companion Volume V, Parts 1, 2, and 3*. London: Heinemann, 1979.

—— *Winston S Churchill Vol. VI: Finest Hour 1939–1941*. London: Heinemann, 1983.

—— (ed.), *Companion Volume VI: The Churchill War Papers, Parts 1, 2, and 3*. London: Heinemann, 1993, 1995, 2000.

—— *Winston S Churchill Vol. VII: The Road to Victory 1941–1945*. London: Heinemann, 1986.

—— *Winston S Churchill Vol. VIII: Never Despair 1945–1965*. London: Heinemann, 1988.

## Major collections

Boyle, P. (ed.), *The Churchill-Eisenhower Correspondence, 1953–1955*. Chapel Hill: University of North Carolina Press, 1984.

James, Robert R. (ed.), *Winston S. Churchill: His Complete Speeches, 1897–1963, Vols 1–8*. London: Chelsea House Publishers, 1974.

Kimball, W. (ed.), *Churchill and Roosevelt, the Complete Correspondence Vols 1–3*. Princeton: Princeton University Press, 1984.

Sand, G. (ed.), *Defending the West: The Truman-Churchill Correspondence, 1945–1960*. Westport: Praeger, 2004.

Soames, Mary (ed.), *Speaking for Themselves: The Personal Letters of Winston and Clementine Churchill*. London: Black Swan, 1999.

Woods, F., (ed.) *Young Winston's Wars: The Original Despatches of Winston S. Churchill, War Correspondent, 1897–1900*. London: L. Cooper, 1972.


## Diaries, memoirs, and monographs

Aga Khan III, *Memoirs of Aga Khan: World Enough and Time*. London: Cassell & Co. Ltd., 1954.

Asquith, Herbert, *Memories and Reflections: The Earl of Oxford and Asquith*, Vols I–II. London: Cassell & Co. Ltd., 1928.

Barnes, John, and Nicholson, David (eds), *The Diaries of Leo Amery, Vol. I, 1896–1929*. London: Hutchinson, 1980.

—— *The Empire at Bay: The Leo Amery Diaries, Vol. II, 1929–1945*. London: Hutchinson, 1988.

Beaverbrook, Lord Maxwell, *Politicians and the War*. London: Thornton Butterworth Ltd., 1928.

—— *The Decline and Fall of Lloyd George*. London: Collins, 1963.

Berman, Richard, *The Mahdi of Allah* [introduction by Churchill]. London: Putnam, 1931.

Bonham Carter, Violet, *Winston Churchill as I Knew Him*. London: Eyre & Spottiswode, 1965.

Bonham, Mark, and Pottle, Mark (eds), *Lantern Slides: The Diaries and Letters of Violet Bonham Carter, 1904–1914*. Phoenix: Orion Publishing, 1997.

Brock, Michael and Eleanor (eds), *H.H. Asquith: Letters to Venetia Stanley*. Oxford: Oxford University Press, 1982.

Butler, R.A., *The Art of the Possible: The Memoirs of Lord Butler*. London: Hamish Hamilton, 1971.

Campbell-Johnson, Alan, *Mission with Mountbatten*. London: Robert Hale Ltd., 1951.

Cantrell, Peter (ed.), *The Macmillan Diaries*. London: Macmillan, 2003.

Colville, Jock, *The Fringes of Power: Downing Street Diaries 1939–1955*. London: Hodder, 1985.

—— *Action This Day—Working with Churchill*. London: Macmillan, 1968.

—— *The Churchillians*. London: Weidenfeld & Nicolson, 1981.

Ferrel, Robert, *The Eisenhower Diaries*. New York: Norton, 1981.

Haldane, J. Aylmer, *How We Escaped from Pretoria*. Edinburgh: William Blackwood & Sons, 1900.

Hamilton, Ian, *Gallipoli Diary*, Vols I–II. London: Edward Arnold, 1920.

Hart-Davis, Duff, *King's Counsellor: Abdication and War—The Diaries of Sir Alan Lascelles.* London: Weidenfeld & Nicolson, 2006.

Lloyd George, David, *Memoirs of the Peace Conference*, Vols I–II. New Haven: Yale University Press, 1939.

Macmillan, Harold, *War Diaries: Politics and War in the Mediterranean.* London: Macmillan, 1984.

—— *Autobiography*, Vols I–VI. London, Macmillan, 1966–73.

Mayo, Katherine, *Mother India.* London: Jonathan Cape, 1927.

Moran, Lord, *Winston Churchill: The Struggle for Survival.* London: Constable, 1966.

Nicolson, Nigel (ed.), *Harold Nicolson: Diaries and Letters 1930–1939.* London: Collins, 1966.

—— *Harold Nicolson: Diaries and Letters 1939–1945.* London: Collins, 1970.

—— *Harold Nicolson: Diaries and Letters 1945–1962.* London: Collins, 1971.

Pottle, Mark (ed.), *Champion Redoubtable: Diaries and Letters of Violet Bonham Carter,1914–1945.* London: Weidenfeld & Nicolson, 1998.

Roosevelt, Elliott (with James Borough), *An Untold Story: The Roosevelts of Hyde Park.* London: Putnam, 1973.

—— *As He Saw It.* Westport: Greenwood Press, 1974.

Shuckburgh, Evelyn, *Descent to the Suez: Foreign Office Diaries 1951–1956.* London: Norton, 1987.

Thompson, Walter H., *I Was Churchill's Shadow.* London: Christopher Johnson, 1951.

—— *Sixty Minutes with Winston Churchill.* London: Christopher Johnson, 1953.

—— *Beside the Bulldog: The Intimate Memoirs of Churchill's Bodyguard.* London: Apollo, 2003.

Weizmann, Chaim, *Trial and Error: The Autobiography of Chaim Weizmann.* New York: Harper, 1949.

Williamson, Philip and Baldwin, Edward (eds), *Baldwin Papers: A Conservative Statesman.* Cambridge: Cambridge University Press, 2004.

## SECONDARY SOURCES

### Selected collections, memoirs, and monographs

Addison, Paul, *Churchill on the Home Front, 1900–1955.* London: Jonathan Cape, 1992.

—— *Churchill: The Unexpected Hero.* Oxford: Oxford University Press, 2005.

Ansari, Humayun, *The Making of the East London Mosque, 1910–1951.* Cambridge: Cambridge University Press, 2011.

Ball, Stuart, *The Conservative Party and British Politics 1902–1951.* London: Routledge, 1995.

—— *Winston Churchill.* London: British Library, 2003.

—— *Parliament and Politics in the Age of Churchill and Attlee: The Headlam Diaries 1935–1951.* Cambridge: Cambridge University Press, 2004.

—— (ed., with Anthony Seldon) *Recovering Power: The Conservatives in Opposition Since 1867.* London: Palgrave Macmillan, 2005.

Bennett, G. H., *British Foreign Policy During The Curzon Period 1919–24.* London: Palgrave Macmillan, 1995.

Brendon, Piers, *Winston Churchill.* London: Martin Secker & Warburg Ltd., 1984.

———— *The Decline and Fall of the British Empire, 1781–1997*. London: Vintage, 2008.

Cannadine, David, *Ornamentalism: How the British Saw Their Empire*. Oxford: Oxford University Press, 2002.

———— (ed.) with Roland Quinault, *Winston Churchill in the Twenty-First Century*. Cambridge: Cambridge University Press, 2004.

Catherwood, Christopher, *Churchill's Folly: How Winston Churchill Created Modern Iraq*. London: Constable, 2004.

Charmley, John, *Churchill: The End of Glory—A Political Biography*. London: Hodder & Stoughton, 1993.

———— *Churchill's Grand Alliance 1940–1957*. London: Hodder & Stoughton, 1995.

———— *A History of Conservative Politics 1900–1996*. London: Macmillan, 1996.

Cohen, Michael, *Churchill and the Jews, 1900–1948*. London: Routledge, 1985.

Cowles, Virginia, *Winston Churchill: The Era and the Man*. London: Hamish Hamilton, 1953.

D'este, Carlo, *Warlord: A Life of Churchill at War 1874–1945*. London: Harper, 2008.

Dockter, A. Warren, *Winston Churchill and the Islamic World: Orientalism, Empire and Diplomacy in the Middle East*. London: I. B. Tauris, 2014.

Farmelo, Graham, *Churchill's Bomb: A Hidden History of Science, War and Politics*. London: Faber & Faber, 2013.

Fishman, Jack, *My Darling Clementine: The Story of Lady Churchill*. London: W. H. Allen, 1963.

Fisk, Robert, *The Great War for Civilisation: The Conquest of the Middle East*. London: Fourth Estate, 2005.

Foster, R. F., *Lord Randolph Churchill: A Political Life*. Oxford: Oxford University Press, 1981.

Fromkin, David, *A Peace to End All Peace: The Fall of the Ottoman Empire and the Creation of the Modern Middle East*. New York, Henry Holt & Company, 1989.

Gilbert, Martin, *Churchill's Political Philosophy*. Oxford: Oxford University Press, 1981.

———— *Winston Churchill: The Wilderness Years*. London: Heinemann, 1981.

———— *World War II*. London: Weidenfeld, 1989.

———— *Churchill: A Life*. London: Henry Holt & Co., 1991.

———— *In Search of Churchill*. London: HarperCollins, 1994.

———— *History of the Twentieth Century*. London: HarperCollins, 2001.

———— *Churchill and America*. London: Simon & Schuster, 2005.

———— *Churchill and the Jews*. London: Simon & Schuster, 2007.

Hastings Max, *Finest Years: Churchill as Warlord, 1940–45*. London: Harper Press, 2009.

Herman, Arthur, *Gandhi and Churchill: The Epic Rivalry That Destroyed an Empire and Forged Our Age*. London: Hutchinson, 2008.

Higgins, Trumbull, *Winston Churchill and the Dardanelles*. London: Macmillan, 1963.

Hyam, Ronald, *Elgin and Churchill at the Colonial Office 1905–1908: The Watershed of the Empire-Commonwealth*. London: Macmillan, 1968.

Irons, Roy, *Churchill and the Mad Mullah of Somaliland: Betrayal and Redemption 1899–1921*. London: Pen & Sword Military, 2013.

James, Lawrence, *Churchill and Empire: Portrait of an Imperialist*. London: Weidenfeld & Nicolson, 2013.

James, Robert Rhodes, *Lord Randolph Churchill*. London: Weidenfeld & Nicolson, 1959.

———— *Churchill: A Study in Failure, 1900–1939*. London: Penguin Books, 1981.

Jenkins, Roy, *Churchill: A Biography*. New York: Farrar, Straus & Giroux, 2001.

Karsh, Efraim, *The Arab-Israeli Conflict: The Palestine 1948 War*. Oxford: Oxford University Press, 2002.

Kennedy, Paul, *Engineers of Victory: The Problem Solvers Who Turned the Tide in the Second World War*. London: Allen Lane, 2013.

Kumarasingham, Harshan, *A Political Legacy of the British Empire: Power and the Parliamentary System in Post-Colonial India and Sri Lanka*. London: I. B. Tauris, 2013.

Lloyd George, Robert, *David and Winston: How a Friendship Changed History*. London: John Murray, 2005.

Louis, William Roger (ed., with Robert Blake), *Churchill: A Major New Assessment*. London: W. W. Norton, 1993.

Lovell, Mary S., *The Churchills: A Family at the Heart of History*. London: Abacus, 2011.

Macmillan, Margaret, *Peacemakers: Six Months That Changed the World*. London: John Murray, 2002.

Manchester, William, *The Last Lion: Winston Spencer Churchill: Visions of Glory 1874–1932*. New York: Little, Brown & Co., 1983.

———— *The Last Lion: Winston Spencer Churchill: Alone 1932–1940*. New York: Little, Brown & Co., 1988.

———— (with Paul Reid), *The Last Lion: Winston Spencer Churchill*. New York: Little, Brown & Co., 2012.

Marder, Arthur, *From Dreadnought to Scapa Flow*, Vols I–IV. Oxford: Oxford University Press, 1965.

de Mendelssohn, Peter, *The Age of Churchill: Heritage and Adventure, 1874–1911*. London: Thames and Hudson, 1961.

Middlemas, Keith, and Barnes, John, *Baldwin: A Biography*. London: Weidenfeld and Nicolson, 1969.

Mukerjee, Madhusree, *Churchill's Secret War: The British Empire and the Ravaging of India During World War II*. London: Basic Books, 2011.

Muller, James (ed.), *Churchill as a Peacemaker*. New York: Cambridge University Press, 1997.

Overy, Richard, *Why the Allies Won*. London: Jonathan Cape, 1997.

———— *The Battle of Britain: The Myth and the Reality*. London: Penguin Books, 2000.

Ramsden, John, *Man of the Century: Winston Churchill and Legend Since 1945*. London: HarperCollins, 2002.

Reid, Walter, *Empire of Sand: How Britain Made the Middle East*. London: Birlinn Ltd., 2011.

Reynolds, David, *In Command of History: Churchill Fighting and Writing World War II*. London: Allen Lane, 2004.

———— *From World War to Cold War: Churchill, Roosevelt and the International History of the 1940s*. Oxford: Oxford University Press, 2006.

Roberts, Andrew, *The Holy Fox: A Biography of Lord Halifax*. London: Weidenfeld & Nicolson, 1991.

———— *Eminent Churchillians*. London: Weidenfeld & Nicolson, 1994.

———— *Hitler and Churchill: Secrets of Leadership*. London: Weidenfeld & Nicolson, 2003.

———— *Masters and Commanders: How Roosevelt, Churchill, Marshall and Alanbrooke Won the War in the West*. London: Allen Lane, 2008.

Rose, Jonathan, *The Literary Churchill: Author, Reader, Actor.* New Haven, Conn.: Yale University Press, 2014.

Rose, Norman, *Churchill: An Unruly Life.* London: Simon and Schuster, 1994.

Russell, Douglas, *Winston Churchill—Soldier: The Military Life of a Gentleman at War.* London: Brassey's, 2005.

Seldon, Anthony, *Churchill's Indian Summer: The Conservative Government 1951–55.* London: Hodder & Stoughton, 1981.

Sheldon, Michael, *Young Titan: The Making of Winston Churchill.* London: Simon & Schuster, 2013.

Taylor, A.J.P., (ed.) *Churchill: Four Faces and the Man.* London: Penguin, 1969.

Toye, Richard, *Lloyd George and Churchill: Rivals for Greatness.* London: Macmillan, 2007.

——— *Churchill's Empire: The World That Made Him and the World He Made.* London: Henry Holt & Company, 2010.

——— *The Roar of the Lion: The Untold Story of Churchill's World War II Speeches.* Oxford: Oxford University Press, 2013.

Walder, David, *The Chanak Affair.* London: Hutchinson, 1969.

Wallach, Janet, *The Desert Queen: The Extraordinary Life of Gertrude Bell.* London: Weidenfeld & Nicolson, 1996.

Wilson, Jeremy, *Lawrence of Arabia: The Authorized Biography of T. E. Lawrence.* London: Heinemann, 1989.

Wrigley, C.J. (ed.), *Warfare, Diplomacy and Politics: Essays in Honour of AJP Taylor.* London: Hamish Hamilton, 1986.

——— *Winston Churchill: A Biographical Companion.* Santa Barbara, Calif.: ABC-CLIO, 2002.

——— *A.J.P. Taylor: Radical Historian of Europe.* London: I. B. Tauris, 2006.

——— *Churchill.* London: Haus Publishing Limited, 2006.

Young, John, *Winston Churchill's Last Campaign: Britain and the Cold War 1951–1955.* Oxford: Clarendon Press, 1996.

# INDEX

# PHOTO CREDITS

Churchill at Chartwell, 1939. Photo: Topical Press/Hulton Archive/Getty Images.

Churchill's broadcast, 1941. Photo: CHAR 09/181B/180, The Papers of Sir Winston Churchill, Churchill Archives Centre, Churchill College. © Winston S. Churchill. Reproduced with permission of Curtis Brown, London, on behalf of the Estate of Sir Winston Churchill and the Sir Winston Churchill Archive Trust.

Winston, aged 18. Photo: Peter Harrington Ltd.

Lord Randolph. Photo: Universal History Archive/UIG/Bridgeman Images.

Jennie Jerome. Photo: The Illustrated London News Picture Library, London/Bridgeman Images.

Winston and Jack with their mother. Photo: BRDW I, Photo 1/8, The Broadwater Collection, Churchill Archives Centre, Churchill College.

Churchill and Clementine, circa 1910. Photo: adoc-photos/Corbis.

Churchill and Clemmie, 1945. Photo: PA Photos.

Illustration from *My African Journey*. Photo: LIB 37, Churchill Archives Centre, Churchill College. © Winston S. Churchill. Reproduced with permission of Curtis Brown, London, on behalf of the Estate of Sir Winston Churchill and the Master, Fellows and Scholars of Churchill College, Cambridge.

Churchill in Pretoria. Photo: BRDW I, Photo 1/18, The Broadwater Collection, Churchill Archives Centre, Churchill College.

Churchill at Deauville. Photo: BRDW I, Photo 1/110, The Broadwater Collection, Churchill Archives Centre, Churchill College.

Churchill and the Pyramids. Photo: BRDW I, Photo 2/83, The Broadwater Collection, Churchill Archives Centre, Churchill College.

Churchill inspecting the Tank Corps, 1915. Photo: © Imperial War Museum, London (Q 34662).

Churchill with General Pershing. Photo: Corbis.

Churchill visiting Bristol, 1941. Photo: Popperfoto/Getty Images.

Churchill accepting a cigar. Photo: Keystone/Alamy.

Allied Forces headquarters, 1943. Photo: Mirrorpix.

Churchill firing a tommy gun. Photo: Getty Images.

Churchill with de Gaulle, 11 November 1944. Photo: BRDW II, Photo 8/10/22, The Broadwater Collection, Churchill Archives Centre, Churchill College.

Churchill crossing the Rhine. Photo: RA/Lebrecht Music & Arts.

Churchill waves to crowds in Whitehall. Photo: Major Horton/IWM/Getty Images.

Churchill and Lloyd George. Photo: Mirrorpix.

Churchill and Lord Halifax. Photo: Getty Images.

Churchill with Stalin. Photo: Lt. Lotzof/IWM/Getty Images.

Churchill with Anthony Eden. Photo: BRDW I, Photo 1/343, The Broadwater Collection, Churchill Archives Centre, Churchill College.

Churchill and Roosevelt at Shangri-La. Photo: courtesy of the Franklin D. Roosevelt Presidential Library and Museum, Hyde Park, New York.

Churchill speaking at a Thanksgiving celebration. Photo: BRDW V, Photo 3/5, The Broadwater Collection, Churchill Archives Centre, Churchill College.

Churchill and President Truman. Photo: Abbie Rowe, National Park Service, courtesy Harry S. Truman Library.

Churchill at the Conservative Party Conference. Photo: Mirrorpix.

Churchill at the Hague. Photo: Kurt Hutton/Picture Post/Getty Images.

Churchill, bricklayer. Photo: Topical Press/Hulton Archive/Getty Images.

Churchill painting in Marrakesh. Photo: M. McKeown/Daily Express/Getty Images.

Churchill in flying gear. Photo: Ullstein/TopFoto.